MANAGEMENT CONSULTANCY IN THE 21ST CENTURY

Management Consultancy in the 21st Century

Fiona Czerniawska

First published 1999 by
MACMILLAN PRESS LTD
Houndmills, Basingstoke, Hampshire RG21 6XS
and London
Companies and representatives
throughout the world

ISBN 0–333–73692–3

A catalogue record for this book is available from the British Library.

This book is printed on paper suitable for recycling and made from fully managed and sustained forest sources.

10 9 8 7 6 5 4 3
08 07 06 05 04 03 02 01 00

Formatted by *The Ascenders Partnership*, Basingstoke

Illustrations by *Ascenders*

Printed and bound by
Antony Rowe Ltd, Chippenham, Wiltshire

The empires of the future
are the empires of the mind

WINSTON CHURCHILL

for Peter

Contents

Preface

Most books aim to propound a single theory or tell a single story. This book is different.

As one of the newest and most volatile industries in a rapidly changing business environment, management consultancy has always evaded analysis and defied prediction.

Had someone tried to speculate, 40 – or even 20 – years ago about the future of consultancy, it seems unlikely that they would have envisaged an industry with the scale and scope that it has today. It would seem foolish, therefore, to attempt to predict how this industry will look over the next two decades. And this book would, indeed, be doomed to failure, if it tried to present a single, coherent vision of the future. But that is not its intention: no one individual or firm has the answer.

Rather than focus on just one potential – and probably erroneous – prediction, it is therefore much more interesting to present a wide range of views – from consultants, clients, suppliers, and industry experts – and to explore the range of possibilities. Will the consulting market continue to grow at its current, almost exponential rate? How could the relationship between consultants and clients change? What are the key threats and opportunities for consulting firms likely to be? What may make one firm succeed while another fails?

The people to whom I talked during the course of writing this book had different answers to these questions. They would not necessarily subscribe to my opinions, nor I to theirs. The point of this book lies in its plurality – in its ability to broaden our understanding of the issues facing this industry, to provoke debate rather than stifle it.

But, although what we have here is speculation, it is certainly not idle speculation. The future has to come from somewhere: consulting firms are what they are today, because ten, maybe 20 years ago, the people who worked in them had at least a sense of how their industry could develop – its future potential. They seized, for instance, the opportunity brought by new technology in order to broaden their role within their clients' organisations. Similarly today, faced with the growing importance of the intellectual economy and the speed with which the business environment as a whole is evolving, there are choices to be made, opportunities to be grasped, risks to be avoided. The ideas put forward here may not be proved true in detail, but we should be in no doubt that they provide the context in which the future *will* happen.

The key question, therefore, is not: which vision is right or wrong? It is: which vision will win?

Finally, it is important to recognise that it is not just the future of the management consultancy market which is at issue here. If intellectual capital is to be *the* key asset of the economy over the next decades, it follows that consulting firms may be *the* major players in every market, not just their own. The future of consultancy will be all our futures.

Acknowledgements

As well as my own views, this book contains the perspectives of many other people, many directly involved in the consulting industry, and others who work with it, rather than inside it. I would like to express my gratitude to them for their willingness to contribute and the openness with which they were prepared to discuss the issues. My thanks also go to: the very large number of people who helped to set up meetings, track down contacts and stretch diaries in order to accommodate me, in particular Tony Tiernan at the Boston Consulting Group and Wendy Millar at Bain & Company; to those who commented on various parts of the draft, especially Francis Quinlan at Hodgart Temporal; and to Stephen Rutt at Macmillan for his continued support.

As always, my husband Stefan has provided help, support and constructive criticism at all stages. Without him, none of this would be possible.

1   Introduction

The irresistible rise of the consulting market

'Management consultancy', the *Financial Times* commented, 'seems to have acquired an unstoppable momentum.'[1] The past few years have seen double-digit growth across much of the industry, with worldwide fees estimated to total more than $60bn.[2]

But the consultancy market is not just significant because it has grown massively (and looks set to continue to grow in the immediate future). It is also increasingly pervasive, moving from organisation to organisation and from sector to sector. Twenty or thirty years ago, using consultants might have been exceptional, but how many major business decisions are made today in which consultants have *not* been involved? Moreover, consultancy these days is not stopping at the factory or office door, it is walking across the threshold into our everyday lives.

In *Dangerous Company*, a study of the impact of consulting firms on their clients, James O'Shea and Charles Madigan (both journalists with the *Chicago Tribune*) noted how – to give one example – the Boston Consulting Group's recommendations for improving the efficiency of healthcare go beyond the bounds of what is normally considered to be consultancy. In particular, the concept of disease management – which brings together medical practitioners and business managers to prevent as much as respond to diseases – looks set to change significantly the doctor–patient relationship in the US. Another illustration of this trend, from the UK, would be the Notting Hill Carnival – Europe's largest street festival – which called in consultants in 1988 when some of the costume makers and performers objected to the way in which the carnival committee was organising the event. James O'Shea and Charles Madigan concluded:

Management consultants often work in shadows, cloaking their missions and client lists in secrecy. But their influence is spreading rapidly and widely as they grapple with social problems that emanate in the workplace.[3]

The issue here is not the pervasiveness itself – there is nothing necessarily wrong with the involvement of consultants in a wider range of socio-economic issues. Indeed, the benefits that consultants bring to their business clients are potentially very valuable to society, if harnessed to these broader problems. The issue is the extent to which we understand the reasons underpinning this trend, and its potential impact.

Consultancy is becoming more pervasive for two reasons. In the first place, it is a trend which reflects the increasing complexity of business. Secondly and partly as a result of this growing complexity, the line which has traditionally separated consultancy advice from management action is becoming blurred.

Of course, it is a truism of business to say that the world is becoming more complex, interdependent and unpredictable – witness the uncertainty around the likely impact on Western business of financial collapses in what were, until recently, 'tiger economies'. Whether you think this growth in complexity is real or perceived, it undoubtedly creates an environment in which consultancy not only flourishes, but necessarily has to move beyond its conventional boundaries. How can you justify undertaking a routine cost-reduction exercise for one company, when it is clear that the root of the problem lies in its network of relations with its suppliers? If business is full of interconnections, it follows that you cannot – as a consultant – limit yourself to one discrete area, because 'discrete areas' don't exist.

This brings us to another characteristic of the emerging consultancy market. Historically, one of the main criticisms levelled at consultants has been that they 'hit and run' – that they submit a report and make recommendations but then leave before implementation starts. Essentially, they have been bystanders at, rather than participants in, the game of business. While this role has often been perceived negatively – a failure of nerve on the consultant's part – it has advantages as well as drawbacks. As organisational distance has given consulting firms objectivity in the past, so getting more involved means that their position as independent advisers is being inevitably compromised. Nevertheless, it has been a feature of the 1990s that clients have become much more demanding about the results they expect their consultants to deliver. Contracts, for example, are increasingly geared around performance-related payment.

Taken together, these trends – complexity, the blurring of client– consultant boundaries and the pressure to produce results – mean that the traditional dichotomies of the consulting market – client/consultant, internal/ external, subjective/objective, advice/action – are starting to disintegrate.

Thus, when the Boston Consulting Group promotes the idea of disease management, it is not just because they have recognised that the efficiency and effectiveness of healthcare delivery is a complex subject which involves understanding the patient as much as the medical infrastructure. It is also because they have realised that they are only going to be able to meet their client's objectives if they can make something happen – in this case, if they can change the way in which people consult their GPs. Twenty – or even ten – years ago, the situation might have been very different: a company like the Boston Consulting Group would have made their recommendations, based on analysis of the facts, which its client would then have accepted or rejected, implemented or stuck on that apocryphal shelf somewhere to gather dust.

To an extent, this – let us say 'old-fashioned' – view of consultancy forced clients, as much as consultants, to be observers: reports were typically high in analysis but low in practical application. Nowadays, clients expect to see 'real' results. Sometimes this may simply take the form of preparing an implementation plan, but increasingly clients want their consultants to *do* something. Moreover, just as previously clients wanted consultants to tell them something new (carry out an analysis of a market, for example, which a client could not have performed itself), now they want consultants to do something which they – the clients – cannot do themselves. The value of outside help lies increasingly in acting rather than advising.

It follows that when a consultancy does something, it is usually something which a conventional client business has not done, or cannot do, alone.

Thus, Andersen Consulting's *Via* World Network is a specialist leisure and air travel consultancy whose mission is 'to transform the travel industry to be more successful by delivering radically new industry processes and removing cost, as well as complexity, from travel product distribution'. *Via* originally grew out a deal in which Andersen Consulting outsourced a client's ticket processing facility and has moved on to offer the same, highly cost-efficient service to other airlines operating in the US. Andersen Consulting did something that its client could not have done independently – develop a low-cost model of ticket processing which could be offered *en masse*.

The pressure to do something on their clients' behalf is starting – and will increasingly continue – to drive consulting firms to move outside conventional business, to become both more pervasive (touching new and different areas of business) and more invasive (taking business where it has not been before).

Ignorance is unlikely to be bliss

In the light of this, it seems extraordinary that we – consultants, clients, ordinary people – understand so little about consulting. As a recent survey in *The Economist* commented:

> The management consultancy business is a tale of mystery and imagination. Nobody seems to know quite what it is, let alone whether it delivers value for money. The consultants do their best to maintain the mystique, pleading client confidentiality and hiding behind terms such as 'value propositions' and 'service offerings'. And yet hard-headed business people the world over are willing to spend millions on consultants' advice. It is hard to avoid the conclusion that, along with that advice, the industry dispenses a little witchcraft as well.[4]

If consultancy is the 'dark art' of business – and one that appears to be becoming increasingly powerful – is it not about time that we started to subject this industry to rather more rigorous analysis?

But why do we know so little?

The reasons are partly commercial and partly cultural. Despite recent moves towards incorporation in some areas, the majority of the largest consultancy firms remain partnerships and are therefore not subject to the same rules on financial disclosure as public companies. While some of the Big Five accounting firms have started to issue annual reports, the amount of publicly available information about the other major firms remains limited. And it is not just primary information of which we are short: because only a minority of the largest consulting firms are traded publicly, there is no body of secondary analysis and commentary produced by investment banks to aid stockholders. Moreover, the situation is not helped by the lack of any regulatory authority: various trade associations exist, but none equivalent to, for example, the International Audit Committee.

The lack of commercial imperative to provide information has been re-inforced by varying levels of cultural antipathy to openness within many of the firms themselves. Client confidentiality may, in many cases, be a legitimate reason to avoid detailed disclosure, but it has also led to a broader-based reluctance to engage in debate about the role and value of consultancy. Tempting though it is to see this lack of discussion as evidence of a conspiracy of silence, concealing the industry's equivalent of Bluebeard's Castle (dungeons filled with the bodies of previous clients, and so on), it is much more likely that the absence of debate reflects the fact that consultancies believe that their efforts should be focused on their clients, not themselves. Consulting firms are not by nature introspective; in fact, it is their commitment to solving client problems that often leaves them with internal inefficiencies. The proper study of consultancy firms is not consultancy.

But perhaps the single biggest barrier to analysing the consulting market is not the scarcity of information about the sector today, but the absence of any history. The role of the consultant has, of course, been around for centuries, but the first consulting firms appeared towards the end of the nineteenth century. Among its early pioneers were Lillian Gilbreth, Arthur Little, Frederick Taylor and Edward Booz: Gilbreth and Taylor had a lasting impact on management theory; Little and Booz established firms which still consult today. McKinsey & Co. and Arthur Andersen were both founded in the 1920s. Between the 1920s and the mid-1980s, the number and size of consulting firms grew, partly organically, partly through merger and acquisition: progress was solid but essentially unspectacular. Three things happened to change this in the 1980s:

- The first factor was the broadening of consulting beyond its core market of the preceding half-century – operations management – to encompass most areas of management, including marketing, organisational design, strategy, and human resource management.
- The second was information technology which, as it has become inextricably linked with management, has accounted for an increasing proportion of fee income.
- The third was globalisation – the extent to which consultants' largest clients were starting to operate on a transnational basis.

To these trends, another was added in the early 1990s – outsourcing.

The changes then, of the past 15 years, have been significant: they were also comparatively unanticipated. There was nothing in the previous 50 years which prepared consultancy firms for these wide-ranging, new services; nothing, even, which indicated that such a change might happen. In just a few years – overnight by the standards of older, more established industries – the whole nature of consultancy had changed. The problem this poses today is therefore twofold. The consultancy firms, as we know them, are barely out of kindergarten: 15 years or so of trends is not much to go on. Secondly, even if we had a longer history to study, it might tell us nothing about the future: in so far as this industry can be said to be characterised by anything, unpredictability appears to be it.

One of the motives for this book is the belief that this situation needs to change, and that it needs to change for two reasons.

The first reason is that, as clients, even as ordinary citizens, we need to understand the impact consultancy is already having and will have in the future. This is true both at the microeconomic level – in terms of the impact a single assignment may have on an individual company – and the macroeconomic level. Does it really make sense, for example, to send our brightest management talent (consultancies are the largest single recruiters of MBA students) to institutions where they will come into contact with a large number of companies but for only a few weeks per company, or to employ them directly in those companies, where their cross-industry experience will be replaced by in-depth knowledge and implementation skills? Why do we have both consultants and managers? Do we need both, but if so, which? Will an economy which is heavily reliant on consultancy be more successful than one based on 'traditional' management? In the short term? In the long term?

> It used to be said that the problem with British Industry was that the nation's best talent was sucked into the City where salaries were better, colleagues more congenial and the lifestyle more glamorous. In the mid-1990s the same applies, but for British read European and for the City read consultancy.[5]

In 1994, the UK government published a rare assessment of the benefits delivered by consultants to central government departments: more than £500m has been spent on consultancy with just £10m in quantifiable benefits (2 per cent of expenditure). By contrast £78m was spent on using civil servants to increase efficiency with £18m in quantifiable benefits (23 per cent).[6]

It has always been difficult to measure the impact of consultancies, not least because only a relatively small proportion of consulting time is spent on assignments which will deliver direct benefits – financial or otherwise. While clients have been exerting greater pressure on their consultants to produce tangible deliverables, the majority of these deliverables are narrowly defined in terms of the assignment itself. Thus, final payment may be linked to the production of a final report or the implementation of a system. It is a rare client – and an even rarer assignment – that attempts to make a link between these outputs and the wider performance of a company in total. Most consultancy contributes to performance only indirectly, either by developing a new strategy or by changing organisational design and processes in order to align them to a new strategy: it is the client who implements the strategy and who makes the new organisation work. Both clients and consultants recognise that the success of a new strategy is dependent on many factors: the consultancy may 'do its job', but the strategy that it has developed – for reasons outside its control – may still fail. This situation makes it easy for anecdotal evidence about the failure of consultancy to emerge (everyone has their story to tell about how a consultant they worked with failed to deliver), but it has made it difficult to produce a more systematic assessment of the consulting industry:

> Consultancies are generally resistant to independent evaluation or systematic monitoring of their work and there is predictably little published, critical examination of their efforts which would enable improved understanding of what works, what does not and why.[7]

But with the trends noted at the start of this chapter, being able to answer the question 'what impact does consultancy have?' is going to be hugely important in the future.

The second reason for improving our understanding of the consulting industry is that – as consultants – we need to know whether the world as we currently know it is going to continue, or whether the trends outlined earlier will result in a major shift in the sector, equivalent to but different from the shift over the past 15 years. Will, for instance, the conventional operational tools of consulting (utilisation, time-based accounting and fees) still be viable where the distinction between consultant and client is breaking down? Will consultancy still be based around highly skilled individuals? Or will commercial pressure increase the rate at which intellectual capital of this nature has to be codified into 'packages' which can be sold to many clients at once and mean that consultancies will become software houses by default? If consultancies become more like their clients, will clients continue to hire them?

Consulting firms have survived – indeed thrived – so far because they have been able to adapt to change as it has happened. It was relatively small firms which encountered the changes of the 1980s – the broadening of services and growing importance of information technology as a source of fees – and it therefore took comparatively little effort to realign their internal organisation in the face of these changes. For the biggest firms, the situation is now very different. All have massive investment in office networks, computer infrastructures and – most importantly – human organisations. Few will find it easy to change as quickly again: some may not be able to at all. In other words, consulting firms are going to need more warning this time around and it follows that they are going to have to start breaking the habit of a lifetime, and look ahead at the future of their own industry.

The objective of this book is to do just that, to see the form that the consulting market, the firms that operate within it and the process of consultancy itself will take in the future. Part I looks at how the way in which trends already visible in the industry may develop in the immediate future; Part II looks further ahead to look at the shape of consultancy in the more distant future, and is based on interviews with the leaders of some of the world's major consulting firms and other experts on the consulting industry.

Finally, it should be emphasised that this book is not just aimed at consultants themselves: the future of consulting is an equally important subject for the companies which buy consultancy, for the managers who work alongside them and the ordinary citizens whose lives are – increasingly – affected by them.

A note on the definition of consultancy

The term 'consultancy' can be – and is – applied to many activities, ranging from strategic advice to computer programming. Is it therefore possible to write a book about 'consultancy' without continually running the risk of making statements which, while valid in one part of the market, may be completely misleading elsewhere?

As a starting point, the definition of consultancy for the purposes of this book is generally in line with that formulated by several US consulting associations in the mid-1980s:

> Management consultancy is an independent and objective advisory service provided by qualified persons to clients in order to help them identify and analyse management problems or opportunities. Management consultancies also recommend solutions or suggested actions with respect to these issues, and help, when requested, in their implementation.[8]

Thus, although IT-related consultancy (that is, advice) is considered here, computer hardware and software development are not; and outsourcing is referred to, but primarily in the context of its implications for other types of consultancy. Where it seems appropriate, a distinction has also been drawn between what could be termed 'business improvement' and strategic consultancy.

Notes

1. *Financial Times*, 19 June 1997.
2. Based on research by the Kennedy Research Group.
3. James O'Shea and Charles Madigan, *Dangerous Company: The Consulting Powerhouses and the Businesses They Save and Ruin*, New York: Random House, 1997, p. 148.
4. *The Economist*, 22 March 1997.
5. *Financial Times*, 20 May 1996.
6. *The Government's use of consultants: an Efficiency Unit scrutiny*, London: HMSO, 1994.
7. John Gill and Sue Whittle, 'Management by Panacea: Accounting for Transcience', *Journal of Management Studies*, 30:2, 1993, p. 288.
8. Sam W. Barcus and Joseph W. Wilkinson, *Handbook of Management Consultancy Services*, New York: McGraw Hill, 1995, p.5.

Part I

Consultancy in the Next Ten Years

2

Changes in the Client–Consultant Relationship

Client attitudes to consultancy in the 1990s

The recession of the early 1990s was the first – and so far only – time that modern consulting firms have encountered any significant decline in the demand for their services.[1] By contrast with other sectors, the problems suffered by consultancies were comparatively light, but they were still sufficient to produce redundancies and insolvencies. The experience was a shock for the industry: accustomed to an environment of continuous growth, consulting firms were poorly prepared for the operational efficiencies required by the new market conditions: many saw a sudden and dramatic fall in profits.

But, if the recession was a shock for the consulting firms themselves, it was more like a shot in the arm for their clients.

Prior to this, it was the consultancies who set the agenda, who dictated the fees and who held the intellectual high ground. While it is certainly true that, by the end of the 1980s, many larger clients, who had by then been exposed to consultancy on an extensive basis, had become more sophisticated buyers, it was not until the 1991–2 recession that clients started to take a much more active control. A combination of lower overall demand for consultancy and the proliferation of new entrants into the market had meant that, for the first time, there was an excess of supply over demand. Greater competition meant that clients could play firms off against each other and negotiate down the fees. More intangibly, a growing sense of frustration among clients at the quality of service they saw themselves receiving, plus – perhaps – the overuse of the word 'consultant' which had come to be applied to anyone from a sales person to an academic – had started to erode the mystique of the consulting industry. It is not surprising, therefore, that numerous business books appeared on how to buy consultancy, or how to get the best from consultants.

Looking at these books, several common themes become clear:

- *Intellectual capital.* One of the fundamental premises of consultancy is that its practitioners add value by bringing a fresh outlook, new ideas and cross-sector experience to clients who might otherwise find it difficult to see beyond their immediate business horizon. 'I really believe in the concept of knowledge transfer', one CEO, interviewed in the *Financial Times* commented, 'if I pay to bring those people [consultants] in, I don't expect them to leave without having transferred their knowledge to my people so that they can move forward.'[2] But one of the criticisms most constantly levelled at consultants is that they fail to do this. Surveys of clients' views of consultants have highlighted the extent to which the latter are perceived to: follow the latest management fad; say what clients want to hear; tell people what they already know; and have little business experience. Essentially all of these complaints come down to a central issue – that consultants are not adding to the intellectual capital of their clients.
- *Making a difference.* A second theme – which emerges partly as a result of the apparent failure of consultants to bring new ideas – has been their perceived failure to 'make a real difference'. Typically, consultants are accused both of writing reports that clients do not understand and therefore cannot act upon, and of making recommendations which prolong their own involvement, thus marginalising the contribution of the client's existing staff. Either way, the net effect is the same: the consultants' activity happens in parallel to the core of the clients' business, rather than having a direct impact on it. The whole assignment is ultimately an exercise in futility. This charge of failing to help clients appears in many guises: consultants are accused of not working effectively with client staff; of following their own agenda; of having preconceived solutions to which they expect clients to conform.
- *Value for money.* Most often, concerns like these translate into arguments over the value for money that consulting offers. At the end of the assignment, what has the client got for its money? When the consultants leave, what have they left behind?

Because it is easy – even fashionable – to cast stones at the consulting profession, it is important not to accept these criticisms at face value, but to try to understand the assumptions which underpin such attitudes – the causes rather than the symptoms of the disease. It will, after all, be these underlying assumptions which determine the demands that clients will make on consultancies in the future, rather than the superficial criticisms.

A first point to note is that, despite this negative feedback, companies continue to buy consultancy. There are three key inferences we can make from this:

- Much consulting work is well delivered and well received, but, as always, it is the problems which people tend to talk about and remember.
- However, the fact that there clearly are problems, and that there is a wide range of anecdotal evidence to the effect that consultants fail to meet expectations, suggest that the quality of consultancy being delivered is at least inconsistent.
- That clients continue to purchase consultancy suggests either that they believe – on balance – that there is likely to be a benefit to their company from employing outsiders or that they see no alternative (they do not have the resources, skills or time to carry out the work required internally).

Consultancy has, therefore, come to be regarded – at least by some clients – as a necessary evil: there are few major business decisions taken today which do not bear the stamp of some consulting firm on them somewhere. At the same time, the actual value received is being increasingly recognised to be an act of faith: neither the consulting firms nor their clients have found it particularly easy to put hard measures to the benefits of assignments. If these two tendencies continue to grow unchecked, if clients feel themselves becoming even more dependent on a service which is of uncertain value, then the chance that problems will occur in the client–consultant relationship becomes high.

To a degree, this conflict is already apparent in the growing number of arguments over fees. Clients want high-quality, intellectually rigorous services, delivered by experienced and committed consultants, but they do not want to pay the earth for it. Despite the consultants' reputation for charging premium fees, discounts, penalty clauses and performance-related fees are all becoming increasingly common. Litigation – or threats of litigation – over alleged failure to deliver is also growing. On the one hand, it is easy to say that clients are no different to ordinary consumers: we all expect more for less these days. When they experience models of operational efficiency, excellent service or good value for money else-where (when they are shopping or travelling, for instance), clients see no reason why their consultants should not be capable of delivering the same combination of service and price. But on the other hand, a more important point may be that clients find it difficult to attach a value – and therefore a cost – to consulting services. They feel they have to buy the service, but they are not sure what they will be getting for their money and, therefore, what fee they should be charged for it.

The symbiotic relationship between clients and consultants

And this tension – between dependency and received value – can only increase. Why? Because this tension is not just the coincidental result of prevailing marketing conditions, but a fundamental product of the consulting industry.

At the moment, the glue that keeps the client–consultant relationship together is the fact that both parties 'buy into' the same business model. Put simply, this model says that every organisation will have gaps in its intellectual capital (translating into a shortfall in creativity, knowledge, skills, time, and so on) which it cannot fill using the resources available to it in-house; consultancies exist to fill these gaps; as the gaps change, so do the services offered by consulting firms. Although it may not feel like it in practice, the relationship between the two is highly symbiotic (Figure 2.1).

This is the model that most clients and consultants have when they commission or work on assignments; essentially, it treats each assignment as an independent, one-off activity. But the problem with this model is that in reality it is not, and cannot be, static. Consulting firms can only continue to survive – let alone thrive – if clients continue to have gaps in their intellectual capital base. The continued appearance of such gaps is driven

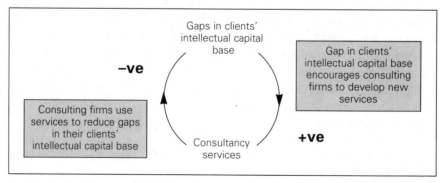

Figure 2.1 The symbiotic relationship between clients and consultants

by two related factors: whether or not the consultants used can actually fill the gap; and the extent to which changing demands on the client's business create new gaps.

To take the first of these points. When – as clients – we consider whether consultants have completed an assignment successfully (that is, whether they have filled the appropriate gap in our intellectual capital), we tend to evaluate them on very specific, usually discrete criteria. This is clearly important, if we are to get any sense of the value for money we have received from the assignment in question, but it does not consider the impact that hiring consultants may have on our organisation overall. Buying in consultants is not only public admission that a company does not have a particular skill, it is also the tacit acknowledgement that it does not need it: the dumbing-down of the organisation is the inevitable by-product. As US academic Eileen Shapiro commented:

> If the managers within the company no longer have the time to think about long-term needs and assess the various techniques available, it becomes easier and easier to abdicate [their] responsibilities ... Then both managers and consultants come to see those inside the company as the 'maintainers' ... while the consultants are seen as the 'change agents' [3]

Hiring a consultant may resolve a specific issue, but it contributes to a mindset which says that the client needs external help because it does not have – or want – the skills internally. In other words, consultants, while they plug some gaps, create other, potentially more significant ones.

Moreover, as business decisions become – at least apparently – more complex, and as the information available to inform these decisions grows exponentially, companies are becoming less and less confident in their ability to take such decisions. Accustomed as we mostly are to thinking of our business environment as uncertain and volatile, it is inevitable that the intellectual capital needs of clients are constantly changing. When two American anthropologists looked at the consulting industry, they were struck by the extent to which this 'preoccupation with newness' created a level of anxiety which was tantamount to the physical stress endured by our earliest ancestors:

> Driven by the furies of a fickle technology, our consuming society flits from one new gadget to another – experiencing along the way the transition, uncertainty, and complexity of future shock. The ambiguity-borne stress that occurred only occasionally in the physical or cultural environment of earlier societies when they suffered some kind of cataclysm has become a constant stress in the contemporary world. [4]

Even if consultants were proving successful at filling all the gaps in a client's knowledge or skills base today, the knowledge or skills required tomorrow could be radically different, inevitably creating new gaps to be filled.

Without question, it has been in the best interest of consultancies themselves to promote the idea that business is becoming more complicated: creating new gaps in clients' intellectual capital is one of the surest ways to guarantee fee income for the future. But, in focusing on this and the dubious ethics of consulting which it implies, we often miss the much more important point. Increasing complexity is the inevitable result of consultancy. The gaps in intellectual capital which each company has are peculiar to that company; there may be common themes, but the precise definition of that gap is – or should be – unique in each case. In the world before consultancy, companies could focus on filling that particular gap, but consultancy brought with it (and was partly a result of) the idea that each company can learn from the gaps of others. By being predicated on the notion that business ideas are transferable from company to company, and from industry to industry, consultancy has helped to spread the idea that there is a 'standard' of intellectual capital which has to be achieved by every company, irrespective of their individual circumstances.

The consulting machine speeds up

These three factors – that filling specific gaps for clients may create much larger ones, the growing complexity of today's business world, and the extent to which consulting firms contribute to it – all combine to increase the gaps in clients' intellectual capital. And because consultancy, like nature, abhors a vacuum, the consulting firms have been quick to offer an increasingly wide range of services to meet this need:

> The cure-all consultancy product becomes more and more attractive to managers as they also come under increasing pressure from their superiors to find new ways of dealing with organisational problems with minimal risk and investment.[5]

While consultancies are falling over themselves to come up with more comprehensive service packages, aimed at being a one-stop panacea for all management ills, it is becoming increasingly unlikely that any of these services will be capable of filling the gaps in a client's intellectual capital.

This is not the fault of the consulting firms themselves: the gaps have become un-fillable. Meanwhile, clients are showing every signs of classic addiction – demanding more and more from their advisers but getting less of a high with each assignment (Figure 2.2). The more value (that is, intellectual capital) clients want, the more intellectual capital they need, the less they can actually be satisfied:

> Consultancy poisoning is an addictive phenomenon, with successive cycles of euphoria and despair … [It] is a malaise arising from lack of self-awareness, abnegation of responsibility for the viability of the organisation, and short-sighted management controls.[6]

If consulting were a brand, we would say that it is being stretched.

The underlying model of the client–consultant relationship is, therefore, in practice much more complex than either side usually acknowledges. Rather than a symbiotic relationship, it is more like a machine where the operational wheels on the cogs do not quite match. The problem is not particularly noticeable when the machine is running fairly slowly, but as it speeds up, that mismatch will become more visible. As clients demand more, and as consultants, in trying to meet these increasing demands, create new demands as quickly as they satisfy existing demands, client satisfaction is going to be much more difficult to achieve.

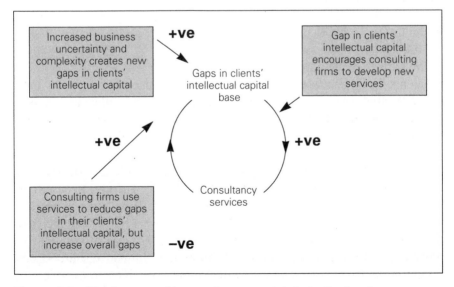

Figure 2.2 The impact of increasing uncertainty in the business environment

Of course, one possible result is that the consultancy bubble could simply burst – that the client–consultant relationship, faced with chronic pressure, breaks down completely, perhaps in a series of catastrophic lawsuits. Alternatively, the incremental weight of evidence to suggest that consultancies do not add value to their clients could be sufficient to tip the balance and make clients revert to using in-house resources for at least some initiatives. The consulting industry could disappear just as quickly as it appeared.

But it seems unlikely that this will be the case: our reliance on consultants – particularly in Anglo-Saxon economies – is now so ingrained that it is difficult to believe that our attitude could change so very quickly. Moreover, we are still unaccustomed to thinking of consultancy *en masse*: as clients and consultants, we tend to think about the issues raised on an assignment-by-assignment basis. Neither consultants nor clients particularly exchange experiences or compare notes. Unlike accountancy or the legal profession, there is no forum in which individual experiences are regularly brought together and analysed.

A more plausible scenario would therefore be that we continue in this cycle. Consultancies will try to fill gaps in clients' intellectual capital which cannot, ultimately, be filled. The faster the consultants put their fingers in the intellectual capital dyke, the more will water start to seep through in other areas. And, because the cycle reinforces itself, what we may find in the future is that:

- the time in which consultants are expected to provide a solution will shrink;
- the gaps they are supposed to fill will grow;
- clients will become harder to satisfy because the gaps in their intellectual capital continue to grow despite the consultancies' input;
- but, despite this dissatisfaction, clients will continue to want consultants to fill the gaps they perceive they have in their intellectual capital.

This is perhaps the essential problem for the consulting industry over the next decade: while clients will continue to buy – even increase their purchase of – consultancy, the client–consultant relationship will become harder to sustain. It also raises significant challenges for consultancies in the future, in terms of their market positioning, sources of competitive advantage, innovation and service development, human resources, and organisational structure. The following chapter provides an overview of the key implications.

Notes

1. There was a recession in the consulting industry in 1970–4 , but its impact was much less noticeable.
2. *Financial Times*, 17 June 1997.
3. Eileen C Shapiro, *Fad Surfing in the Boardroom: Managing in the Age of Instant Answers*, Reading, MA: Addison-Wesley, 1996, p. 211.
4. Warner Woodnorth and Reed Nelson, 'Witch Doctors, Messianics, Sorcerers, and OD Consultants: Parallels and Paradigms', *Organizational Dynamics*, Autumn, 1979, p. 17.
5. John Gill and Sue Whittle, 'Management by Panacea: Accounting for Transcience', *Journal of Management Studies*, 30:2, 1993, p. 288.
6. John Brandon, 'Where Consultants Fall Down', *Management Today*, May, 1988, pp. 112–19.

3

Consultancy in the Next Decade? An Overview

What are the implications of changing client needs?

In the preceding chapter, we looked at how clients' expectations from consultants may grow in the future – in terms of speed and scope, as much as scale. Such pressure will pose a significant challenge to the consulting industry: as the 'machine' starts to operate more quickly, there is a danger that consulting firms will be unable to satisfy the demands being made on them without significant changes to the way in which they work.

Before analysing the detailed implications for consulting firms, we need first to understand at a high level how this core trend – the increased, ultimately unserviceable, demand for new intellectual capital – will make itself felt across the consulting industry as a whole.

The time in which consultants are expected to provide a solution will shrink

Consultancy 'time' has mushroomed since the mid-1980s: the average assignment has got longer; consulting firms are spending more time and resources nurturing what they hope will be long-standing relationships with major clients.

There are two factors which are driving this trend:

● The first factor is external to the consulting industry. The past ten years have seen a massive shift in the consulting world towards delivering technology-related services; technology has provided much of the impetus behind the industry's growth. Technology-related projects, especially where they involve implementation, can be very long (the scope and therefore duration of SAP assignments being a particularly clear example of this).

- The second factor is internal. As we noted in the introduction, consultancy since the 1991–2 recession has been characterised by a shift from advising to doing: and 'doing' takes longer than advising. What the recession brought home to many consultancy firms was the need to have a smaller number of big projects, rather than a large volume of much smaller ones. Consultancies have therefore seen it to be in their long-term, as well as short-term, interests to expand the scope of new assignments where possible. Having a long order-book (something which consultancies have historically found it difficult to do) has become a priority.

But technology, and clients' expectations, are changing. Where once a company would have spent considerable in-house time on developing their own tailor-made software, most accept that they can buy a ready-made package from a professional software house. Although many companies are still in the grip of major software implementations, our attitudes are changing. Ten years ago we believed that we should adapt software to match our internal processes: nowadays we accept that it is probably quicker, cheaper, and ultimately more effective to adapt our processes to a given package. We want faster results – because the organisations we work for want faster results. We want to fill the gap in our intellectual capital, tick the task off as 'done' and move on to the next issue as quickly as possible.

In terms of the client–consultant relationship, this means that clients' demands are likely to become much more polarised. The need for tangible results means that there will continue to be, as now, a market for very large-scale consulting assignments, where the distinction between 'advising' and 'doing' is increasingly blurred. But, at the other end of the spectrum, we will probably also see a distinct shift towards shorter, more discrete assignments which focus on a specific problem/solution, a trend that will put consultants under intense pressure to provide a service which can solve all the client's issues within a fairly short space of time. And because these assignments will be equivalent to waving a magic wand, clients will expect the solution offered to be both new and visibly innovative. This is 'Holy Grail' consulting – the belief (on both the consultants' and the clients' side) that there is a fast and comparatively simple solution to what may in reality be a very complex problem. The consultancies with the most innovative idea which promises the fastest results will win the work. Clearly, some segments of the consulting market will be more resistant to this than others: it is difficult, for example, to see how strategic consulting in particular, where the value to clients is derived from creating a solution to a unique set of circumstances, could be replaced by predetermined ideas. At the same time, for the sectors of consultancy where *having* a solution takes precedence over *developing* a solution in the client's eyes, this trend poses a significant threat.

This growth of this type of consultancy clearly has ramifications for the way in which consultants work with clients: working with someone, or 'in partnership' with them, takes time. The whole idea of process consulting takes time. As clients focus increasingly on obtaining a fast return, it seems likely that many consulting firms will be forced to shift away from process and back towards analytical consulting. It also has two major implications for the way in which consultants work with each other:

- First, in order to be able to produce a stream of new ideas, within increasingly tight timescales, consulting firms will have to become immensely efficient at knowledge-sharing. Already, most of the large firms (for whom, given their number of staff and geographical dispersion, knowledge-sharing is a much more significant issue than it is for a very small company) have made considerable investment in the networks and systems needed to facilitate the flow of ideas around their respective organisation. But a knowledge-sharing culture has not come easily, especially in organisations – and partnerships are good examples of this – where knowledge has been synonymous with power. One solution has been to develop an infrastructure which sits above any local divisions: hence the attraction of the idea of a global firm – internally as well as externally. But in an environment where clients' patience is declining, globalisation probably represent only one part – the long-term part – of the solution. As a result, it seems probable that consulting firms will have to explore other options which generate new ideas rapidly, either by diversifying (effectively acquiring new intellectual capital) or by creating networks of themselves with other complementary consultancies.
- Second, the emphasis on knowledge and analysis, rather than process, seems likely to change the skills required to be a consultant and, indeed, the role of the consultant within the consultancy process. To firms who have prided themselves on being 'people' companies, this may seem like sacrilege. But you only have to scan what is available today on the Internet to appreciate the extent to which information (management theories, models, and so on), which used to be the almost exclusive concern of consultants, can now be directly accessed by clients. ERNIE,

the Ernst & Young Web-based subscription service, allows users to access 'packages' of the firm's intellectual capital in their own terms and own time, and they do so without interfacing with actual consultants. Some types of consultancy are, after all, only an intermediary between clients and the intellectual capital they require, and it seems unlikely that it will be exempt from the process of dis-intermediation – the removal of the middle man – which is already prevalent in sectors like insurance. Consultancy can be hugely expensive: if clients have the option to take a cheaper (and quicker) route, it seems likely that many will opt to do so. In this scenario, the consultant's role will change: rather than be a facilitator or project manager, they will become knowledge-gatherers, responsible for codifying intellectual capital for future sale.

The client–consultant relationship will become more difficult to sustain because the gaps in clients' intellectual capital will put consulting firms under intense pressure

The fact that clients are likely to want simpler solutions with innovative content and fast results does not mean that they are going to narrow the scope of what they ask their consultants to do or lower the demands they make. In other words, as general business uncertainty increases, the 'gap' which clients want consultants to fill will be bigger. This will translate itself – as it has already started to do – into the application of hard business measurements to consultancy assignments: consultants will be asked to 'improve profits' or 'increase sales', rather than deliver a report or implement a system. This trend will drive a further change – again, one which is already observable – in which consultants have to 'do' more and 'advise' less, simply in order to achieve the goals set by their clients. This pressure will clearly conflict with the probable move away from process consulting: a tension that means that, although consultants will do more, they will actually spend less time transferring knowledge or trying to get organisational buy-in for their ideas. In other words, consultants will start to become managers of, rather than assistants to, a client's staff. It follows that the distinction between client and consultant will not only start to disappear, but that it will become irrelevant to most clients. Clients will want the job done, and will become increasingly uninterested in who is actually doing it. Consultancy and outsourcing will become indistinguishable.

Client dissatisfaction looks set to grow – fuelled partly by the economic model of consultancy described above, but also by the growing sophistication and expectations of consultancy buyers. The blurring distinction between client and consultant will also mean that the former will no longer hold the latter in awe (something, which despite denials, generally remains true today).

In practical terms, it is likely that client loyalty will decline. There is already evidence that the largest clients are 'cherry-picking' consultants, based on the specific requirements of a particular assignment, a process which has played a significant role in opening up the market to small, specialist consultancies and freelance consultants. In the future, it seems probable that this same mindset will be adopted by medium-sized clients – those who currently still seem to prefer the 'one-stop' approach to buying consultancy.

From the perspective of the consulting firms, this has four significant implications:

- It means that assignments are likely to involve a combination of consulting firms, with each being picked as a specialist in a particular area. Consortia bids for work are therefore likely to become much more common.
- In an effort to retain some degree of loyalty, consulting firms will explore different incentive programmes. These may range from the corporate (tiered access to specialist seminars and suchlike for long-standing or high-spending clients) to the personal (offering partnerships to departmental heads who outsource their function to the consulting firm). Who knows, they may even start offering air miles.
- The third implication is that the consulting firms will need to differentiate themselves from their rivals much more effectively than at present. Currently, the consulting marketing is highly homogeneous (how else could mega-mergers even be contemplated?), with all the major firms offering what are effectively the same services to the same client base. Only the smaller, niche firms have a clear positioning in the market. But if clients are to buy consultancy on a much more 'cherry-picking' basis, it will become essential for each firm to set out its particular strengths.
- Fourthly and finally – and perhaps most importantly – a combination of enforced co-operation on assignments and the pressure to differentiate will mean that consultancies are more likely to form complementary alliances between themselves (initially between the biggest and smallest firms, but increasingly between at least parts of the bigger firms). The result will be the emergence of consultancy eco-systems – self-supporting networks of consulting firms, aimed at meeting specific client needs.

Being dissatisfied will not, however, stop clients feeling that they should call in consultants. Rather the growing pressure of environmental uncertainty, and a habit of mind which presupposes that there are certain skills which a business does not have internally, will mean that clients become increasingly dependent on consultancy input. Furthermore, by setting their consultants ever more material performance goals, clients will implicitly be off-loading even more of their problems onto their nominal advisers. By asking a consulting firm to increase sales, for example, there will be a temptation for the client to shift significant business responsibility to the consulting firm. This is, after all, what happens every time a company hires consultants at the moment: the difference is one of degree only.

An implication of this is that, while clients become less loyal to consultants, they will expect their consultants to be more loyal to them (a function of the paranoia usually closely linked to dependence). Consultancies may therefore find themselves excluded from working with particular companies or in particular sectors, and certainly less free to transfer a service delivered to one client to another.

An overview of the consulting market in the future

Bringing all these detailed implications together, we can start to develop a picture of how the overall consulting market is likely to look in the next decade, to supersede the model which most of us have about the market at present (Figure 3.1).

The key driver of demand for consultancy services is the gap clients perceive in their intellectual capital (however this is translated in practical terms). These perceived gaps are being constantly increased by:

- the uncertainty of the business environment in which most of them operate; and
- the complexity of those environments – something which is largely driven by the volume of new management ideas available to companies, ideas which only become available because consulting firms promote them from sector to sector.

There are three major characteristics of the increased demand for consultancy:

- clients will want innovative thinking;
- but they will not want to have to wait years before that innovative solution has an impact; and

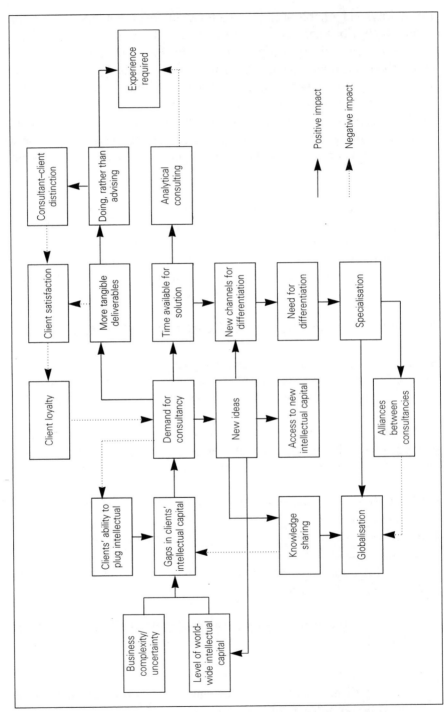

Figure 3.1   The dynamics of the future consulting industry

- they want to set more ambitious and more tangible goals for their consultants.

An immediate impact will be the continued rise in client dissatisfaction, as clients develop greater – and more measurable – expectations which they give their consultants increasingly little time to achieve. A less direct impact is that clients will – even more than they do at present – be subscribing to an attitude which says that they do not (cannot) have the intellectual capital that consultants bring them. By doing so, clients will be increasing, rather than decreasing, their dependence on consultants.

For the consulting firms, the implications are enormous.

The pressure to produce innovative thinking will, as noted above, mean that knowledge-sharing becomes perhaps the crucial internal function of a consultancy. And, where internal knowledge-sharing does not generate a sufficient number of new ideas to meet client needs, then it seems inevitable that consulting firms will look at ways of acquiring this capital externally, either through global integration of their member firms or, increasingly, by diversifying through acquisition. The moves by the biggest consulting firms to buy legal and PR firms would appear to be an early symptom of this trend. The reduced attention span on the part of clients will mean that consulting firms have to find faster ways of developing and delivering solutions, something which is likely to lead to the resurgence of analytical consultancy (as opposed to process consultancy), but also to more emphasis on doing, rather than advising. As, to an extent, these two trends are contradictory, the future model of consulting work may well turn out to be one in which the consulting firms develop (analytical) solutions off-site and then take responsibility for implementing them: the opportunity – or indeed, incentive – for knowledge transfer will be considerably reduced. Consultants will not simply start to 'do' more: they will be telling clients' staff what to do. This tendency will be exacerbated by the greater demands for results being made by clients.

There are two, less direct impacts to these trends. The first is that reduced 'time to solution' and the greater emphasis on analytical consulting will mean that consulting firms will start to explore new, faster (and lower cost) channels to their clients. The second is that, as the consultants do more, and advise less, the distinction between them and their clients – between insider and outsider – becomes less clear. Given that one of the main reasons for purchasing consultants (at the moment and in the future) is that they are outsiders who can bring fresh and objective intellectual capital to their clients, the blurring of the client–

consultant distinction seems likely to contribute further to clients' growing dissatisfaction.

Increasing dissatisfaction will, inevitably, rebound on the consultancies themselves and on the demand for consultancy services. However, rather than immediately translating into reduced demand, dissatisfaction is more likely to lead to reduced client loyalty, as clients seek out the specialist consultants who fit their precise needs. For the consulting firms, this will mean having to work with their sometime competitors on the same assignments. It will also force these firms to promote their specialist intellectual capital more clearly and invest in it more heavily.

Factors which are likely to dampen demand are the lack of division between consultants and their clients ('If they're the same as us, why should we hire them?') and, perhaps most importantly, the emergence of new channels (such as the Internet) which may make some aspects of the conventional consulting process redundant. But consultants should not be too worried: offset against this is the growing uncertainty and complexity of the business environment which means that, however effectively and quickly clients try to fill the gaps in their intellectual capital, new gaps open up daily.

Many of the seeds of this model are already apparent: the embryonic use of the Internet; the investment in knowledge-sharing; the increasing number of disputes with clients. But there are two ways in which this future will feel fundamentally different from the present. The first is a simple question of degree. Although we may see early signs of many of these trends, they will become considerably more material in the future: clients' patience will be noticeably thinner; the pressure to innovate will be much more intense. The second is a much more significant issue, and one which follows on as a direct result of the overall increase in pace. Most of the arrows in Figure 3.1 indicate that the factor to which they relate has a positive impact on another factor. Thus, clients' increasing unwillingness to wait for results means that the emphasis on analytical consulting will increase. However, there are some factors where the impact is negative, and these flow back into the overall model causing tension and conflict. In summary, these are:

- As the demands clients make on their consultants grow, satisfaction will fall; in anything other than a knowledge-based market, this would dampen demand. But, as the more clients use consultants, the less equipped they are to survive without them, demand will, in fact, go up – even in the face of growing dissatisfaction. The client–consultant relationship, which is already under some strain, will become much more volatile and unpredictable.

- Dissatisfaction will inevitably have a knock-on effect on client loyalty, with clients increasingly likely to pick and choose consultants on a much more precise basis. By forcing consultancies to differentiate themselves and specialise more than has hitherto been the case, the role of an 'umbrella' firm will be significantly weakened. Networks of smaller firms and individuals may provide a more sustainable operating structure in this new environment. But, at the same time, the pressure to share knowledge more effectively will be just one impetus towards globalisation and mergers. The mega-firm will be born at a time when its whole rationale has been significantly weakened.

- Having to bring new ideas to clients ever more quickly will mean that consultancies are increasingly forced to explore new ways of capturing and delivering their intellectual capital. But in the process of doing this, it seems likely that they will be cannibalising their own product: as consulting know-how becomes available from other sources (for example, incorporated into software), the incentive for clients to consult the originators will decline.

- The dual shift towards analytical consulting and doing will pose serious problems for consulting firms in terms of people management, with activities potentially being polarised between the two different – potentially contradictory – approaches.

It is the ability to handle these tensions which will separate the winners from the losers over the next ten years.

The following chapters of this book look at the implications of this model for consultancies in much greater detail, taking each of the factors identified:

- *Innovation.* Consultants have a poor image when it comes to innovation (remember that joke about a consultant being someone who takes your watch and tells you what time it is?). How will consulting firms ensure that they are capable of supplying the continuous stream of new ideas clients will be demanding?

- *Knowledge-sharing.* This is not something traditional partnerships were designed to do and the experience so far is that they have not proved particularly adept at making the transition to the brave new world in which information is open and accessible to all. How will the successful consultancy of the future be making best use of its corporate knowledge?

- *Access to new intellectual capital.* Convergence between sectors looks set to be one of the driving forces in business over the next two decades.

Consultancy will be no different, as firms supplement their attempts to develop new ideas and share knowledge on an internal basis. What areas should consulting firms consider diversifying into? And what are the opportunities and threats involved in doing so?

- *Alliances.* As clients' needs become more specific and fast-moving, and as intellectual capital becomes more specialised, consulting firms will have to forge alliances (with other consultancies, and with non-consultancies) in order to survive. Who is already allied to whom? How and why should this change in the future? What impact will alliances have on the firms on the outside?

- *Differentiation.* If clients are going to 'cherry-pick' their consultants with greater precision, promoting the differences between firms is going to become a strategic imperative. The consultancy market is notoriously homogeneous: how are consultancies going to grapple with this issue? What are the risks in not doing so?

- *Specialisation.* Hand in hand with the notion of promoting specialisms comes the idea of developing them. How should consultancies be looking to change the way they recruit and develop their staff? What are the implications of employing highly specialised individuals? Will there be any role for the generalist in the future? And what are the ramifications for the structure of consulting firms – if clients are buying an individual expert, what role does the organisation have?

- *Globalisation.* It is the biggest trend of the late 1990s, and one of the main pressures for 'mega-mergers'. But what will a 'global firm' really look like in practice, if we think ahead? Which approach to globalisation will have won out? And will it really matter?

- *New channels.* The Internet and other forms of networked intellectual capital probably pose a significant threat to at least parts of the consulting industry over the next 20 years. What form will this threat take, and how should consultants respond?

- *Experience versus brainpower.* In his typology of client work,[1] David Maister proposes: 'brains' (whose strap-line is 'hire us because we're smart'), 'grey hair' ('hire us because we have been through this before; we have practice at solving this type of problem'), and 'procedure' ('hire us because we know how to do this and can deliver it effectively'). Analytical consulting will push firms towards the 'brains' end of the scale, but doing so will make them need more of the 'procedure': what they will not need is the 'grey hair' – the people who, at the moment, contribute a significant proportion of revenues. The implications of this are enormous at all levels – on consultants themselves and on the firms which have to manage successfully the transition to this new operational environment. How will the industry cope with the change? What will be the critical success factors in this very different future?

- *Analytical consulting.* Approaches to consulting have always swung between process and analytical consulting. Since the mid-1980s, the stress has firmly been on process consulting and this is one of the factors which has led to significantly larger assignments. But will clients' desire for an innovative and fast solution mean that the pendulum swings back – perhaps decisively – in the other direction? If so, what are the implications of this for firms which have focused almost exclusively on the process side? What impact will it have on niche consultancies, who have historically been more analytically inclined?

- *Doing rather than advising.* When we say that clients are going to do more and advise less, what does this mean in practice? What kind of things will consultants be doing, and how will they manage and control the process? The division between clients and consultants has not just been one of the essential rationales for hiring the latter, it also underpins many of our views about the ethics of this as-yet-unregulated industry. In what way is the client–consultant relationship likely to change, and what are the implications of this change?

Notes

1. David Maister, *Managing the Professional Service Firm*, New York: Free Press, 1993, pp. 4–5.

4 Innovation: The Over-production of Truth?

Ideas can be dangerous

Even practising consultants admit that it is some time since their industry has been seen as a hotbed of innovation.

Clearly, there are always exceptions that prove the rule. The strategic consultancies retain a reputation for innovative thinking, and one which they increasingly promote through articles and books, and specialist consultancies may also have a good reputation in their chosen fields. But by and large, the words 'consultancy' and 'innovation' do not often appear in the same sentence together. As the *Financial Times* commented, the consulting industry should be asking itself

> why so few eminent 'thinkers' … have emerged from the high powered firms in recent years. Consultants may be too busy with the nitty gritty to produce the 'big ideas', yet they have largely ceded the 'guru' field to business school academics, many of them with little hands-on experience.[1]

As this comment implies, the problem for consulting firms has been an economic one. The consulting industry is predicated on the fact that intellectual capital is a transferable commodity: that an assignment for one client yields commercially viable ideas, skills or processes which can be reapplied to another, even in a different sector. Without this ability to extrapolate experience or process from one company to another, from one sector to another, consultants would have nothing to sell. Moreover, because they would effectively be starting afresh with every assignment, they would have to charge clients the earth for selling it. What many of the more operationally focused consultancies excel at is in transferring 'formal' knowledge – that is, knowledge which has been codified as the result of previous assignments – from client to client. But this type of knowledge is not the same as creative thinking. As the academic, Mats Alvesson, has pointed out in relation to the consulting profession:

> creativity stands in an ambiguous relation to formal knowledge. One could argue that pure knowledge and creativity to some extent are contradictory.[2]

In fact, consulting firms have probably spent more management time and effort worrying about 'reinventing the wheel' than they have about being innovative, because the former has a direct impact on the profitability of the firm. Consulting firms make money because they reapply their learning – and the more often they reapply it, the more money they earn – not from being innovative.

Moreover, as the market for very large-scale consulting assignments has grown over the past ten years, the temptation to be innovative has receded further. To win and, indeed, deliver large assignments – almost all of which are implementation-focused – consulting firms have to have a track record in carrying out the complex tasks involved. Large-scale assignments are all about doing well what you have already done before: in this context, innovation is not so much irrelevant as a positive danger.

In many large and medium-sized consulting assignments, the innovative elements are confined to 'visioning workshops' and are separate from the process of doing that has to be tried and tested. But this often means that the balance of the assignment is tipped in favour of the process, rather than the content of what is being done. It is therefore hardly surprising that consultancies have tended to position themselves as experts in one or other of these roles – a distinction which has been mirrored by a tendency among clients to split the two roles, bringing in different consultants for each role.

All this works – and will continue to work – while clients continue to make this distinction; while they continue – implicitly at least – to believe that innovation and implementation are mutually exclusive, and while they accept that much of the consultancy done to them has been done to others before them. But it breaks down when clients start to blur the distinction, when they demand: first, innovative solutions which involve doing as much as thinking; and, second, implementation solutions which are also innovative in their approach. This blurring is – as we noted in the previous chapter – already becoming apparent, driven by growing demand from clients that consultancy should yield tangible benefits. As a result, clients in the future are likely to want innovative consulting services (on the grounds that past services will often be perceived to have failed to deliver the necessary goods) but services which are sufficiently concrete that they can still be sure they are worth buying. Of course, some clients will continue to buy innovative thinking; of course, others will want to buy implementation skills where the emphasis is on tried and tested approaches, not radical new ideas. But many clients will want to have their cake and eat it – to combine newness with increased certainty of success. Moreover, the increasing rapidity with which management ideas appear and disappear will also mean that one such idea is not enough – clients will want and expect a constant stream of such ideas. Ironically, this attitude of mind is being fuelled by consulting firms themselves – 'ironically' because it will call into question some of the most fundamental operating and marketing tenets of the consulting industry. To quote the *Financial Times* again:

> Ask a consultant on either side of the Atlantic what the hot topics are in the profession today, and before long innovation will come up. It will sometimes be bracketed with strategy, sometimes with change management. The general thesis is the same: that after a decade of concentrating on efficiency, companies now find it hard to come up with new ideas to expand their business.[3]

For consulting firms, this future environment holds two immediate challenges: the speed and effectiveness with which they can generate new ideas, and their ability to convert these ideas into concrete 'products' which answer clients' need for greater guarantee of success.

However, a third challenge arises as the result of these first two. Traditional consulting has delivered highly tailored services with minimal efficiency – the modern equivalent of an eighteenth-century craftsman producing a Chippendale chair. The quality is usually high, but the process of producing it is slow because the skills involved cannot be automated. Prior to the increased competition of the late 1980s, efficiency was not an issue, due to the high fees which consultants were able to charge. As competitive pressures have grown, the established consulting firms have all made efforts to increase efficiency, with varying degrees of success; overall, however, the nature of consulting has made it difficult for consulting services to be mass-produced. The antithesis of this is the software industry. Once the initial – and considerable – investment has been made in developing the software, the final product can be mass-produced in almost no time and at almost no cost. Yet consultants and software packages effectively fulfil the same function, although they do it by very different means. They both allow clients/users to do things that they could not otherwise have done, by filling gaps in their intellectual capital. Consultants do this by bring new ideas and skills to bear on their clients' problems; software, by providing tools (and – with CD-ROM databases and the Internet – increasingly knowledge) to which their users would not otherwise have access. From this perspective, software poses one of the biggest threats to traditional consultancy in the future. In fact, software's erosion of conventional consulting markets can already be seen in the tax advisory market. A decade ago, clients might have called in a tax adviser to help out with the tax computation, a function now performed by tax software packages. Tax consulting has, as a result, moved further up the advisory food-chain – offering increasingly strategic tax planning ideas – but software continues to snap at its heels in the form of increasingly sophisticated tax management tools. How long can the tax consultant manage to stay ahead?

It is comparatively easy for software manufacturers to encroach on tax advisory work because the latter is already neatly 'packaged' for consumption, if only because it has to be directed towards certain common problems. Because it is 'pre-packaged', the process of converting the tax consultant's intellectual capital into a series of rules, and thence into a computer program, can be very fast. By contrast, management consultancy, precisely because it is conventionally tailored to individual client needs, has been more difficult to codify. But, in a world in which consulting firms are trying to produce many more ideas and to convert them into tangible 'products' from a client's perspective, the division between management consultancy and software will be less clear-cut. As consulting firms produce more 'products', so will they provide software companies with the starting point of a new software package. Once again, there is some evidence that this is already happening to a limited extent. A few years ago, you might have sent your staff on a time management course (perhaps you still do), but many of the skills taught on these courses are now embodied in time management packages. It seems likely that, if a technique like business process re-engineering were to be invented in ten years' time (and, undoubtedly, something along these lines will be), then at least part of the consulting service – perhaps even all of it – will be based around a software package.

Given client demands for more, and more concrete consulting services, it seems inevitable that the distinction between consultancy advice and software will be less clear. Software, after all, offers consulting firms the solution to both problems – speed and tangibility. However, it also poses a considerable threat. If all consultancies are going to do in the future is churn out new, packaged ideas, how long will it take for them to be perceived to be commodity producers, much like software manufacturers? This is the Catch-22 of clients' simultaneous demands for speed and

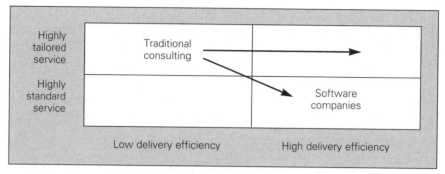

Figure 4.1 Two evolutionary paths for the consulting industry

tangibility. In an ideal world, consultants need to move from producing tailored but inefficient services – the Chippendale chair-maker – to producing tailored but efficient services (see Figure 4.1). The danger is that they will not be able to make the move from inefficiency to efficiency, without also moving from a tailored product to a standardised product – the software manufacturer. But, if their clients want to have their cake and eat it, consulting firms are going to *need* to square this particular circle.

Generating more ideas more quickly

Innovation – as we noted above – has never been consultancy's strong point:

> Management consultants like to portray themselves as anonymous aides-de-camp devising winning strategies for the generals of free enterprise in the war of the bottom line. They wrap their products in elegant brochures, erudite book jackets, or the colourful pages of the *Harvard Business Review*. But strip away the pontificating prose and ubiquitous graphics and a simple formula for the successful consultant remains. Devise an idea, repackage it, give it a catchy name, then sell the something in a new wrapper to another client. Few would like to admit it, but that is what the consultancy business is all about.[4]

But, faced with an environment in which clients are considerably more hungry for ideas – and, given past bitter experience – more cynical about many of the consulting ideas which pose as 'new' – consulting firms will have to do more than relabel the contents of their existing wine-cellars. The hunt for new ideas will be on – and on a serious scale.

There are two strategic options available: consulting firms can either become more innovative internally, or they can purchase their innovation externally.

The majority of consulting firms – large and small – have historically adopted the former approach, either by setting up specific 'R&D' groups or by trying to engender a creative environment. The 'skunk group' approach has the advantage that it allows people the opportunity to think creatively, without also having to worry about maintaining billable hours. It also allows the consulting firm to ring-fence the creative activity so that it does not interfere with its mainstream operations – delivering formalised knowledge to clients. But a knock-on effect is to make it difficult to integrate any of the creative thinking back into the mainstream practice: in other words, being innovative remains at best a marginal activity. Developing a creative environment might resolve this issue – although it might also, for that reason, pose a threat to the profitability of the consultancy. If everyone is going around creating new ideas, then who is responsible for bringing in any sustainable profits? Moreover, 'being creative' as a strategy may work effectively for smaller consultancies, whose organisation is probably more flexible and who are culturally happier to take risks, but it may well be impossible for the larger, more established firms, most of whose culture is built around successful – low-risk – approaches to delivery.

Faced with obstacles to generating ideas internally, it seems likely that some consulting firms in the future will turn to the second option – acquiring new ideas externally. This is, after all, just a more extreme and visible version of what happens already. Consulting firms complain a great deal about the lack of potential recruits for their industry, a problem caused as much by their high staff turnover rates (often up to 25 per cent per year) as it is by changes in demographics or educational standards. New recruits are currently the means by which consulting firms acquire new intellectual capital. With the shift – in most firms – away from graduate recruitment, consultancies are increasingly looking for people who have skills, experience and ideas; who can demonstrate the implementation of ideas in their organisations. Once the recruit has joined, his or her ideas are incorporated into proposals and assignments, gradually being subsumed into – and also refreshing – the collective intellectual capital of the firm. However, this strategy has its weaknesses. First, consultancy companies are running out of new recruits (an issue which is covered in more detail later); thus, the conventional well of ideas is beginning to run dry. Second, even if a consulting firm could recruit all the people that it needed (to carry out billable work), then this might not meet its requirements for new ideas. If it recruited enough people to supply the ideas it wanted, then the firm might well end up with more people than it could actually occupy on billable work.

The answer to this dilemma – although it goes against the grain of much consultancy thinking – will be to divorce the idea from the person. Thus, rather than recruit a person to get an idea, the consulting firm will simply buy the idea and sell it to clients, probably in the meantime hiring someone else to deliver the idea. This distinction between idea and person has several advantages. Clearly, it means that the consulting firm is not burdened with an additional member of staff, whose skills as a consultant may be limited. But, more importantly, it also allows the consulting firm to maintain the distinction between creativity and delivery on which much of its internal operations and profitability is dependent.

Indeed, the seeds of this trend are already apparent. The links between business schools and consultancies are becoming closer and more numerous. It also seems likely that consulting firms will hire management gurus as associate partners. Ironically, they will be outsourcing the development of their intellectual capital to academics and specialists, just as many clients have already outsourced the development of their intellectual capital to consultancies. To meet clients' needs to have more new ideas, consultancies will, in effect, be setting up back-to-back agreements with their suppliers of intellectual capital, ones which guarantee a certain number of ideas, probably at a pre-specified price and delivered at a specified time (because one of the problems consultancies have encountered with internal innovation is that its costs and delivery dates are notoriously uncertain). Although such 'contracts' will essentially be invisible from the client's viewpoint, the role of the consultant will have changed from being a manufacturer of new ideas, to an intermediary – a conduit of ideas to their clients – reliant on other companies, institutions or individuals finding and supplying them with those ideas. At the moment, most consulting firms head-hunt for new recruits: in the future, they look set to head-hunt for the best ideas (Figure 4.2).

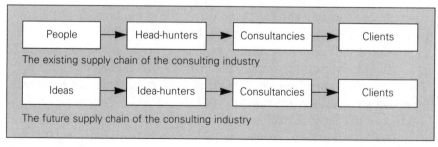

Figure 4.2 The existing and future supply chains in the consulting industry

Converting ideas into consulting products

However, having access to a constant flow of ideas only solves half of the consultancies' problem: the other issue is to ensure that these ideas appear concrete and capable of delivering results in their clients' eyes. Of course, neither of these idea-attributes can be measured objectively: substance is, like beauty, in the eye of the beholder.

The clearest way to understand what is likely to constitute substance is to look at an example of a 'substantial' product in the past. Business process re-engineering was launched in the early 1990s, initially on the back of a seminal article by Michael Hammer in the *Harvard Business Review* and subsequently through Hammer's book with James Champy,[5] published in 1993. Its spread was rapid and spectacular: a 1993 survey in the UK estimated that 21 out of the FT100 companies were already engaged in re-engineering projects.[6] But, as for almost any successful product, there has been a significant backlash over the past few years for a variety of reasons. While some clients credit BPR with significant improvements to their efficiency, for many others, the promise of BPR has failed to materialise in practice. Moreover, the focus of business since the 1991–2 recession has switched away from cost reduction to demand creation, leaving BPR behind. Whatever its current state, the lessons of BPR for consulting firms are considerable. It was bought by hundreds of clients, for millions of dollars, for two principal reasons. First, BPR had a definite methodology which was *sufficiently* different to other services (there has been a long-running and ultimately irrelevant debate about whether BPR was actually *new*) to acquire a distinct hold in clients' minds. There were techniques, tools, diagrams – all of which contributed to a feeling of substance. Second, perhaps more than any other management technique in the past 20 years, BPR had a public – even popular – profile. By reading about BPR in the same way that they read about finance and accounting, clients started to associate the former with the established practices and formal procedures of the latter. Clients could feel they were buying something.

But there were two other factors which contributed strongly, if more indirectly, to the success of BPR – and which apply more generally to all successful consulting 'products'. The first was the emergence of language as a tool which consulting firms could actively use to create an impression of substance; the second was the extent to which BPR touched a raw nerve in the contemporary business world.

Taking language first. More than any other industry, consultancies are blamed for coining new business jargon (and then charging for it), as this comment from *The Daily Telegraph* illustrates:

Just as there is a danger of being hoodwinked by specialist management jargon, so there is the possible hazard of being unjustly deterred when the racket of buzz-words conceals genuine benefit. A classic target for the sceptics might be corporate cultural change. What with its core values, mission statements, workshops and benchmarking, it sounds like classic consultant-speak degraded by psychobabble.[7]

Perhaps the most exciting or terrifying aspect of consultancy – depending on whether you are on the inside or the outside – is the extent to which it is possible to 'make things up': because as yet comparatively little investment is required to translate a project for one client into a methodology for several (although this may change in the future as management consultancy becomes increasingly technology-dependent). This is not to suggest that this 'making things up' is a worthless process – much of the benefit of consultancy work comes from the passing of concepts and ideas from client to client, and from industry to industry – but it does bring home the extent to which consultancy, of all service industries, is the most dependent on language.

Language has always been important in management consultancy, arguably more so than numbers, despite the fact that the majority of the leading consultancies evolved out of accountancy firms. Consultancy was, in effect, the response of those accounting firms to a shift within business from numbers to language which is evidenced by the prevalence of mission statements, business books and so on. Indeed, just as accountants could not exist without numbers, consultancies could not exist without words. When business made those evolutionary steps, in the first place, into standard accounting practices, and from there into language, it was acknowledging that it was possible to think about business in abstract terms. It was recognising that, although every business may be different and may still depend heavily on the skill of the individual who manages it, some parts of its operations are common to all commercial organisations and can be discussed independently of the specifics of the enterprise. If it were not possible to establish standard formulae for profits, or analyse the efficiency of a process (rather than just describe it), then accountancy and consultancy would not exist, as both are founded on this basic principle.

However, consultancies were not simply the beneficiaries of this trend: they also unquestionably contributed to it, by disseminating new ways of doing and thinking, all of which were dependent on language. Consultancy services were language based, not only because that was the nature of the market, but as a matter of survival: if consultancies could not sustain the notion that it was possible to have theories about business – that it was possible to talk about it – then consultancy itself had no future. Consultants have – quite literally – to keep talking.

Let's now look at the second factor – the extent to which BPR touched a specific raw nerve of the business community in the early 1980s. A 1994 study on BPR by a UK academic concluded that a significant factor in its rise was not its (actual or perceived) newness, but the fact that it captured the *zeitgeist* of the time. Just as Frederick Taylor's ideas on scientific management appealed to a society increasingly interested in scientific measurement (the early part of the twentieth century also saw the development of statistics, the theory of IQ, and so on), BPR appealed to the 'American dream', quoting Hammer and Champy:

> The alternative is for corporate America to close its doors and go out of business ... Reengineering isn't another imported idea from Japan ... Reengineering capitalizes on the same characteristics that made Americans such great business innovators: individualism, self-reliance, a willingness to accept risk and a propensity for change. Business Reengineering, unlike management philosophies that would have 'us' like 'them', doesn't try to change the behaviour of American workers and managers. Instead, it takes advantage of American talents and unleashes American ingenuity.[8]

For consultancies today and in the future, the history of BPR teaches that a 'product' is defined in four ways:

- it has perceptible substance to it, notably in the form of a written methodology;
- it is heavily promoted, so that clients are aware that it 'exists' before consultancies try to make them buy it;
- it is articulated through specific language, which gives the product an identity of its own; and
- it is linked – intentionally or otherwise – to wider business and cultural concerns.

At the moment, a consulting product succeeds or fails depending on the extent to which it accidentally exploits one or more of these features. In the future, as clients demand an increasing number of new ideas, each of these four attributes will need to be developed consciously and systematically – something which has significant operational implications for consulting firms, most of which do not, as we noted earlier, have a good track record for innovation on a commercially viable basis.

Avoiding the commoditisation of ideas

However, there is a real danger that the process of consultancies taking an ever-increasing number of ideas to clients devalues the ideas – if there are so many around, how can any of them be any good? Most of us already have a fairly cynical attitude towards new management ideas, living as we do in an environment where the 'velocity of fads' – as one American academic described it[9] – is constantly increasing. Producing too many ideas is potentially as dangerous as producing too few:

> The man of knowledge in our time is bowed under a burden he never imagined he would have, the over-production of truth that cannot be consumed. For centuries man lived in the belief that truth was slim and elusive and that once he found it, the trouble of mankind would be over. And here we are in the closing decades of the twentieth century choking on truth.[10]

How can consulting firms manage this risk? There are two immediate options:

- *Clearer ideas/products hierarchies.* Ideas/products tend to be commoditised where they come individually: a group of a dozen ideas/products looks uninteresting (and low value), but a structure of one or two central ideas, with a series of sub-ideas coming from them – an idea/product hierarchy – looks both significant (it is easy to see what the key messages are) and substantial (the sub-ideas make the overall idea look more concrete). Consultancies will therefore need to take a much more structured view of their intellectual capital. At the moment, this is usually allocated to broad service or sector categories, with little integration between these categories. The past couple of years have seen the emergence of 'meta-services' which do attempt to bring together several services under one heading – Price Waterhouse's focus on shareholder value is a good example – but it will take time to change the habit of many established consultancies' lifetimes, of seeing ideas and services as discrete units, sold and managed separately.
- *Launching collections of ideas/products.* Ideas/products are also devalued where they appear in the marketplace haphazardly. We all like to think that we are sophisticated consumers, uninfluenced by advertising, but the Hollywood blockbuster is evidence enough that there is an association in our minds between significant publicity and 'must-be-seen' films. And the same logic applies to consulting products. Currently, they not only emerge randomly but with little

publicity. If consultancy firms are to recoup the return on their investment in products and establish their dominance in particular niches, systematic and substantial publicity around formal product launches will be a prerequisite. Rather than allowing products to hit the market one by one, consulting firms should be seriously considering launching their products in co-ordinated groups – 'collections' even.

Most consulting firms have already recognised that innovation will be one of the most important drivers of success in the industry over the next decade. But this recognition is only the start: resolving the sourcing of these new ideas and converting them into commercially viable products, without also opening the door to new entrants, poses a far more significant challenge.

Notes

1. *Financial Times*, 12 September 1995.
2. Mats Alvesson, 'Organizations as Rhetoric: Knowledge Intensive Firms and the Struggle with Ambiguity', *Journal of Management Studies*, 30, 1993.
3. *Financial Times*, 19 June 1997.
4. David Maister, *Managing the Professional Services Firm*, New York: Free Press, 1993, pp. 147–8.
5. 'Re-engineering Work: Don't automate; Obliterate', *Harvard Business Review*, July–August, 1980.
6. J. Woudhuysen, 'Engineers of a Fresh Approach', *Marketing*, June, 1993.
7. 19 December 1994.
8. Michael Hammer and James Champy, *Re-engineering the Corporation: A Manifesto for Business Revolution*, London: Nicholas Brearley, 1993, pp. 1–3, quoted in Keith Grint, 'Re-engineering History', *Organization*, 1, p. 194.
9. Richard T. Pascale, *Managing on the Edge*, London: Penguin, 1991, p.19.
10. E. Becker, *The Demise of Death*, New York: Free Press, 1973, p. x, quoted in Andrzej A. Huczynski, 'Explaining the Succession of Management Fads', *The International Journal of Human Resource Management*, 1993, p. 456.

5 Managing Existing Intellectual Capital

The survival of the most knowledgeable

Since the beginning of the 1990s, there is probably no area which has received more attention and investment in consulting firms than knowledge management. If we include the technology which makes knowledge management possible, then the investment runs into hundreds of millions of dollars. There is not a major firm today which does not have a sophisticated infrastructure for sharing its knowledge on a global basis and which does not actively promote this facility when selling its services. Ernst & Young has its Centre for Business Innovation; Booz-Allen & Hamilton, Knowledge On-Line. 'I think there's a big difference today with the major firms', Tom Barron, the Vice-President of Shared Services at Dun & Bradstreet (and an ex-consultant) observes. He notes that:

> the information flow is now technology-based and global. McKinsey knows as much in Tokyo about how they do XYZ-type projects as they do in New York. A decade ago, it was all in the heads of individuals. The only way [a client] ... got good services from Price Waterhouse was for Price Waterhouse to get the right people in a room, find the last ten reports and noodle around. It wasn't very productive for the client.[1]

Several factors have driven this investment: the need to eradicate operational inefficiencies (reinventing the wheel for each assignment); the availability of knowledge management technology; the fact that many clients have been making similar investments; and the need for consulting firms to strengthen their credibility by being able to demonstrate 'codified' knowledge.

It is therefore hardly front-page news to say that knowledge management will continue to be a major issue for the consulting industry in the foreseeable future. However, the factors driving interest in it are likely to change. As we noted previously, clients' growing demand for new ideas and the extent to which many consulting companies (the exceptions being the small number of firms that have a history of, or cultural predisposition towards, innovation) will have to turn to external 'idea-providers' will both mean that effective knowledge management will stay high on the corporate agenda. So too will the increasing pressure from clients to deliver results within shorter and shorter time-frames: having ready access to a body of existing and/or newly created knowledge will clearly be essential to meeting clients' expectations in this area.

But there are two factors which could make the future of knowledge management significantly different to its past, or even its present. First is the idea that the consulting industry is a machine that will be running faster and faster over the next decade, as clients demand more from it, and as the consulting firms have to update their operations in response. Newly installed, still not fully integrated into the assignment delivery process, the process of knowledge management in most firms is likely to come under increasing strain as the cogs of the machine have to turn more and more quickly. For this reason, consulting firms will have to supplement their current approaches to knowledge management with new tactics. The second factor is that knowledge management will become a means – not so much to be a leading player in the consulting market – but to survive.

Let's look at two hypothetical consulting companies. Both companies have knowledge management systems, both are working on similar projects aimed at (for example) cutting the cost of research and development in the pharmaceutical industry. Both draw on previous work in the sector to do this, but Company A does so more efficiently than Company B, allowing it to complete its assignment first. Moreover, Company A is also both more efficient and more effective at taking the output from this assignment and incorporating it in its knowledge management system, making it rapidly available for use with other clients. This means that when the two companies compete next for a similar piece of work, Company A has an advantage – a better body of knowledge to draw on. And each time Company A beats its rival – and it will do this more and more, as its advantage grows – it builds up its base of knowledge, further increasing its chances of continuing to win work in the future. A virtuous circle is created, in which Company A's critical mass of knowledge attracts additional knowledge, thus constantly strengthening Company A's competitive advantage. Ultimately, Company B is pushed out of this particular market. Replicate this across multiple markets, and Company B goes out of business.

Of course, it is this type of doomsday scenario which has driven much of the recent investment in knowledge and knowledge management tools, but it has been rarely true in practice because the services offered by consulting firms have been comparatively heterogeneous and fragmented, making it comparatively difficult for one company to lay claim to one 'area' of knowledge on a sustainable basis. However, a very clear example has been the rise of SAP-related consultancy, where a sizeable and quite distinct market emerged in the early 1990s, from which less successful players have been increasingly excluded.

SAP was the brainchild of four ex-IBM employees, who formed their own company in 1972 to develop their vision of a completely integrated software package capable of handling most business processes, at a time when most business processes were handled by separate systems. The idea of being able to provide all parts of an organisation with a standardised information system and access to the data they need was reinforced by BPR's focus on demolishing internal barriers. In 1997, the company's revenues (up more than 60 per cent) were more than DM 6 billion, with profits of DM 1.67 billion.

But, for clients, SAP comes with a health-warning: the cost.

> Consultants will camp out at your company, installing applications for your special needs, training your people, and working out the bugs in your system … With the consultants' clock ticking, a major, corporation-wide implementation can be staggeringly expensive.[2]

From the perspective of consulting firms, SAP-related consultancy is an object lesson in the importance of establishing early footholds in new knowledge markets as they emerge. As the market for SAP consultancy suddenly burgeoned in the early 1990s, only a minority of consulting firms recognised the potential. Those that did were quick to recruit the few trained SAP consultants available and to win assignments with clients which helped them to build up critical mass, in terms of both numbers of people and intellectual capital. By the time the second wave of entrants had materialised, the first-wave companies had already established a hold on the market which was difficult to break. In an almost textbook example of the idea of 'increasing returns' within the economy,[3] those firms with SAP expertise went from strength to strength, effectively creating knowledge-based barriers to entry, even in a market where demand continues to outstrip supply.

Staking a claim: knowledge ceases to be common land

SAP-related consultancy is also a good illustration of how the growing pressures for vastly improved knowledge management will affect consulting firms. At the moment, it is the exception which proves the rule of a fragmented industry. However, the success of the firms offering SAP services has been such that we are likely to see the model repeated more often in the future. We are already seeing firms 'laying claim' to areas of intellectual capital in an effort to establish an early dominance and keep later entrants at bay. But the SAP model will encourage them to stake out larger and larger territories in the hope of securing medium-term income.

The image of the wild west has been frequently applied to the Internet – anarchic, un-policed and inhabited by prospectors. Perhaps with consultancy, the appropriate analogy would be with Britain just before the industrial revolution. Despite the emergence of very big consulting companies in physical terms (number of employees, fee income, and so on), the services offered remain very fragmented: consultants tend to operate out of small, specialist business units; production – because it is always tailored to the needs of individual clients – is relatively inefficient; the emphasis is on the skills and experience of the individual consultant. But SAP-related consultancy is more of a factory operation. Clearly, each implementation is still customised for clients, but the software itself ensures a degree of uniformity in the implementation process. And uniformity means that people can be trained for the job – the reliance on the specialist skills of individual consultants is much less. SAP is the consultancy market's equivalent to mass-production. Faced with these two models – the small group of jobbing craftsmen against the factory-like scale of SAP implementations – it is not difficult to see the way consulting firms are likely to evolve.

While some 'claims' are already being made, the bulk of the 'land' which makes up the intellectual capital of management remains comparatively uncharted. We associate certain ideas with specific individuals or organisations (for example, we may know that the experience curve was an idea first promoted by the Boston Consulting Group, or we may connect Tom Peters with customer service excellence), but most management theories have tended to be too amorphous and too readily transportable from company to company to allow us to make many such concrete connections.

The challenge for consulting firms in the future will be to change this. There are five main ways in which this will happen: essentially, consulting firms will:

- become much more conscious of their existing intellectual capital and the way in which it (potentially) differentiates them from their competitors;
- spend time and effort in attempting to value their intellectual capital, partly in order to protect it, partly to justify investing in it;
- increasingly use legal means to establish and defend their rights to particular areas of intellectual capital;
- try to secure their position as the putative owners of some areas of intellectual capital by forging alliances with the producers and consumers of that capital; and
- generate public awareness that they 'own' specific intellectual assets.

Taking the first of these, it is probably fair to say that there is no consulting firm in the world today which has a comprehensive understanding of its intellectual assets. For new, small or highly homogeneous companies, there will be an intuitive sense of what these assets are, but for the more diverse, long-standing companies, the gap between what they know they have and what they actually have is immense. In most of this second type of firm, intellectual capital only becomes visible when it is written up as a case study of an assignment or when it is converted into more general application, perhaps in the form of a marketing brochure. This inevitably means that much of a firm's true intellectual capital never gets out of the head of the consultant who thought of it. To combat this problem, many firms have recognised the need to appoint support staff who are responsible for going from consultant to consultant, assignment to assignment, in order to gather and record intellectual capital which could be exploited by other parts of the organisation. This is, however, an essentially bottom-up approach and one which is unlikely to yield 'big' ideas. It is therefore likely that firms in the future will need to carry out top-down audits of their intellectual capital on a more formal basis, just as a decade ago they might have been investing in a registry of physical assets.

But knowing what intellectual assets are available to an organisation will be only half of the issue: equally important will be knowing what these assets are worth. But, for an industry which is fundamentally based around intellectual capital, extraordinarily little thought has been put into the idea of valuing it. To the extent that this issue is recognised at all, it is reflected in the growth projections of individual business units, yet even these fail to recognise the *potential* value of these intellectual assets.

Once a company has been able to assign a value to its intellectual capital, it will be able to understand which areas it needs to protect most.

Historically, litigation over intellectual property in the consulting industry has been comparatively rare, for two principal reasons: first, because the importance of intellectual capital has only been recognised comparatively recently; second, because the nature of consultancy work – ideas – has made it difficult to assert intellectual property rights. Unlike manufacturing goods, management theories and ideas cannot be patented. They can be copyrighted but this has done little to prevent a competitor stealing the idea, changing it fairly cosmetically and then relaunching it.

However, this situation is starting to change, both in terms of the overall legal framework and in the attitude of the consultancies themselves. In 1995, KPMG launched an 'economic value management' (EVM) practice, headed up by three professionals from the company which developed 'economic value added' (EVA), Stern Stewart – a company that KPMG was auditing at the time. The lawsuit, filed by Stern Stewart the following year, alleged that it was more than people who had crossed to KPMG, but that client lists, computer disks and a laptop had also gone. KPMG retaliated by charging Bennett Stewart, Stern Stewart's co-founder and senior partner, with libel and slander. The battle split the consulting industry. On the one side, there was the acceptance that good consulting ideas will inevitably be copied – not always to the detriment of the originating firm. As James Champy, who has watched many other firms copy his business process re-engineering ideas, remarked:

> To try to stop other people from using your ideas is very small-minded. It benefits the firm that's come up with concepts to have them accepted broadly in the market place.[4]

But, on the other side is the growing recognition that consultancies will have to protect the most valuable core of their intellectual capital in the way that manufacturers protect their inventions, or pharmaceutical companies their drugs. A few years ago, you could not patent software, only copyright it; now you can patent it – a change which potentially has immense implications for software developers. Today, it is barely possible to copyright a consulting idea; but how long will it be before we can patent these? Perhaps the intellectual capital market of the future will be a very polarised one, with a large body of existing knowledge being freely available (not least because ownership has become almost impossible to establish), but with small areas (consultancy's equivalent of Microsoft's source code) being fiercely protected.

The marginalisation of informal knowledge

However, this shift towards formalising a consulting firm's existing intellectual capital will have another, unintentional effect. It is inevitable that even the most stringent approach to auditing a firm's intellectual assets will miss some areas of knowledge, especially less formal, less easy to articulate thinking. It is, for example, much easier to record and reuse a methodology for improving a supply chain than it is to explain the process by which an individual consultant helped a client understand their core values and convert these into a meaningful mission statement. This second, more informal intellectual capital tends to have four attributes:

- it involves thinking or work carried out by an individual rather than a large group of people – managing other people is one of the key ways in which knowledge shifts from being informal to formal, from being internal to external;
- it tends to be focused on 'intangible' areas – culture, ideas, behaviour – knowledge is easiest to formalise when it is most closely linked to tangible goods (a supply chain being a particularly clear example);
- it also tends to relate to 'new' areas of business – the more mature the consultancy service, the more likely it is that the thinking around it can be (indeed, probably already has been) 'methodologised'; and
- it relates to a known issue – bringing together a company's intellectual assets which relate to supply chain strategy is comparatively easy because the supply chain is widely recognised to be an important issue to clients; good ideas on an unknown subject are unlikely to be seen as intellectual assets.

Of course, the services that consulting firms offer change continually, so that, over time, the more informal ideas which have these four characteristics gradually evolve into more formal services, carried out by a team of people rather than an individual. Even the most familiar and formalised consulting services, such as business process re-engineering, were young once.

But it is not the fact that the intellectual assets of a consulting firm will be at a different stage in their development cycle which is at issue here. What matters is that, by auditing and establishing ownership of their more formal assets, consulting firms will be creating a much more significant distinction between formal and informal knowledge. By investing in the former, they will effectively be marginalising the latter.

Will this matter? Faced with the alternatives of staking their claim for specific intellectual assets or going under, a consulting firm would probably say that this is a price worth paying. To all intents and purposes – it could be argued – these assets are already marginal as their contribution to fee income is slight, if not invisible.

But we also need to recognise that these informal assets are often the formal assets of the future, and that, if they are totally marginalised, the chances of them surviving the evolutionary process are much lower. By focusing on formal knowledge, it is possible that consulting firms will cut themselves off from their future knowledge base. They will find themselves stuck in an intellectual rut, unable to develop organically because they have not established any process to nurture new and unfamiliar ideas. In other words, effective knowledge management runs the risk of stifling creativity and innovation.

Moreover, consulting firms depend on informal knowledge more than they may care to admit in public. Mats Alvesson, a Swedish academic, has studied the relationship between formal and informal knowledge in consulting firms. Consultants, he argues, like to promote an image of applying formal knowledge and acting rationally in order to minimise the impact of ambiguity in social experience:

> Ambiguity [in the business environment] calls for a well-articulated and persuasive language in order to convince outsiders – and perhaps also insiders – that the [knowledge-intensive workers] have something to offer worth paying (in many cases a lot of money) for and attributing authority to.[5]

According to Alvesson, almost all of the intellectual capital of consulting firms is informal knowledge; formal knowledge is effectively a marketing ploy. To counter both of these issues, consulting companies will need to look more closely at how they foster and protect their informal thinking.

The implications for clients

But if this will be the situation for consulting firms, what are the implications for clients? The consulting industry does not survive on growing intellectual capital, but on transferring it to its clients. What will the impact of this greater division between informal and formal knowledge be on clients?

In June 1997, the *Financial Times* brought together a group of senior executives to discuss the best ways of managing consultants. A constant theme throughout the discussion was the need to ensure that consultants passed on their knowledge to their clients, if the latter were to receive any lasting benefits from the assignment. 'I really believe in the concept of knowledge transfer', said one,

> if I pay to bring [consultants] in, I don't expect them to leave without having transferred their knowledge to my people so that they can move forward.[6]

Asked what they would do to promote knowledge transfer, several stressed the need to 'disengage the external consultants before the project is done', so that in-house people could take over the work. Knowledge transfer has always been associated with good consulting practice:

> Good consultants leave their clients as early as possible to ensure that the client does not become dependent on the consultant. Rather like the doctor or dentist you make the patient well preferably with preventative activities and responsibilities undertaken by the patient himself and then let the patient get on with his life. It is the same with good consultancy.[7]

But how will knowledge transfer work, in an age when ownership has become a serious, even contentious issue?

Already, at least in contractual terms, most consultancies try to protect themselves against clients or competitors making money from their ideas. Effectively, clients are able to use a firm's ideas but they do not own them: the intellectual capital resides with the firm. In practice – as the KPMG/ Stern Stewart dispute illustrates – protection is considerably harder to come by. Because most firms tend to focus on the revenue they will earn from assignments in the short term and because the intellectual capital content of these assignments remains largely uncodified, instances of abuse remain rare. But as these two factors change – as consultants become more aware of the long-term value of their intellectual capital – it seems likely that they will expend more effort trying to regulate the transfer of knowledge to their clients.

It is a dilemma already facing firms that put some of their intellectual capital on the Internet. Even for 'extranets' (where access is restricted to a small number of chosen clients, often on a subscription basis), consulting firms have to find a balance between giving away some know-how –

otherwise, no one would find the site worth visiting – and giving away too much. One solution is to 'trade' intellectual capital. Instead of giving away knowledge for free – or for a nominal charge – consulting firms can ask clients to give back some of their own knowledge. Clients can be asked to register their areas of interest, the major problems they are facing, or the critical business decisions they will be making. All of this information can help the consulting firm target its services much more effectively, sending information to the people most likely to be receptive.

It is, therefore, not just the internal knowledge of consulting firms that will be important in the future. The knowledge those firms have of their clients will also be hugely valuable. We should expect to see complementary firms sharing information they have on their clients. We should also expect that such information will be shared between consulting firms and merchant banks, advertising agencies and other business-to-business organisations, in much the same way that retailers and manufacturers are starting to share information today. Knowledge will not be a monologue, but a series of dialogues between consulting firms and other organisations – something we will explore further in the following chapter.

Notes

1. Interviewed in the *Financial Times*, 16 June 1997.
2. *Fortune*, 2 October 1995.
3. See W Brian Arthur, 'Increasing Returns and the New World of Business', *Harvard Business Review*, July–August, 1996.
4. Quoted in *Fortune*, 18 August 1997.
5. Mats Alvesson, 'Organization as Rhetoric: Knowledge Intensive Firms and the Struggle with Ambiguity', *Journal of Management Studies*, 1993, p. 1013.
6. *Financial Times*, 16 June 1997.
7. Max Eggert and Elaine van der Zeil, *The Perfect Consultant*, London: Arrow Business, 1995, p. 33.

6

No Consultancy Is an Island: Alliances and Networks

Faced with the need to manage more intellectual capital, from more disparate sources, more effectively than ever, it seems sensible to ask the question: will the consulting firm of the future be able to survive on its own?

This is both an unfair and a fair question. It is unfair in the sense that the history of the consulting industry has been one of merger and counter-merger: few consulting firms – the major strategy firms are notable exceptions – have had any pretensions to 'survive on their own'. Indeed, the smaller a consulting firms is, the greater the imperative to link up with complementary organisations. 'Rather than having informal arrangements to cross-refer work with a handful of other firms', *Management Consultant International* noted in April 1997, 'an increasing number of small consultancies are grouping together into more tightly managed networks.' Alliances between specialist consulting firms enable them to compete with their larger, more generalist rivals for sizeable assignments in terms of both their specialist expertise and their lower cost base. Alliances, for the consulting industry, are nothing new.

But this is a fair question, if we look more broadly at the way in which the business environment as a whole is changing. You do not have to be Peter Drucker to know that the conventional boundaries between sectors are collapsing. A combination of many factors – ranging from declining government regulation to the need to exploit an existing customer base – has meant that retailers are becoming banks, that car insurance companies will sell you cheap electricity, that software companies are looking to be media giants. Just take a look at these three comments, all about different takeovers in April 1998:

- 'We would use our ability over time to market to the customer base of each business the product and service ability of both.' (Lord Wolfson,

the Chairman of Great Universal Stores, on its bid for UK catalogue
store chain, Argos)

- 'Our UK units will benefit from opportunities to cross-market to the
  approximately 3 million frequent users of NCP facilities and the 3.5
  million members of Green Flag.' (Henry Silverman, the CEO of US
  company, Cendant, on its takeover of NCP and Green Flag, UK
  companies respectively providing car parking and breakdown services)
- 'To date the Stanley Gibbons database has been under-utilised ... We
  need to learn the precise requirements of our customers and to start
  meeting those needs.' (Walter Goldsmith, Chairman of flower delivery
  company, Flying Flowers, on its takeover of philatelist Stanley
  Gibbons)

Alliances and mergers have always occurred: what is new is that these
are now happening across traditional sector boundaries. Rather than
solidifying existing industry structures, these alliances are creating new
industries. These are industries that straddle different parts of the
conventional value chain. Instead of looking to ally with organisations for
the purposes of vertical integration, companies are looking either to make
alliances across the value chain (so that, for example, a company like
Flying Flowers, whose core competence is managing customer
relationships, looks to perform the same function in a different part of the
retail market), or to by-pass traditional links in the value chain.

What is also new is that the nature of competition appears to be
changing as a result of the alliances being formed. There has always been
a paradoxical relationship between collaboration and competition. In
theory, collaboration will increase an organisation's ability to compete
(because it strengthens its core competencies), but at the same time,
collaboration (especially among companies in the same sector) reduces the
need for direct competition. But this, as US academic Benjamin Gomes-
Casseres has pointed out, is changing:

> In the modern world of large firms, global businesses, and advanced
> technologies, the relationship between these two processes is much more
> complex. The type of business rivalry emerging in this environment grows out
> of the very dynamics of collaboration. Simply put, business rivalry now often
> takes place between sets of allied firms, rather than between single firms.[1]

Similarly, at the start of *The Death of Competition*, consultant James
Moore tells the stories, first of ABB Asea Brown Boveri, which develops
its strategies around the future needs of its customers, and, second, of a

restaurant which opened up near to ABB's new headquarters in Canada, and which succeeds by offering high-quality food to the local executives based in companies like ABB. Both stories have the same message – competitive advantage comes from co-operating – not competing – with other organisations. 'This is the new paradigm in strategy-making', writes Moore,

> the basic idea is simple: Understand the economic systems evolving around you and find ways to contribute ... In the new economic environment, many otherwise great businesses fail, because the context around them changes, rending them unimportant or obsolete ... The new paradigm requires thinking in terms of whole systems – that is, seeing your business as part of a wider economic ecosystem and environment.[2]

If we look forward to the future of consultancy, it would be hard to find a more apt description of one of the key issues facing consulting firms. For all the alliances and mergers that have taken place within the industry, it remains the case that consulting in the past has been an isolationist activity. Although the origin of large firms often lay in the amalgamation of smaller ones, even the most integrated firms continued to be run on a highly individualised basis, with partners responsible for their own fiefdoms. During the recession of the early 1990s, it became apparent that a firm which comprised small, comparatively autonomous business units was not well equipped to withstand increasingly intense competition. The large consulting firms responded by launching programmes designed to break down internal barriers and develop a common sense of purpose. For smaller firms, the solution lay in linking themselves to other small firms or to large companies in other industries, notably hardware and software suppliers. However, the motivation in both changes has been essentially a defensive one: strength in numbers, not putting all your eggs in one basket, and so on. Implementation has often been grudging, and its results variable.

But the challenge of the future will be a quite different one. Co-operation, networking, business 'ecosystems' (to use Moore's terms) all provide two unparalleled opportunities for consulting firms:

- to develop a wide range of new services and take these to different markets; and
- to form mutually supportive groupings that will be able to change the nature of competition both inside and outside the consulting industry.

Why network?

There are four fundamental reasons why the consulting firms of the future will be looking to create ecosystems of their own:

- the need for new types of intellectual capital;
- the chance to create instant critical mass in new or emerging markets, and then take control of them;
- the pressure for consulting firms to specialise and differentiate themselves more effectively from their rivals; and
- protection.

Accessing new types of intellectual capital

We have already noted that clients of the future are likely to be far more voracious in their demands for new intellectual capital: they will not simply want more new ideas, but a steady stream of them, providing tangible assurance that they are not falling behind their competitors. One solution to this – discussed in the previous chapter – will be for consulting firms to manage their intellectual capital much more effectively. But the same demand will also drive firms to look for partners who can provide new, complementary intellectual capital. Moreover, as client industries converge, the intellectual capital to which they want access may well be outside the normal reach of a consulting firm. In the future, they may need the intellectual capital of, for example, an investment bank, just as some firms have recently decided that they need the intellectual capital of legal firms.

Using instant critical mass to take control

Purchasing new intellectual capital, or acquiring it via alliances or mergers, will not just be important on the micro – individual client – level. Rather than taking time to develop a new service or access a new market organically, acquisition will provide an almost immediate *entrée* into new areas. Rather than going in unprepared, the consulting firm will have the fully fledged expertise to make an immediate impact.

This impact will, in turn, be essential if a firm is to establish dominance of the market concerned. It used to be the case that the markets for specific consulting services emerged gradually, often over some time. Perhaps it is a management culture of increasing instant gratification; perhaps it is simply the fact that we have much better access to information than we had ten, even five, years ago: whatever the reason, we seem to live now in a world in which consulting markets are created almost instantly. The opportunity for a firm to build up its expertise is already shrinking fast: in consulting parlance 'you have to hit the ground running'. Being able to play the leading role in these markets – rather than simply have a bit part – will be crucial, if only to justify the level of investment required to enter it. And having a leading role will be dependent on getting on stage first. Forging alliances which provide instant new services will be the key way in which a consulting firm can be first to market, and can then use its pre-eminent position to control the development of the market. Alliances, in effect, will give consulting firms the chance to create, not just new services, but entire new markets.

Creating greater differentiation

Most consulting firms – large and small firms alike – are bad at making choices. This stems partly from a desire to remain genuinely responsive to client needs (clients therefore decide for consultants what the latter's future services and markets will be), and partly from having inclusive decision-making processes which, while strong at creating consensus, are weak when it comes to making difficult choices. For this reason, many of the alliances formed in the consulting industry in the past have been the products of opportunist instinct rather than a well-honed strategy. The result of this – and this is something that we will be exploring in greater depth in the following chapter – is that most consulting firms have failed to differentiate themselves.

Creating alliances represents a partial solution to this so far intractable problem. Consulting firms are just starting to wake up to the idea that there are only a finite number of possible combinations or networks. Make the wrong choice now and you could see yourself excluded from lucrative markets in the future. Make the right choice and you will have created a powerful barrier to entry. In effect, alliances provide an important opportunity for resolving the branding and differentiation issues which haunt the industry at the moment.

But with only a certain number of alliances to develop – like land to carve up – it is clear that consulting firms will need to make much clearer, more consistent choices than they have in the past. If you end up with 50 alliances, but spread across as many sectors or services, then your efforts will have been wasted. Consultancies, therefore, will need to choose the ground for which they wish to stake a claim: will they ally with a company that offers synergistic services into established markets, or will they link up with someone who can give them access to a new market?

Protecting oneself

Alliances, in the consulting industry, have tended to be defensive. As was noted above, the economic impact of the recession was one of the key drivers of mergers in the early 1990s. But alliances have played a defensive role in other aspects as well. A survey by *The Economist*, back in 1988, ascribed a recent spate of acquisitions to the fear of lawsuits and the desire to fend off challenges to the partner ownership system. Earlier experiments with different types of ownership structure, the survey pointed out – such as when Booz-Allen & Hamilton floated part of its equity in 1969 but saw its share perform worse than expected – had not been a success.

In the immediate future, however, it is likely that alliances will play another type of defensive role. We have already discussed how being able to access and own intellectual capital reserves will be one of the key determining factors of success over the next few years. But asserting ownership and litigation represent only one way for a consulting firm to establish and defend its intellectual assets. *De facto* control can be achieved where a firm is prepared to create alliances between itself, the originators of the intellectual capital (or parts of it) and the consumers of it (clients) – in effect, vertical integration of the intellectual capital value chain.

The emergence of a new segmentation

'We are all increasingly into each other's business', said Jon Moynihan, the Group CEO of PA Consulting, in 1995.[3] 'There is little sign of any doubt about the big is beautiful philosophy', reiterated *The Guardian* three years later:

> senior solicitors envisage a future of service organisations combining all the functions of law, accounting, audit, actuarial services, corporate advice, insolvency and fraud investigation. The separate professions will go the way of butchers, bakers and candlestick-makers in the age of Safeway and Tesco.[4]

But how will convergence – 'being into each other's pockets' – affect the consulting industry? In two ways: first will be the impact of consulting firms moving into new consulting and non-consulting markets; second will be the converse to this – the impact of non-consulting companies coming into the consulting market.

You can – and people have – cut the consulting market in many different ways. But, for the purposes of understanding the impact of convergence, we could see the 'core' market broken up into four main areas: specialist firms, strategy houses, 'traditional' consultancies and the large accountancy-based practices. Around the edges of this core lie several tangential groups: academics, non-consulting companies that have launched consulting firms, systems integration houses, hardware manufacturers, outsourcing providers and – increasingly – other professional service companies: law firms, PR agencies, and so on (see Figure 6.1).

Let's look first at the way in which consultancies have used alliances and acquisitions to move into new sectors, both inside and outside the traditional consulting market.

Taking a representative cross-section of this activity (summarised in Table 6.1), several consistent strands emerge. Almost all proactive activity stems from the accountancy-based consulting practices. These – the most voracious of firms – have been using alliances and acquisitions to diversify

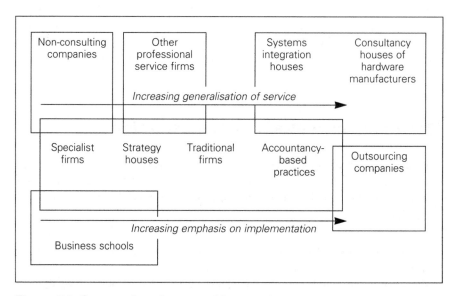

Figure 6.1 Segmenting the consulting market

(into new consulting and other professional services markets) and to strengthen their position in IT-related consultancy, with links either to systems integration or software houses. There are, however, some significant exceptions to this rule who prefer to establish joint ventures with clients than with other professional service firms. By contrast, the strategy houses and traditional consulting firms have tended to rely on organic growth.

If we turn to look at the new entrants, we can see a trend from the late 1980s starting to repeat itself, with non-consulting firms, simultaneously attracted by the industry's high level of profitability and driven by a belief that they should spin off non-core activities, launching their own consulting firms. This thinking also applies to other professional service firms, as well as non-professional service firms; 1996, for example, saw the launch of a consulting division by one of Europe's largest agencies, Euro RSCG Wnek Gosper. 'It's taking what we have been good at', commented the company,

> understanding brands and understanding consumers – and feeding it into the business planning process at an earlier stage … [in order] to take brand-orientated beliefs further up the business chain.[5]

Although still rather low-key, if the late 1990s follow the pattern of the late 1980s, we should expect to see this kind of venture becoming increasingly popular.

So what does all this suggest in terms of the structure of the consulting market in the future? Without a doubt, it makes it considerably more complex and less clear-cut than at present – not simply because of the type of convergence outlined here, but also because the absolute number of spin-off companies and joint venture organisations looks set to proliferate. If we extrapolate current trends, it seems likely that the quite diverse networking activity of the early 1990s will give way to more concentrated activity, around the accountancy-based firms in particular. Other professional service firms, seeking to enlarge their share of board-level advice, will find themselves most closely allied with the strategy houses. Specialist consultancies will be focusing on consolidating their comparatively immature markets, by teaming up with similar companies in order to acquire market share (much as compensation and benefits consultancies are doing at present). But the accountancy-based consultancies look set to become the hubs of the alliance networks of the future, the central points of the 'ecosystems' envisaged by James Moore (Figure 6.2).

Table 6.1 Convergence across the sectors of the consulting market

	Business schools	Non-consulting companies	Other professional service firms	Specialist consultancies	Strategy houses	Traditional consultancies	Accountancy-based practices	Systems integration houses	Software/hardware manufacturers	Outsourcing companies
Business schools										
Non-consulting companies										Mellon Bank joins with MCI Systemhouse to outsource accounts payable and receivable services
Other professional service firms				Omnicom, the global marketing group … Barra, US company advising the investment management industry …						
Specialist consultancies			Omnicom, the global marketing group, moves into brand-related consultancy by acquiring UK-based Newell and Sorrell. Barra, the US company advising the investment management industry, forms a consulting subsidiary, Barra Strategic Consulting		Strategy implementation firm, Renaissance Solutions, buys UK strategy firm, Coba Consulting			Renaissance Solutions buys US systems house, International Systems Services, and subsequently merges with The Registry, a US company providing IT support and consultancy		
Strategy houses	Booz-Allen & Hamilton establishes link with Insead covering research and joint projects									
Traditional consultancies										

Accountancy-based practices	C&L forms alliance with University of Michigan Business School to provide a leadership training service for clients	E&Y establishes joint venture with Agricultural co-operative Farmland Associates. E&Y also joins forces with Xerox to provide consulting and systems services to large financial services companies. Andersen Consulting teams up with New Brunswick telephone provider, NBtel, to market the Internet-based Interactive Phone Store	C&L merges with Kwash Lipton and acquires Compo Consulting Group, both US benefits consultancies	C&L buys Autofacts, US automotive specialists. KPMG forms alliance with marketing research company, Total Research, to develop customer satisfaction measurements service. PW acquires Danish supply chain management specialists, Peter Matthiesen	PW buys LVS, a Russian systems integration firm. D&TCG buys Source (Fr). C&L acquires Kinesis, UK-based IT implementation and document management company	PW forms an alliance with US software company, Alcar Group, to co-operate on projects to enhance shareholder value and with US-based Siebel Systems, specialising in sales software. C&L forms alliance with the Indus Group, a specialist software company in the energy and process sectors. E&Y acquires French software company, Heclas. KPMG creates joint venture with Microsoft and network provider, Cisco Systems
Systems integrations houses					Technology Solutions Company buys technology implementation firm, HRM Resources	
Software/hardware manufacturers						SAP forms joint venture with software and IT services company, Software
Outsourcing companies						

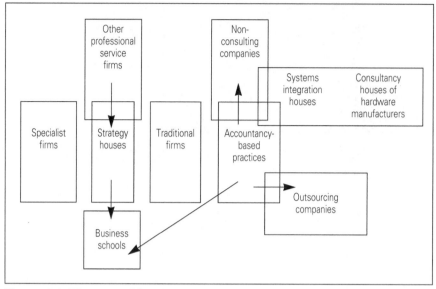

Figure 6.2 The consulting 'ecosystems' of the future

How is it that accountancy-based firms will be most likely to exert this type of gravitational pull? Three reasons suggest themselves:

- these firms are already beginning (consciously or unconsciously) to work in this way, as even the sample of ventures in Table 6.1 indicates, and will therefore have a head-start on other companies;
- their existing size gives them an immediate advantage, not least in terms of being able to make acquisitions; and
- from the point of view of many prospective partners, accountancy-based firms have one huge advantage – the asset that is their range of contacts within client organisations (strategy houses, which perhaps command a large proportion of board-level relationships, will be attractive for the same reason, but perhaps more so to other professional service firms, who will be battling for increased share at this level of the organisation, than to hardware and software manufacturers and outsourcing providers, who often require relationships at multiple levels within the organisation).

But does this mean that the consulting market of the future will be even more of an amorphous – sometimes impenetrable – jungle than it is at present? Probably not, because rather than being a homogeneous mass of comparatively indistinct services, these ecosystems, although complex, will be quite clearly differentiated. We might see one for, say, pharmaceutical clients in which a consultancy company, a group of hospitals, a market research agency and the makers of sophisticated computer modelling software all come together to offer advice on cutting down the amount of time and money spent on the research and development of new drugs.

The segmentation of the consulting market in the future is unlikely to be drawn around 'sectors' as we see them today, or even around specific service types: it will be drawn around issues.

Notes

1. Benjamin Gomes-Casseres, *The Alliance Revolution: The New Shape of Business Rivalry*, Cambridge, MA: Harvard, 1997, p. 2.
2. James E. Moore, *The Death of Competition: Leadership and Strategy in the Age of Business Systems*, Chichester: John Wiley, 1996.
3. Quoted in the *Financial Times*, 12 September 1995.
4. *The Guardian*, 7 March 1998.
5. *Management Consultancy International*, December, 1996.

7 Branding and Differentiation

Try this test: Which major consulting firms, in their 1996 reports, said:

- 'We are committed to proving value to our clients and achieving our vision of being recognised as the professional services firm that contributes the most to its clients' success'?
- 'We are meeting the market place by changing and evolving – doing what it takes to serve our clients and provide them with value that can't be found anywhere else'?
- 'Our strategic intent is to create value for our clients and to bring competitive advantage to their activities'?
- 'We are an organisation that is committed to working together to deliver value. Our clients gain the greatest benefits from the firm when we work together with them and for them'?

The answers do not to jump out of the page, even for a seasoned observer of the consultancy market (but, if you are interested, the answers are: Ernst & Young, Andersen Consulting, Coopers & Lybrand (prior to its merger with Price Waterhouse) and KPMG).

Differentiation is already one of the most serious issues facing the consulting industry, and it is likely to become an even more serious issue over the next few years.

The single most important factor driving this growing need for differentiation is client loyalty – or rather, the lack of it. Clients often see consultants as part of an indistinguishable mass:

> A chief executive officer recalled being confronted recently by platoons of pinstriped consultants who were all MBAs, who all had clients in the Fortune 100, and who all claimed success at solving the same problem: 'In all honesty, I couldn't tell the difference among them. They all talked the same game and they all made sense. It was almost the flip of a coin.'[1]

In fact, when you start to think about it, it is hard to find an industry that outsiders perceive to be more homogeneous than consulting. True, clients may distinguish between certain segments (IT implementation versus strategic consultancy, for instance), but, with a few notable exceptions, they tend to view the firms within each segment as largely undifferentiated. The situation seems ironic:

> Why, if management is primarily about creating differentiation – in product design, strategy, etc – its own sector often recruits the same people, develops identical services to cash in on the latest fads ... and uses the same tired marketing and public relations techniques to promote its different practitioners, McKinsey and Andersen Consulting apart, there is little distinguishable branding in an industry that virtually invented the term.[2]

But why should this be the case? One possible reason is that consultants have tried hard to mirror their clients – by working in partnership with them, by trying to anticipate and meet their needs, and so on. This is essentially imitative, rather than innovative, behaviour, and it applies on both the micro and macro scale. When several consultancies decide to bid for a specific assignment, they attempt to tailor their way of working to the client's individual needs (indeed, one of the most common sources of client dissatisfaction is that consultants do not do this enough). It therefore follows that, in their effort to win the work involved, the approaches adopted by the different consulting firms converge: the bigger the assignment, the greater the formality with which client needs are laid out – the more likely it is that this convergence will happen. And it therefore also follows that the trend towards more, larger-scale projects has had the effect of further homogenising the consulting market.

On a more macro level, the intangible nature of consultancy services breeds similarity. BPR would not be BPR if the only two firms offering it as a service approached assignments very differently; equally, TQM could not exist if there was no agreement about what it involved. Consulting firms therefore have to deal with peculiarly inelastic product definitions: it does not take much to stretch the BPR process into something that would not be conceived of as BPR.

To an extent, this represents an opportunity for consulting firms. It means, for example, that products can be altered and recycled relatively quickly and easily (hence the criticisms that BPR was just traditional cost-reduction consultancy in a new guise). However, the inelasticity of consulting services also makes it much more likely that the consulting market will be homogeneous. If it does not take much to fragment a particular line of business, then it is in the interests of consulting firms to ensure that as little fragmentation takes place as possible. In other words, if a new service line emerges (and we are talking here particularly about the segment of the market that deals in consulting 'products', not those that rely more on a creative process), it makes sense for all the consulting firms that want to offer it to their clients to develop a consensus about what this service should look like. Of course, each firm will develop and promote its individual variations on the central theme, but the core product will be – has to be – the same. Moreover, with barriers to entry and levels of investment still very low compared to many other industries, imitation makes much better economic sense than innovation: if one firm sees another doing well at a particular new service line, there is little to stop them launching their own version (there are, as yet, no patents to infringe).

But these underlying economics are starting to change. It has always been the case that the wider a service was offered, the more likely it was to be commoditised – partly as a result of greater availability (any old consultant can do this), partly as the product definition became untenably stretched. As consulting firms become faster at gathering and acting on market intelligence, and become more efficient at developing their own, often look-alike services, so this process of commoditisation will speed up. Ten years ago, a leading-edge consultancy service had a shelf-life of perhaps five years; today, two years is probably more typical. Differentiation is important because it is one of the key means by which consulting firms can break out – and be seen to break out – of this vicious circle.

In 1990, Andersen Consulting changed the face of marketing in its industry by launching a series of high-profile, highly visible publicity campaigns – everything from television advertisements to hoardings. Almost overnight, a sector that had always derided the need for such activity saw that 'professionalism' and 'marketing' were not mutually exclusive concepts. The messages of the firm's campaigns were clear and simple: 'metamorphosis in a world of change', for instance, where a slowly crawling snail was transformed into a fast, hopping frog; 'are all your talents working in concert?', where different works of art come to life to form a new, harmonious picture. The images are very resonant – people and animals made to change shape by the classical gods in Ovid's *Metamorphoses*, Pygmalion's statue stepping down from its pedestal. Rather than specific services, these advertisements speak of values and commitment – and their message does not stop with the conventional marketing mix. As Andersen Consulting partner Jim Murphy commented:

Most important is something that we don't own, our clients own, it's in their head, and that is our promise to them as an organisation … It comes to life not only in advertising, literature and signage, but how people act on the job, how we sell, what kind of clients we have, what we do. All of this has to be part of the built-in culture. It comes out of our training, the acculturation process. The idea of what Andersen Consulting stands for as a brand is put in front of all our employees.[3]

The image continues – the works of art do not only come to life in the television advertisement, but every day, through the way that Andersen Consulting's employees behave.

But it is not just the message here which is important. Equally so, was the fact that the firm was prepared to say it, at a time when its competitors were considerably more reticent. Like its consultants, the confidence implied by advertising in such a high-risk manner 'brought to life' the underlying message.

But differentiation is an area in which the majority of consultancies have little expertise; moreover, very little work has been done to understand the issue, either from an academic or business perspective. In 1990, Neil Morgan carried out a study of the marketing departments of professional accounting firms. The emphasis, he noted, fell rather on exploiting what a firm already had, rather than developing new services, on defending, rather than extending market share. The resulting picture is of companies trying to promote their image, but almost in isolation from the rest of the industry. Thus, although issues such as professional reputation, image and service excellence were top of the marketing agenda, these were all aimed at proving the worth of the firm itself, not at differentiating it from its competitors. Advertising came bottom of the list. The marketing departments were, he concluded, nothing more than glorified corporate communications teams: 'the marketing department's input into and control over the firm's marketing strategy is relatively small'.[4]

The extent to which consulting firms need professional marketing and sales experience has always been a contentious issue. Traditionally, consultants, like lawyers and accountants, have seen themselves as above this kind of activity: a good firm sold business through its reputation and the recommendation of its clients, rather than as a result of an advertising campaign. However, a minority of firms, recognising that the best practitioners may not always be the best sales people, have employed a direct sales force. And the proportion of firms taking this approach has risen as companies who have prior experience of sales and marketing in a conventional sense (such as IBM) have entered the consulting sector.

The challenge of the future, therefore, lies in two parts: creating a differentiated brand and changing the structure and culture of the consulting organisation in order to sustain it.

Creating a differentiated brand

The traditional approach to differentiation within the consulting industry has been specialisation. It has, for example, been by emphasising their new ideas or in-depth experience in a particular field that new entrants have been successful in carving out niches for themselves. Established, broader-based firms have responded in kind, typically by promoting specific services: 'growth through specialisation' became the strategy of more than one consultancy in the early 1990s.

But there are two major problems with the idea of using specialisation to differentiate.

The first is that specialisation itself does nothing to promote a brand: rather the opposite, it leads to fragmentation. Time and money have been spent designing frameworks which bring these different elements together, but the exercise is a structural one – the whole never adds up to more than the sum of the parts. For many companies, this external image has been the mirror image of internal fragmentation, with firms split into a myriad of separate business units, each of which is pursuing a quasi-autonomous strategy. Without clear internal goals and values, it has been almost impossible to develop a more coherent external image, let alone a brand.

The second problem is that the specialisms that are being used as a source of differentiation are prone to change. Everyone – consultants and clients alike – would recognise that consultancy is, and has to be, a fast-moving business. Intellectual capital does not require the massive R&D budgets of, say, a pharmaceutical company; nor does it – unlike a car manufacturer, for example – need a huge assembly line to be constructed. In order to operate effectively in the intellectual capital market, consulting firms need to be immensely responsive to changes in their clients' demands, and fragmentation is one way of dealing with this issue. Large, hierarchical firms are like oil tankers – once set in a direction, they take time to change course (and the huge, but temporary, losses incurred by companies like IBM are a testimony to this). By contrast, an organisation that is composed of many small units, each of which is very focused on their immediate markets, can change course much more quickly. Of course, the downside is that the fragmented organisation is less good at moving in a single direction – which is part of the explanation why more fragmentary organisations are less effective when it comes to a stable environment. Consultancies, therefore, need to change their specialisms in order to survive, but, as a result, it becomes difficult for the specialist image being promoted to add up to a sustainable brand.

Creating a differentiated brand in the future will require a different approach. It will involve firms identifying and promoting the values embedded in their organisation, and using these values to attract clients with similar values. When Harley Davidson wanted to turn around its business after years of declining market share and falling quality, it began to exploit its position as the only motor-cycle manufacturer in the US by promoting traditional American values – liberty, individuality, small town community, and so on. It stressed American craftsmanship and originality over that of foreign imports. When it held a bikers' rally in a town, it would organise events with a local charity, have its executives turn up on their bikes and generally try to 'live the vision'.

Imagine applying this technique to a consultancy. First of all, we might go through an exercise to understand what our values are and how they differ – and can be seen to differ – from our rivals (many firms have done the first part of this exercise, but not the second). We might, for instance, discover that one of our core values was being able to respond very quickly to any request for help from a client. Considerable effort – not captured in the organisation's formal reporting measurements – was being put into pulling together proposals and resources at very short notice. As a result, our client base tended to be biased towards companies that needed help in a hurry, for example in response to a hostile take-over bid. Second, there would be the question of translating these core values – responsiveness, help when you most need it – into a promotional campaign, and ultimately a brand.

It is one of the axioms of marketing that intangible services are most effectively promoted via tangible substitutes. Thus, rather than tell us how good their people are, the reports of consulting firms have tended to give us pictures of real people; equally, rather than just claiming that their assignments have yielded positive results, they have shown real clients talking about real benefits. But the process has tended to stop there: very few consulting firms have managed to create any more substantial an impression, or any more concrete a brand. Indeed, simply because these firms have relied on people – staff and clients – to embody the brand, there is a limit to the extent to which the values they are trying to embody will appear different. People – especially in written reports – tend to sound and look the same. Thus, not only (as we observed earlier) are the propositions of consulting firms undifferentiated, but so are the mechanisms which they adopt to promote them.

In terms of creating a differentiated brand, therefore, there will be two key challenges for consulting firms in the future:

- First, they will need to identify values within their organisations which will set them apart from their competitors, and which will attract and retain employees.
- Second, they will need to find new (or at least different) ways in which they provide concrete evidence externally of these internal, intangible values.

It is probably harsh, but honest, to say that most consulting firms have not been strong on values. If we accept that there is an analogy between what a doctor does to an individual patient and what a consultant does (or could, or should do) to a company, then we can see how far short the latter fall of their potential image of 'business healers'. In the public mind, consultants are probably closer to lawyers – corporate ambulance chasers – who exploit client problems for their own profit.

However, the consultancies of the future will have to be big on values. And not just any values. It will not be enough to say 'we're client-focused', 'we work in partnership with you' or, indeed, 'we add value to you'. To create a differentiated brand, the values of the future will also need to be differentiated.

Consultancies have tended to think of themselves as having one asset: people. More recently, they have begun to see that the knowledge that these people have – the firm's intellectual capital – is also an asset. Business books, journals and articles have already become some of the most important weapons in the consultant's armoury, and we should expect them to become even more important in the future. As a result, it is highly likely that the largest consulting firms will attempt to secure their position on the intellectual high ground by buying or launching business publishing houses and by allying themselves to business schools in order to gain access to a constant source of research material. A combination of increased investment and more intense competition for this intellectual high ground will mean that consulting firms have to become considerably more focused in terms of promoting their intellectual assets. For the minority of firms already trying to exploit this opportunity at the moment, air time is allocated pretty much on a first-come-first-served basis, with comparatively little thought being put into promoting a firm's key intellectual assets on a more systematic basis. In the future, no doubt, this will change, with consulting firms using journals, books and related media on a much more strategic basis. The fight to win a client's business will start, not at the door of their offices or on the first page of the proposal, but long before the client invites a consulting firm to bid for an assignment.

If consultancies are starting to review their intellectual assets with a view to using them more effectively, there remain other 'assets' which consulting firms have yet to recognise, let alone exploit.

Foremost among these under-utilised assets are the relationships these firms have with their clients. While the overall trend in the industry may be away from client loyalty on a corporate scale, almost all consultants strive to acquire and retain the trust and confidence of clients on an individual basis. That software suppliers – for example – want to forge alliances with the major consulting firms is evidence of the extent to which these relationships are enormously valuable. Consulting firms often have access to the board of a company in a way in which no software manufacturer could hope to have, and using consultants as a conduit for their products is therefore hugely important.

Attempts to realise the value of these relationships have tended to remain at the individual level – typically, a partner is asked to facilitate the introduction of a colleague to a client. But this is in stark contrast to other sectors, notably financial services and retailing, where it has been recognised that an organisation's relationship with its customers needs to be understood and exploited on a much more systematic basis. Saga, a British company which has traditionally organised holidays for retired people, has used its customer base (and their loyalty to its brand) to move into new areas such as insurance. Also in the UK, as the electricity industry is opened up to competition, utility companies have been looking to create alliances with organisations with complementary customer bases (the Automobile Association and trade unions, for instance) so that each can cross-sell to a much wider base. As the division between sectors blurs, having 'ownership' of a group of customers will become a competitive advantage.

Although they have yet to appreciate or act on it, the same applies to consulting firms. They – especially the largest, more established firms – *potentially* have access to a highly valuable database of contacts, areas of interest, and so on. The problem is that it currently exists only in people's heads: yes, a firm is likely to record the names and addresses of clients; yes, they may also keep a check on what client bought what service; but no firm has yet really managed to capture the mass of informal, unstructured knowledge about clients' likes and dislikes, future interests, career ambitions, and so on – which, collectively, represents its most valuable information on clients. Of course, many clients will not want to purchase all their consultancy from one firm, but these types of relationship marketing activities will significantly improve a firm's overall sales effectiveness.

Like corporate values, this is something that will have to change in the future, for a consulting firm to survive, let alone thrive. We should, therefore, expect to see firms:

- investing much more in developing sophisticated client databases, which track informal, as well as formal, information on clients;
- using this information to target – much more systematically than at present – new services on specific clients – the consulting equivalent of one-to-one marketing;
- creating loyalty programmes which are designed to cement client relationships;
- using the quality and nature of their client bases to differentiate themselves (for example, old established companies versus young and thrusting entrepreneurs); and
- forming mutually beneficial alliances with other companies, whereby each organisation can cross-sell its services to the other's clients (linking up with an investment bank would be a good example).

'Owning' clients will be central to the strategy of consulting firms in the future, but it will not be the only thing they will want – or need – to own. If intangibility is a block to differentiation, then it is partly because it is difficult to own ideas or services in the way that, say, Coca-Cola can own its product. It is like a philosophical proof: a tangible asset can be owned; if you demonstrate that you own an asset, then the asset must be tangible. There is a – perhaps apocryphal – story about Orange, the UK mobile phone operator owned by Hutchinson Telecom. When it came to the launch of the service, the company told its advertising agency that it wanted to 'own' something that nobody else owned. The agency responded by saying that an organisation could not own an image or a value, but it could own a colour – hence the name. Similarly, consulting companies need to be able to demonstrate ownership if they are to create any sustainable differentiation: intellectual capital and client relationships are part of this, but consulting firms will still need their equivalent of a colour – something which creates an immediate, positive association in the marketplace.

Part of that 'something' will be language. Consulting firms have always relied heavily on language. After all, what is consultancy if it is not language? Moreover, consultants have used language – most obviously in the form of management jargon – as a means of establishing their credentials, of differentiating themselves from their clients at least. Consultants, as the writers of one recent academic study on the consulting process put it, have 'discursively constituted identities':

> [These] are not fixed but must be constantly reinforced; they are stable only so long as the interlocking network of implicit and explicit agreements which supports them holds together; they are not settled once and for all but are the object of on-going discursive modes. This is why we have argued that consultancy practice necessarily entails the exercise of power, in the endeavour to construct others' identities and interests, and through the exclusion of rival views of problems and solutions.[5]

At the moment, a key obstacle which is preventing consultancies from differentiating themselves more effectively is that they all talk the same talk. As we saw at the beginning of this chapter, they all use the same phrases and words. Again, it is a degree of nervousness which underpins this situation: the language they use is the language of management consultants – if they did not talk like that, then they would not be consultants. The consultancy that succeeds in establishing its own vocabulary stands to gain a tremendous competitive advantage. It goes all the way back to the client quoted at the start of this chapter: the majority of consultants do share the same background and it is not easy to change this. But if we can get them to use language differently – if we can create a linguistic asset for our business – then we have a quick and effective way of differentiating ourselves.

Building an organisation and culture which sustains the brand

But none of this matters, if we cannot make it stick. We can create a radically differentiated brand, supported by ground-breaking advertising, but its impact will be negligible (it could even be negative) if we cannot sustain this image internally and externally.

In the majority of consulting firms, the marketing function has been chronically under-supported and under-funded, while the marketing process is undertaken by practising consultants. The typical marketing department has therefore been little more than a glorified corporate communications team, with most of the 'real' selling and marketing being handled by consultants themselves. Professional sales and marketing skills have, explicitly, been seen as antipathetic to the consulting ethos and, implicitly, as a threat to the traditional power bases of partners and senior consultants. But the latter are too fragmented a group to be able to create, let alone sustain, an over-arching brand (and it is no accident that the firms with the more established brands are those with the larger and better funded marketing teams).

This problem remains largely unresolved, but it is likely that this conventional distinction between (superior) chargeable and (inferior) marketing staff will have to change. Indeed, some of the more established firms have just started to experiment in this area; and some of the newer firms have worked in this way since their inception. We can expect to see a significant growth in the numbers of people employed in these areas, perhaps hampered only by the difficulty of recruiting good people with this very particular set of skills.

But this change is only likely to succeed if the wider organisation changes, not only so that the consultants work more closely with these new teams, but also that they recognise the importance of the brand which is being created and work to deliver on the promises it makes. Consulting firms differ hugely in the extent to which they can act as one mind: some, like Andersen Consulting, have made a virtue out of their cohesiveness, others, like Coopers & Lybrand, have prided themselves on a more individualistic outlook. But much more important than these cultural variances is the extent to which consultants are cynical about their own profession. Positive values have not tended to feature highly in consulting organisations. Too many consultants believe their own bad reputation, and too many people have often been under too much pressure to extract fees from clients who do not, in reality, need the service on offer. In fact, this does not necessarily make consulting any more or less amoral than other companies (many of us buy things we do not need). A differentiated brand will only be possible if it is underpinned by a cohesive value system – something that most consulting firms will find difficult to realise in practice.

Perspective 7.1 Francis Quinlan, Hodgart Temporal

At the time the Andersen Consulting campaign was launched, the benefits of spending so much money on above-the-line advertising – in an industry which is historically based on individual client–consultant relationships and especially in a firm (such as Andersen Consulting) where the target market segment has always been very tightly defined – were questionable. But what Andersen Consulting wanted to do was to change the frame of reference in what was a largely undifferentiated, accountancy-oriented market. Rather than being seen in the context of the other Big Five firms, the comparison it wanted its clients to make was with companies like IBM. It wanted to redefine the market, to establish itself as the brand leader, and to build awareness, not just among immediate clients, but also among the next generation of future clients. It was a courageous decision, and one that has set the pace for the rest of the industry over the past few years.

But, looking into the future, it is important to recognise that this type of high-profile brand building is only one part of a successful brand strategy. While the marketing of other know-how businesses may provide some inspiration, professional service firms will need to recognise that they are unusual because their offerings are wholly intellectual products – unlike Microsoft, for instance, whose intellectual capital is articulated through the tangible software that it produces.

Effective brand strategies for a consulting firm must have three components:

- *Level 1 – The signage.* This is the conventional level of signalling and communications which many think of as the sum of branding: the logo and house style; the level and style of external awareness-building programmes which, by virtue of consistent use, the market associates with the firm.
- *Level 2 – The market positioning.* This is how clients see the firm in relation to market needs and competitor offerings. It encompasses the types of client it typically services, the kinds of service it offers and how it offers them, and the type of value it yields its client. Many – probably most – firms lack clear positioning, though effective branding demands it.
- *Level 3 – The character of the firm.* This is the persona of the firm, which may be indicated by Levels 1 and 2 branding but which is best exemplified by the behaviour of its people. Where they demonstrate a consistency of approach, informed by a common mindset or a cohesive frame of reference, they can both reiterate and extend the firm's identity and market positioning. Where they don't do this, they give the lie to the firm's desired branding.

Of these three levels, it is thus the third which is most powerful, but also the one that is least exploited by consultancy companies at present. Those with the sharpest branding at this stage tend to have their market positioning clear. Many large firms, however, continue to have a fragmented image – the product of multiple mergers and the acquisition of many smaller firms: you cannot really claim to have a brand in these circumstances, except in terms of superficial signage. As the largest firms improve their branding over the next few years, what they will actually be doing is improving the clarity and consistency with which the market perceives them and distinguishes them from their competitors.

This move towards corporate branding will mean that the personal 'brand' of individual partners becomes less important. This will be in sharp contrast to very small firms, the brands of which will continue to be determined by the individual owners/managers. For firms in the middle, we are likely to see two types of brand strategy: the niche company, which may be quite sizeable in practice, but whose brand comes from its very targeted positioning in the market, and the whole raft of generalist firms that are not famous for anything – firms which grew out of a small number of client–consultant relationships and which have never been able to develop a clear positioning. Most consulting firms probably fall into this category. Does it matter that these firms will not find it easy to develop a brand? Yes, because their size is not providing them with any competitive advantage over their much smaller rivals.

Once a firm has established a clear brand identity, the next challenge will be to sustain it. Again, the primary focus here will need to be on people – particularly their recruitment and development. Some long-established firms have an advantage here if they have consciously pursued consistent personnel policies. Andersen Consulting, though a young brand, has had a significant advantage, too, because it has inherited and refined Arthur Andersen's early investment in firmwide methodologies and training, which in turn allowed it to bid for major projects involving hundreds of people who had never previously worked together. It remains to be seen how and when the other consulting firms are able to catch up. In the future, as IT and changing industry boundaries mean that organisations converge, this ability to be able to redeploy a consistent skill-set in different – and rapidly evolving – sectors will be fundamental to success.

Buyers of consulting services will always be looking for particular types of input: some for innovative ideas, perhaps to take forward themselves; others for a complete solution which is guaranteed to work. But the implication of this, from a branding perspective, is that clients will more and more ask the question: 'what are you famous for?' in seeking likely service providers, even before they ask for a credential statement. If the reply is that they are widely known, have a well-recognised signage – the client will respond: 'so what?' If the reply is that they have a clear market proposition vis-à-vis their competitors, this may well be enough to qualify them. But true competitive advantage will lie with those firms which have people capable of solving the problem, able to work in a consistent way, and backed by an organisation that can deliver these solutions through a cohesive and distinctively characteristic frame of reference.

Francis Quinlan has long experience of working with professional firms. Prior to joining Hodgart Temporal he was for 12 years Director of Marketing for Arthur Andersen where he became a partner. During this period he developed the firm's successful marketing programmes in the UK and Europe and took a leadership role in the firm's global marketing strategy. He also worked on the development of Garretts, Andersen's associated law firm, and provided marketing consultancy to clients of the firm from time to time. Previously, he has worked in consulting with one of the leading international practices, in marketing management in several business sectors, and has taught marketing strategy at two business schools.

Founded in 1990, Hodgart Temporal is a strategic and management consultancy that specialises in advising professional firms in Europe. Hodgart Temporal's services are directed at enhancing the competitiveness and performance of their clients. Areas of specialisation include: strategy formulation and development, market and client research, remuneration and performance, organisational reviews, quality reviews, management training and development, profitability analysis and mergers. Hodgart Temporal's approach is based on a deep knowledge of how professional firms operate, their culture and their values. Hodgart Temporal has worked with some of the largest firms in their respective professions as well as a wide range of medium-sized and smaller firms and the firm is currently advising a number of partnerships about their international development. Offices are located in the West End and their US associate, Altman Weil, is based in Philadelphia with further offices across the US.

Notes

1. Danielle B. Nees and Larry E. Greiner, 'Seeing Behind the Look-Alike Management Consultants', *Organizational Dynamics*, 1985, p. 69.
2. *Financial Times*, 12 September 1995.
3. Quoted in *Management Consultant International*, January, 1996.
4. Neil A. Morgan, 'Professional Accountancy Firms and Marketing', *The Service Industries Journal*, 1990.
5. Brian P. Bloomfield and Ardha Daniel, 'The Role Of Management Consultants in the Development of Information Technology: The Indissoluble Naute of Socio-Economic Technocal Skills', *Journal of Management*, 1995, p. 40.

8

Specialisation

Some things don't change much:

- 'In the end, everyone should meet on (and fight over) the same patch – one that combines the merits of generalist and specialist.' (*The Economist*, 13 February 1988)
- 'The consultant of the future will be a specialist not a generalist, hungrier than ever before, better able to operate at boardroom level, more able to articulate the skills he has to other business units and better able to price jobs sensibly.' (Bob Simm, then head of KPMG consulting practice, in 1992[1])

Consultancy has always been a balance between generalisation and specialisation. Even in the smallest, most focused firms, the specialist consultant has been expected to complement his or her specific skills with a broad understanding of the business environment as a whole. Indeed, it is often this combination that has been used to distinguish 'consultants' from that lower breed of outsider, the 'contractor'. Somewhere along the line, the ideal of the 'T-shaped' consultant was born: someone who was capable of generalist knowledge across a wide range of areas, complemented by an in-depth understanding of one specific area.

The arguments for specialisation and generalisation are like those for outsourcing versus in-sourcing: fashion seems to swing in favour of one and then the other; the death of one is announced only for it to be suddenly resurrected the following year. Will this oscillation continue in the future, or should we expect to see a decisive move towards one approach?

To be able to answer this question, we first need to examine the drivers for and against each approach.

On the generalist side, the main factors have been: credibility and the need, first, for flexibility and, second, cohesion. Taking credibility first:

the ability to think broadly has not just been a distinguishing feature between a consultant and a contractor. It has also been a means by which consultants ensure that they are perceived to be – at least – their clients' equal (specialisation being the consultant's advantage over the client). It is the consultancy equivalent of general management. Just as a client company will put its most valuable staff through a career development programme which is designed to give them the necessary skills and breadth of exposure to allow them to progress to senior management positions, so a consultancy needs to ensure that its consultants can hold their own at board level by demonstrating comparable credentials. The importance of generalisation in consultancy is therefore directly correlated with the perceived importance of the concept of 'general management' to business.

But, if generalisation is important in terms of credibility, it is considerably more important internally. Ensuring that its consultants have some degree of general business understanding gives a consulting firm the flexibility to identify opportunities for new business, to change focus where a specific skill becomes redundant and – conversely – to move resources to areas of high demand. Put at its simplest, generalisation creates flexibility, and flexibility creates profits.

Furthermore, flexibility provides a degree of cohesion. There is relatively little 'glue' holding consultancy organisations together: few firms are held together by strong brands, established products or – even – long-standing client relationships. Staff turnover among consultants may be as high as 30 per cent, but, even over the course of the average 3–4 year stint with a particular firm, much of a consultant's time will be spent out on clients' sites. Specialisation leads to organisational fragmentation, and generalisation is one of the few offsetting factors that consulting firms have at their disposal. Giving up their generalist characteristics could also endanger their ability to get people to work together.

This raises the important issue of synergy. Are consulting firms synergistic? What can the 'mega-firms' do that small consultants cannot? In the consulting industry – unlike, say, manufacturing – synergies do not necessarily give rise to economies of scale – as evidenced by the fact that the fee rates for small consultancies are often much lower. The advantages of size lie in the level of investment possible, global reach, flexibility of resources and the ability to address client issues from multiple directions. But all these advantages become much more difficult to realise without generalisation. Generalisation, therefore, is the essential channel for synergy: without it, the different parts of consulting organisations would not be able to talk to each other, let alone work together.

What then are the factors that push consulting firms in the opposite direction – towards specialisation? By contrast with generalisation – which is fundamentally driven by internal needs – the pressure for specialisation comes from external sources: the need to be able to deliver added value services and to demonstrate a differentiated positioning in the marketplace. Specialisation is one of the primary means by which consulting firms distinguish themselves from their competitors (a point which was covered in greater depth in the previous chapter).

In a market in which management theories often look homogeneous and innovative ideas can be copied almost instantly, depth – rather than breadth – of experience has become essential in clients' eyes. Being able to field, not just a national expert, but an international expert in a specific area is already a critical success factor in winning some types of new business. This pressure from clients is fuelled by several factors: the declining role of the general business manager, the increased complexity of almost all areas of management which means that functional directors have to be experts as much as co-ordinators, and perhaps a growing cynicism about management theory. In a world where the value of an intangible service is a hotly debated topic, being able to demonstrate specialist know-how is tantamount to proving your worth. There are few clients who would be prepared to pay a lot of money for a generalist, however good: there are many who already are paying a great deal for specialists with particularly in-depth understanding of an area of specific relevance. Part of the reason for this is obvious – a specialist has the skills the client organisation lacks – but other parts are more subtle. Clients perceive specialists as able to provide a solution that generalists – clients themselves, in effect – cannot provide for themselves. Having a specialist skill implies a special solution. Buying specialists also puts the client in control: it is the client who has defined the problem and identified the kind of expertise required to resolve it. By contrast, generalist consultants have a greater opportunity to set the agenda.

Of course, it is possible to be too black and white about this, especially where the next few years are concerned. There remains a small number of immensely influential clients – the CEOs of major corporations – who will undoubtedly continue to value the holistic perspective and wide range of business knowledge that a top strategy consultant brings. Focusing on a specialist skill could be detrimental in this area of the market because it might well compromise the more lateral view being provided.

But, with the exception of this type of consultancy, it seems reasonable to say that the pressure to specialise is mostly driven by external factors, and the pressure to generalise, by internal ones. Clearly, these are interrelated – it is as much in the consulting companies' interest as their clients' that they can wield the specialist skills to carry out an assignment. But, that being said, it is important to recognise that the interests of consulting firms and their clients are not entirely convergent on this issue. Clients want specialisation: consultants want to give them specialists, but cannot afford to have an organisation that is solely made up of specialists who are likely to be much less flexible than their generalist counterparts.

So, if these are the pressures that mean that many consulting firms swing to and fro between generalism and specialism, where should we expect the pendulum to stop in the next 5–10 years? Assuming that market forces play their part, there can be no question: specialisation will win. The issue, therefore, is how will the majority of firms – especially those without any differentiated market position or a clear sense of where they add specific value to their clients – adapt to this situation? While greater specialism may resolve difficulties in some areas – notably improving the value for money that clients perceive and creating greater differentiation – it will inevitably exacerbate others – flexibility, and internal cohesion and synergy.

Solving the problems of specialisation?

Flexibility

Flexibility is essential to the consulting industry. It allows firms to move resources from declining to expanding markets with minimal upheaval. It means that the skills and intellectual capital it has amassed in one sector can be redeployed in another. How will consulting firms cope with the reduced flexibility that accompanies specialisation?

The first step will be to recognise it as a problem. At the moment, the combined generalist/specialist option – that 'T-shaped' consultant – has been a means of avoiding the issue. In the absence of any structural balance between the two approaches, it has effectively been the responsibility of individual consultants (aided by the relevant training) to reconcile them. But, as that personal balance becomes harder to maintain – indeed, as there is less of an incentive to maintain it, as career development will depend on specialisation rather than general business knowledge – firms will have to take on greater corporate responsibility for finding a solution.

One approach would be to encourage consultants to be generalists up to a certain grade/seniority and to specialise thereafter – making explicit what happens in many firms implicitly. The problem, however, will be that the economic advantages of specialisation – as partners/directors try to leverage their very expensive time with specialised support – will put pressure on the organisation to start the process of becoming specialised sooner rather than later. Thus, specialisation will, over time, start at more and more junior grades: except in the most homogeneous of consulting firms and markets, the level of generalisation will be difficult to control and sustain.

The more heterogeneous firms may find it easier to employ more freelance consultants – 'free agents' as they increasingly call themselves in the US, so that flexibility is maintained through multiple short-term contracts instead of employing large numbers of people on a permanent basis. This is a model which makes particularly good sense if we accept that the turnover rates of intellectual capital are likely to increase. Rather than accepting that a consultant has a shelf life of 10–20 years, we may need to recognise that the equivalent shelf-life in the future may be less than five years and that, rather than stay with a consulting firm for a long period, a consultant needs to move in and out, recharging his/her intellectual capital either by working in industry or by formal training. Effectively, this route allows market forces to solve the problem for the consulting firms, because individuals – in order to ensure their continued employability – will adapt to changing environments much more quickly than any institutional training programme could. Rather than 'T-shaped' consultants, we will essentially have consultants who are just the stem of the 'T', but are likely to be several such 'stems' over the course of their working lives.

However, while this model makes for enormous and self-sustaining flexibility, it will not be easy to manage. If consultancies are increasingly struggling to attract the best people from what they see to be a dwindling pool of qualified resources, then surely a system in which they are having to negotiate for all of these people all of the time will leave them considerably more vulnerable to being unable to meet demand when required? Consulting firms will need a new human resource model to be able to deal with this issue – something which few firms have even started to consider.

Internal cohesion and synergy

In *Managing the Professional Service Firm*, David Maister points out that collaboration and co-operation across (internal) boundaries is preached internally, and is fervently desired, but is hard to accomplish. Not because of bad management, but because of the complex managerial task of reaching for the benefits of both local autonomy and collaborative action. [2]

The essential problem, he argues, is that the work of professional service firms has always to be adapted to the needs of its local market and a local, largely autonomous business unit is the best way to do this. The corporate body, therefore, is driven by coalitions between these business units, rather than by any push from the centre. If the centre is to add value, then it comes, first, from helping the local practice perform its function more effectively and, second, from targeting those clients which may be beyond the reach of any one local practice (such as multinational clients).

The impact of specialisation on a firm's ability to 'network' value around its organisation will be threefold. In the first place, as the specialist areas become more clearly defined – 'deeper', if you like – and the divide between specialisms greater, it is inevitable that different agendas will start to emerge. It will also become harder to identify a common strategy which is more than the sum of its individual parts. Second, and as a direct result of these divergent strategies, the value the centre is able to add gets less: looking at the world from a centralist, generalist perspective will not help these individual business units. Even centralised functions, such as training and career development, may be much less relevant, as each specialist area will have its own needs. Much more helpful to the specialist business unit – and this is the third and most important effect of specialisation as a whole – will be to be able to link up to its parallel units in other parts of the world. In other words, the extent of integration by specialism within global consulting organisations will be much greater than at present, where the national firm structure often tends to come between the local specialist group and their counterparts elsewhere (Figure 8.1). Thus, the specialist team dealing with, for example, supply chain management, will forge links with other supply chain management teams.

Being reliant on people and intellectual capital, consulting firms are fluid, self-adapting organisations. As it becomes clear that the greatest value to be added comes from the closer collaboration of groups of people across the world who are working in the same specialised field, the structure of the firms will adapt to accommodate this. Thus, the role of the national, even that of the international firm, becomes subsumed into the specialist structure. Clearly, in practice, this may apply to some specialisms more than others, but, overall, we should expect to see this kind of model emerge.

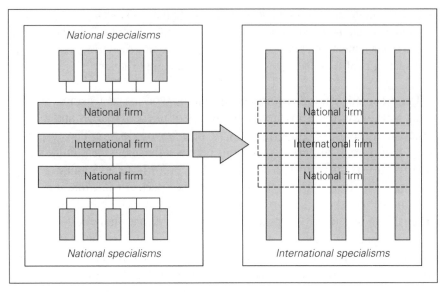

Figure 8.1 Creating the specialist firm

As a model, it obviously poses a serious threat to the one-firm concept: inter-specialism networking is both harder to achieve and – from the point of view of the specialists themselves – increasingly irrelevant; the specialist sub-brands may start to compete with a firm's overall brand. Most significantly, it may change the rules of competition within the industry. As we discussed in the previous chapter, competition between consulting firms occurs on many fronts, largely because the distinctions – at least between the major firms – are slight. By contrast, niche players have a tremendous advantage because they can develop clear – specialist – reputations in their chosen markets. As the specialisms within generalist firms emerge much more strongly, there will be fewer points of overlap and the level of direct competition will decline. This changing competitive landscape begs a further question: to what extent will the collaboration between specialist areas go beyond the boundaries of single firms? After all, it follows that if the greatest synergy within a firm will be between similar, but geographically dispersed specialisms, why should this synergy stop at the gates?

This will undoubtedly be a thin-end-of-the-wedge issue. As clients' demands become more precise and the level of specialisation deeper, individual business units will start to look for additional skills. Some of them will find what they need through organic staff development or recruitment, but others will create links with similar groups of specialists elsewhere. The number of firms operating in each specialist market will decrease: competition will be between groups of related specialists, rather than between individual firms. Over time, we may even see quasi-monopolies emerging in some areas, especially where the specialism itself is new and resources comparatively scarce. In order to make an impact on the market, and to meet demand they stimulate, the specialist groups from different firms, together with complementary niche players, may well have to work together. From a profitability point of view, this is unlikely to be a problem: it may even be a more profitable structure than the one we have today. But it clearly makes it more difficult to hold a multi-disciplinary firm together. With 'value' travelling up and down the specialist groupings, not across them, the glue that keeps such firms together is necessarily weaker.

What, then, will be the role of the centre? Will there be a role? Or will consulting firms simply switch to this much more vertically differentiated, even fragmented structure? In so far as the centre does have a role, it will be in managing the risks of structures like the one envisaged here.

An area where the input of the centre will be crucial will be in the management of the portfolio. Most multi-disciplinary firms subscribe to the idea of portfolio management, although very few have made it work in reality. But it seems likely that the managing partners of the future will have to take a much more proactive role in deciding in which specialisms to invest. The generalist core of consulting firms will become much more like a holding company, whose function is to maximise the overall value of the asset for its stakeholders in acquiring, developing and disposing of specialist areas. The holding company provides a useful analogy: it will become less important to employ practising consultants in the centre, both because the role of the centre will be closer to investment management than consultancy and because, as a generation of specialists grows up, it will become increasingly difficult to find individuals with the *breadth* of experience to manage the service portfolio in its entirety. It also follows that, if you no longer need consultants to run a consultancy, anyone can – and probably will – start doing it. It will be logical, in the future (and once various regulatory issues have been resolved), to find investment banks and other asset management companies running, not so much consulting firms, but groups of consulting services, operating in parallel under some sort of corporate brand. We should expect to see non-consulting companies with strong existing brands exploiting those brands by offering consulting services. This has already happened to a degree within the hardware and software markets (IBM, for example, has a consulting practice which is able to exploit its parent's brand). But how long will it be before we have Coca-Cola or Virgin Consulting?

Change, however, is likely to be slight and incremental, as one specialism after another gradually establishes stronger vertical, rather than horizontal, links. It does not, therefore, spell the sudden end of the multi-disciplinary firm, although it certainly makes the latter's role a more challenging one. Instead, what we should expect to see is that the managing teams from such firms take on a more detached, holding company-style role. While other asset management companies might be looking to enter the consulting market, consulting companies – having acquired a taste for asset management – may well find themselves taking on non-consulting assets.

Notes

1. *Financial Times*, 21 October 1992.
2. David Maister, *Managing the Professional Services Firm*, New York: Free Press, 1993, p. 329.

9

The Changing Balance of People and Technology

Re-engineering the raw material of consulting

Some food for thought:

- A survey in the *Financial Times* in January 1998 showed that consultancies are the largest single recruiters of MBA students. But, within three years of being recruited, almost a third of these people had moved on.
- One estimate suggests that a total of 250 000 new recruits will be required by the industry by 2000.[1]
- Assuming an average salary of $80 000, recruitment agency fee of 25 per cent of salary, and $10 000 for induction, the recruitment bill for a big consultancy is something in the region of $50m per annum. And this probably just covers attrition: firms that plan to expand will be spending far more.
- In 1998 *Fortune* reported that first-tier consulting firms were, in fact, offering $92 000 to new graduates.

Many organisations pay lip service to the idea of being a 'people business', but it is hard to conceive of an industry which is more genuinely dependent on its people than consultancy. The core consulting process has involved experienced individuals reapplying their skills in new situations, thinking on their feet, and working closely with their clients' people. And it has been heresy – until very recently – to suggest that it could, or should, be otherwise.

People have been *the* source of fundamental strength to the consulting industry, translating what could so easily be – and often is – seen as irrelevant management theory into concepts and working practices that clients initially understand and ultimately value. You only have to scan the annual reports and promotional material prepared by consultancies to see how important the people factor is: intangible services are made concrete by including pictures and thumbnail sketches of the consultants involved.

The rapid growth in consultancy since the early 1970s has happened (indeed, been facilitated by) a time in which demographic trends have been highly favourable to the industry. First, with the baby-boom generation, there have simply been more people entering the labour market; second, the number of women entering the labour market has also risen; third, as access to higher education has eased, the number of people with degrees has also grown. Of these trends: the baby-boom is over – the proportion of people aged between 25 and 34 in both the US and UK has been falling since the mid-1980s; the number of women entering the economy has largely plateaued; only the number of people with degrees continues to rise. 'Consultants have a big people problem', announced *Fortune* in 1998:

> It's an incredible thought: The world doesn't have enough consultants. But there is a problem – a big one. Consulting firms, even the largest and most prestigious, face an acute shortage of their principal asset – people.[3]

One solution – and it is also the one on which most consulting firms are currently focused – is for consultancy to make itself more attractive for potential recruits, to make sure that it maximises its share of the highest quality parts of the labour market. In the first place, this will probably mean changing the recruitment profile, perhaps to recruit older and much more experienced people (the cut-off point, especially for the strategy houses, remains the early thirties), perhaps to recruit people from very different backgrounds (astrophysicists rather than business school graduates). Second, it may also mean that consulting firms have to take into account the shift in attitudes among a younger generation of recruits, people who may be looking for a more balanced lifestyle, rather than the ambitious and dedicated recruits who characterised the 1980s. It seems likely, also, that consultancy firms will need to change their own organisational structures to accommodate this preference for more flexible working – job-sharing, a greater number of freelance consultants. The relationship between the firm and these 'semi-detached' employees may be quite different, with individuals not only taking responsibility for their career development but funding it as well, as consultancies become less and less prepared to invest in training where they know that the recipient is likely to leave in less than five years. Consultancies will still provide training – indeed, one can foresee that they will provide more and more as the educational system fails to deliver recruits of the level required

– but it may be that it is the individual consultant who pays for it, motivated by the need to keep their individual CV up to date.

But, whatever the solution tried, attracting and retaining people more effectively is unlikely to be the complete solution. Perhaps there is a single, perfect solution that, when it is found, will genuinely create a sustainable competitive advantage for the winning firm, that one firm will find a strategy which means that its rivals become chronically – fatally – under-resourced.

But it seems more likely that such changes, as they are made, will be mimicked by competitors. Changes in the culture and management of firms take time to have an impact – time enough for other firms to catch up. Changing the way consultants manage their people asset is unlikely to be enough to solve the underlying problem of scarce resources.

The end of the people model?

But, while consultancies are 'people businesses', their reliance on people also has its drawbacks:

- people may enable growth, but they can also be an obstacle towards greater profitability;
- consistent high-quality output is hard to control; and
- finally, while consultancies may be clinging to their existing ways of working, clients are exploring new approaches and these may set their expectations in the future, forcing consulting firms to change.

The people model and limitations to profitability

But the number of people a consultancy has does not just drive its top line, it controls the bottom line as well.

Profitability across the industry is determined, not just by the extent to which consultants are 'utilised' and their individual fee rates, but by the ratio of staff to partners or directors. But, irrespective of the relative profitability of firms across the industry as a whole, the fact that time and materials tend to be by far the dominant source of income means that the extent to which an individual firm can improve its profitability is limited. Unlike a software firm, for example, a consultancy cannot obviously develop something and then produce it at virtually no extra cost. Unlike merchant banks, consultants have not charged premium sums for passing on information about, say, an opportunity to a potentially interested party. Consultancies can – and do – put up their daily rates, but their profitability is still restricted by the number of hours their staff can work.

In an environment where companies – particularly high-tech companies – are earning super profits by exploiting their intellectual capital in different ways (patenting a specific gene is a good illustration), it cannot be long before consulting firms start to look actively at alternative methods of generating profits. Just because the operational model they have had has worked to date, does not mean that it is going to be a sufficiently effective model going forward.

People and quality

The problems with the people model do not stop with limited profitability, but extend to the way in which consulting firms are exposed to risk. It has always been difficult to control the quality of people. With all the methodologies in the world, a consultancy could still not guarantee to clients that the quality of what they receive will be consistent across the board. A manufacturing company can produce identical ball-bearings, but rewind the tape, and every consulting project will turn out slightly differently.

In the 1960s and 1970s – the golden age of fact-based consulting – inconsistency was probably not too much of an issue: problems in the course of the assignment could be eclipsed by the brilliance of the final report; results could be caveated. In any case, consultancy was a serial process – as a consultant you moved from one assignment to another, barely getting to know the client and certainly not around long enough to be known by them. Longer-term strengths and weaknesses – indeed, individual characters – tended to remain hidden. But the emergence of IT-related and process consulting exposed consultants to longer assignments in which it was much more difficult to standardise behaviour, let alone quality. Since the late 1970s, consulting projects have grown in scale, scope and criticality. Given this coincidence of more visible inconsistency with the growing strategic importance of consultancy assignments, it is hardly surprising that clients have become increasingly prepared to protect their interests. Although most cases continue to be settled out of court, litigation by clients is on the increase.

From the liability perspective, finding some means of being able to deliver more 'shrink-wrapped' services has become an increasingly urgent task. As assignments become longer and more complex, the problem can only escalate. Consulting firms need to be able to make a transition similar to that of software houses, moving from bespoke development to offering packaged solutions which can be tailored, mostly cosmetically, to meet a client's individual specifications. Like packaged software, this type of consultancy will be pre-tested; generally bug-free; controllable; and so on. Whatever is involved in it, it seems likely that people will play a more limited role than at present.

Changing client expectations

To these two internal limitations of the people model – the need for increased sales and profits, the risks involved in relying on people – we should add a third, external reason which is likely to drive change.

We have already cited the example of software companies that have found what is, in effect, a new model for generating profits: invest massively in developing a software package which can be manufactured and distributed almost for free. Both information technology and the information stored on it are clearing the way for new ways of working. The Internet is already having a significant impact on airline ticket purchasing, for example. Under a process called yield-management, airlines can change the price of tickets depending on the demand; unsold tickets can be auctioned. Travel agents are just one of many groups which are being 'dis-intermediated' as customers make their purchases direct from the supplier or manufacturer.

Consultants' clients are living in an environment where some of their fundamental assumptions about pricing, channels to market, even delivery mechanisms are changing hugely. The fact that consultancy is highly dependent on people (rather than technology) has, to an extent, buffered the industry against these trends, but the insulation will wear thin relatively soon. Clients will be looking to consultancies to match the upheaval that they themselves are facing, in much the same way that global clients have expected their consultants to develop global operations. They will, in effect, be looking to consultants to exploit the same new technologies and channels available to them. Why should a bank offering PC-based banking not also expect their advisers to offer PC-based consultancy? Why should a retailer which has moved into home shopping not expect its consultants to offer a comparable service? Ten, or even five, years ago, there was immense scepticism that consumers would be willing to buy these kinds of products by telephone or via a computer: should we not expect consultancy to have to make a similar shift, improbable though it may currently seem?

Looking for new human resource models

All these factors – the inherent disadvantages of the people-based model of consulting, plus the changes in the external environment – make it likely that consultancies will, over the next decade, have to experiment with a whole series of alternatives to their existing *modus operandi*. As the senior partner of one firm acknowledged:

> In part we will see an evolution to not just human-based consulting, but to innovative ways to package and use knowledge differently. With the growth rates in consulting over the past five years, there won't be enough people. We have to change the labour component and at the same time increase the value added to the client.[4]

But perhaps the solution does not lie with managing people differently.

Clearly, improving the way in which consulting firms use technology and collate their intellectual capital via knowledge management systems (two areas of key investment at the present) suggest ways to leverage the shrinking human asset more effectively. Another strategy has been to specialise in specific areas (obviating the need to recruit across the board) and to focus on those service areas (notably in IT-related consultancy) where it has been possible to develop a standardised approach. IT assignments provide a regular source of income which can be used on training and development, and investing in new products. And, because IT-related work is a more homogeneous market than traditional consulting markets, it is easier to develop standard training courses and methodologies that reduce the need to recruit specialised people and minimise the risk of problems. As a result, the ratio of partners to staff is much lower than for less IT-orientated firms.

But IT-related consulting alleviates the people problem only marginally, by allowing relatively unskilled people to be trained rapidly in standard procedures. A more substantial advantage can be gained by converting some of the IT expertise which has built up in these companies into software. Andersen Consulting has its Centre for Strategic Technology Research; PricewaterhouseCoopers has its Advanced Software Engineering Centre.

However, it is a strategy which is not without risks. Potentially, technology cannibalises consultancy by converting what used to be the expertise of an individual into software which can be used by clients themselves (Figure 9.1). When a consulting firm develops some new intellectual capital – a way to optimise R&D expenditure, for example –

it does so with the aim of increasing sales. If the service proves very successful it may find itself with too many clients and not enough consultants to do the work (one of the classic limitations of the people model in practice). To overcome this, it may convert part or all of that intellectual capital into a software package (in this case, perhaps a computer model which carries out the actual process of optimisation). Doing so will allow the firm to earn higher than normal profits, because it will be able to carry out more 'consultancy' with fewer people. But higher profits will, in turn, attract other players, notably software houses which would then develop their own 'packaged' version of this service. By incorporating the new application into their existing software (as a special module, say) the software company will be able to tap into an existing client base much more readily than the consulting firm: if an organisation already has the software company's financial package, they will probably be interested in a new module which will both reduce their R&D budgets and can be easily and cost-effectively integrated with their existing systems. Coming from the software company, which will not be burdened with the development costs of having to think up the idea in the first place, the software package will also be cheaper. In the battle between the two, the software house will probably be the victor: clients will continue to buy the idea, but not from the consulting firm – which is, effectively, back to square one.

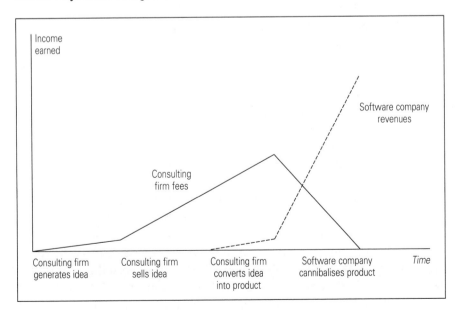

Figure 9.1 Cannibalising the consulting market

Providing the consulting firm can continue to generate new intellectual capital, this scenario will not prove disastrous, but once the speed with which those ideas can be generated falls behind the time it takes to convert them into software packages, consulting firms will be facing a market in which their ideas are cannibalised, almost before they have taken them out to clients.

It is probably an inevitable development – in fact we can already see signs of it in some very specialised areas of consulting. For example, some types of tax review, which only a couple of years ago would have been done by a team of tax specialists, can now be done much more effectively by computer models. Computerised benchmarking tools are also only automating what until recently would have been conventional consulting assignments. If the situation is here to stay, then the imperative for consultancies will be to try to take control of the process, to initiate and manage the conversion of their ideas into software by allying themselves closely with software houses, even acquiring their own software houses. It seems inevitable, therefore, that the distinction that largely exists at present between consultancy and software will start to blur significantly.

Consulting on the Internet

But perhaps the most important new opportunity – and one that consulting firms have barely started to consider – is the Internet.

Current approaches vary: some sites contain high-level marketing information only, while others are taking a much more interactive approach, providing clients with benchmarking tools where they can assess their performance in specific areas relative to a database of other organisations. Many firms are already using the Internet to create seamless email links with their clients, effectively removing one of the more visible barriers between clients and their advisers.

But the Internet offers three key opportunities to consulting firms. In the first place, it can be used to give clients access to consulting know-how without having to go through the process of hiring actual consultants. This will probably take the form of a database that will be available on a subscription basis, and be aimed at smaller clients for whom a full-scale consulting assignment would be prohibitively expensive. Ernst & Young was the first of the large professional services firms to sell its consulting services over the Internet. ERNIE was launched in May 1996, and aimed at providing advice to small to medium-sized companies, especially the fast-growing among them. It is a subscription-based service that enables users to address questions to consultants under a small number of broad category headings. These questions are forwarded on to an expert in the specific area and an answer returned within two days. Users can download the proprietary information they require and browse through a database of answers to frequently asked questions.

The second key opportunity is that the Internet can be used as a means of delivering relevant information to a highly targeted audience. As well as the 'pull' technology of facilities such as ERNIE, consultancies will be able to 'push' specific information to the people to whom it will be of most interest. Having got – for example – clients to register their interests, consulting firms will be able to send them information which is precisely relevant to their needs. Moreover, once someone has entered their interests – and, most importantly, received useful information in exchange – there will be little incentive for them to pass on those same interests to another consulting firm. Thus, the firm which secures information from clients first is likely to retain these clients, providing again that it gives them something worth being loyal for. As the consulting firm and its clients exchange more information, a much more detailed profile of the latter's interests and concerns will emerge, increasingly enabling the consulting firm to distribute precisely targeted information. Nor will the benefits stop here. Having built up a very detailed relationship with its clients, the consulting firm will be able to act as an intermediary, passing on other information – from third parties – in which the client is likely to be interested. Clients will gain, as they will have a source of increasingly relevant information, which has been tailored to their exact needs. Third party suppliers of information will gain, because their 'product' will be reaching the people it most wants to target. And consulting firms will gain, because they become the 'owners' of the client, able to broker mutually beneficial deals on their clients' behalf. For some consulting companies, this way of doing business may prove more profitable than conventional consulting; thus, we should expect to see a migration of traditional consulting firms into the 'information-broking business'.

This relationship leads on to the third advantage of Web-based activities for consultants. Clearly, it can be used, not just to send clients useful information, but to target the marketing of consulting services much more effectively. 'One-to-one' marketing could resolve the doubts many consulting firms have traditionally had about proactive marketing. It would enable them to use traditional marketing techniques (such as mailshots), but tailor them to suit the interests and history of each individual client. Each client would, therefore, receive a letter or brochure which is designed to appeal to them on a very precise basis – including the types of services in which they are known to be particularly interested, perhaps even in the style which they tend to prefer. It would be the information age's answer to the practitioner who conventionally visited each of his or her clients to discuss their needs on an individual basis. Once again, other companies – retailers, banks, manufacturers – are already experimenting with this type of communication strategy: it is only a matter of time before consultancies start to realise its particular potential in their industry and adopt the same approach.

Perspective 9.1   Pauline Bickerton, founder and director of MarketingNet

The Internet presents consulting firms with two huge opportunities. In the first place, it could provide them with a much more intelligent channel for managing client relationships; second, it will allow them to represent their expertise in new and more accessible ways. Consulting firms at present have barely scratched the surface of what is possible in these respects.

At the moment, a client looking for advice from a large consultancy has to navigate through a whole series of internal obstacles: Who should they talk to? What department are they in? Are they the real specialists in a particular field or will someone else in another office be a better person to talk to? These hurdles are symptomatic of the extent to which organisations are broken down into functional units. For a client, who needs to move from one functional area to another, the journey can be especially difficult. Developing an effective and interactive Web site challenges these internal divisions: for it to be successful, you need the continued input of the whole organisation. Doing this is not easy: many people will feel threatened by having to make themselves and their skills quite so accessible, but for the firms that manage the transition, the benefits will be enormous. You can foresee sites that play the role of 'virtual sales people', taking potential clients through a series of intelligent question and answer sessions in order to clarify their needs and to identify the person most suitable to handle their enquiry. Rather than trying to leave telephone messages, becoming frustrated at lack of feedback or simply feeling confused, clients will know exactly where they are in the process and exactly what will happen next. Rather than both the client and consultant being uninformed about each other's business, an Internet-based process will allow them to exchange and refine information throughout the process. At the moment, a potential client is at the mercy of the consulting firm when they try to make contact: an Internet-based process will put them much more in control.

One of the key ways in which the Internet is already changing business is to make an organisation's or an individual's knowledge much more public: we are entering an age where companies will have to be much more open and proactive in highlighting the intellectual assets that give them competitive advantage.

For consulting firms, this will probably mean having to experiment with 'surgery'-style approaches in which experts are available on-line at specific times to deal with queries from existing and potential clients. Culturally, consulting firms have been circumspect about giving away their intellectual capital, but their reputation and credibility in the future could depend on the extent to which they make their ideas accessible in this type of interactive forum.

Although this kind of approach still centres on the individual expert, its long-term effect will be to strengthen the brand. As more and more information becomes available it will be the overall quality and accessibility of information from the firm in total that will become important. The Internet, therefore, will shift the balance in consultancy marketing, away from the individual expert, and much more towards the collective knowledge-base.

Both these trends – the 'virtual sales person' and the collective knowledge-base – will mean that the consulting firm of the future will need to rely much less on the individual consultant going out to talk to clients in order to win new work. Ten years ago, we all might have thought that the idea of dealing with a bank via a touch-tone telephone would be too unwieldy and impersonal to work: now it is part of our everyday lives. Who says that consultancy won't be sold almost wholly across the Internet in the future?

Pauline Bickerton is a founder and director of MarketingNet. She is also the co-author of *Cybermarketing: How to use the Superhighway to Market your Products and Services* (Butterworth–Heinemann, Oxford: 1996). MarketingNet is a creative marketing agency specialising specifically in bespoke marketing for the Internet. Founded in 1995 and based in the UK, it provides a wide range of clients with technical development and support, combined with specialist marketing consultancy.

Notes

1. Kennedy Research Group.
2. *Fortune*, 13 April 1998.
3. *Ibid.*
4. *Management Consultant International*, June, 1996.

10 Globalisation

Globalisation – from solution to potential problem

For the past decade, globalisation has been *the* panacea for consulting ills – clients' and consultants' alike.

Initially, globalisation was justified on the basis that clients, who were themselves operating on an increasingly transnational basis, expected their advisers to do the same. 'The major clients are looking for consultancy support on a global scale', reported *Director* magazine as long ago as 1989:

> An international company now, for example, wants an information technology network designed and implemented throughout its entire empire, not just in one country. And it wants a consultancy that can mobilise specialists all over the world quickly and that can do the job ... At the moment these demands are restricted to a small number of clients, but of course, it represents a large chunk of business.[1]

In an interview a few years later, John Harris, then European President of Booz-Allen & Hamilton, explained that their strategy was based on a recognition that:

> our clients were moving into pan-European markets, that globalisation was an emerging management issue and that our ability to provide technology and implementation services was a basis for competitive differentiation. Our response to this situation involves operating on a pan-European basis, assigning industry and functional specialists to client teams and drawing upon resources in the US and around the world. One of our priorities is to concentrate on clients who are global competitors.[2]

Globalisation has been a source of growth for consulting firms. Clients looked to consultancy firms to provide the skills and knowledge to give them a competitive edge in their global markets. With technology, political and regulatory environments changing radically (European monetary union being a good example), consultancy firms were able to develop multiple service lines around the strategic and operational implications. Globalisation became a question of credibility: how could a consulting firm advise a global client if it was not global itself?

However, the past few years have seen a growing acknowledgement that the rationale for global consulting firms is as much internal as external. First, the recession of the early 1990s highlighted the extent to which having a genuinely global network of resources allowed a firm to move consultants out of areas or markets which were recession-hit and into more buoyant economies. This is the model that many strategy houses have used for decades. Here, the worldwide sharing of resources is underpinned by transnational profit-sharing: thus, when one part of the world is in recession, the firm can refocus on regions which are less affected; if there is a problem with one country, it is in the interests of all the countries to resolve it. Second, much of the infrastructure required by consulting firms to support expansion (intellectual capital, knowledge-sharing, technology, and so on) is already proving highly expensive: pooling investment across countries will be a fundamental means by which the capital is raised for future expenditure of this nature.

Of the Big Five firms, Andersen Consulting is widely perceived to have led the way in terms of global integration, helped by its 'one-firm' culture, but the other firms are now rapidly following suit by restructuring their consultancy practices and expanding (either organically or through merger/acquisition) into new countries. A cursory survey of activity during 1997 shows, for example, Price Waterhouse strengthening its presence in Russia and South Korea, Coopers & Lybrand in Finland and Hungary, Ernst & Young in India and Japan, Bain & Co. in Brazil, and Gemini Consulting in Switzerland.

Progress is being made, in some areas, and by some firms, more than others. But for the majority of consulting companies there is still a long way to go before the ideal of the global firm, as it is being talked about today, becomes a reality. National firms continue not to co-operate; cultural difficulties and domestic loyalties are still major barriers; performance measurements still encourage the traditional, quasi-feudal perspective. For the largest firms, there are decades of mergers and acquisitions to overcome; for the smallest, the logistical pains of establishing a viable foothold in an overseas market are as difficult as ever.

Globalisation – as a major strategic and operational issue for consulting firms – is unlikely to go away within the next ten years.

The remaining challenges of globalisation

But, at the same time, it is difficult to believe that the approach taken by consulting firms to globalisation will remain unchanged. Despite the progress made towards globalisation, the consulting industry has yet to go through the major industry shift similar to that, for example, which the advertising industry experienced during the early 1990s when it tried to make the move from domestic to transnational operations.

Although now ten years old, Christopher Bartlett and Sumantra Ghoshal's guide to creating the transnational company, *Managing Across Borders*, remains one of the most respected studies on the challenges of globalisation. But Bartlett and Ghoshal's focus was primarily on manufacturing and consumer service companies. What if we were to try to apply today the lessons they drew from these sectors to the consulting industry? They identified three fundamental barriers to 'transnationalism':

- strategic barriers, where a company had difficulty breaking through the management bias that had built up over decades in order to recognise the new opportunities of a global trading environment;
- organisational barriers, where the structure of a company undermined any attempt to introduce cross-border working;
- cultural barriers, where the outlook of an established group had, over time, become accepted as the organisation's institutional norm, preventing a more diverse operating environment becoming accepted.

Of these three obstacles, it is the third – perhaps surprisingly – that is likely to pose the greatest challenge to the globalisation of consulting firms. The first two issues are widely recognised and largely dealt with, but the third remains to be grasped effectively. This is because the cultural shift which should underpin the process of globalisation is not about 'simply' switching from one culture to another, perhaps from having a national, comparatively closed environment to having a much more open operation. It is about switching from having one dominant culture to accepting multi-culturalism – 'legitimising diversity' in Bartlett and Ghoshal's words. In successful transnational companies, according to their estimation:

Management not only recognised the importance of the complex and changeable external forces affecting operations, but tried to reflect those characteristics internally through the development of an organization with multidimensional perspectives.[3]

Yet most consultancies would pride themselves on their flexibility and on their ability to respond quickly to changing demands from clients. Why is it, then, that culture may be such a potential barrier? Essentially, it is because flexibility and diversity are not necessarily the same things – tempting though it is to see them as such. The flexibility of consultancy, in which an assignment for one client can be analysed into rational, discrete 'methodologies' that can subsequently be applied to other clients, is the quintessential product of the Anglo-Saxon economies. Other – notably continental European and Far Eastern – economies place much greater emphasis on integration (rather than fragmentation through analysis), experience (rather than method) and community (rather than individual). As Charles Hampden-Turner and Fons Trompenaars argue in *The Seven Cultures of Capitalism*:

> The whole consultant culture is American; the very idea of sending a wise individual to mend a group is an individualistic concept.[4]

In fact, it would be possible to argue that flexibility and diversity are mutually exclusive, so far as consulting firms are concerned. In order to continue meeting client needs – in order to continue to be flexible – consulting firms need some degree of operational coherence. Think how difficult it is to pull together a team of consultants, not all of whom speak English as a first language. Now overlay this with the idea of bringing together people who have very different preconceptions about, say, organisational redesign. The process by which a consulting firm responds to clients' needs – their flexibility – has to become slower as a result. This is because the flexibility of a consulting firm does not come from taking a pre-existing idea and changing it, but from pulling together several pre-existing ideas into a new synergistic whole and one which meets the needs of an individual client better than any one idea in isolation. Consultancies win assignments – usually – because they can integrate their ideas more effectively than their rivals, not because they are more innovative. Clearly, globalisation should provide a wider, much richer source of ideas that can be pulled together for clients – indeed, this is essentially the benefit that firms are seeking when they go down the globalisation road. But there is a real risk of anarchy: consultancies will have more ideas from which to choose, but less ideological coherence – fewer 'rules' – about how they should be integrated. Why should a French approach to an issue be any better than, say, a Korean?

The push towards globalisation in the future will need to address this issue. How do you balance having access to new ideas – multi-culturalism – with having a single approach to bringing these ideas together and applying them? How do you balance creativity with control?

There will undoubtedly be longer-term solutions, as we bring up a generation of children who are infinitely more comfortable with the differences and ambiguity of a globalised environment. In the short term, however, different options will have to be explored.

The emergence of the global 'super-firm'?

Nor are the problems of globalisation confined to this one issue. So far as the consulting industry is concerned, it is also already apparent that the costs of complete integration – people, processes, systems, strategy, and marketing – will be unacceptably high in many instances. An incremental approach will be needed, one which prioritises specific areas for investment. Some services will become more global than others. One firm might, for example, choose to make its pharmaceutical practice global, but leave its banking practice on a national footing; another might prefer to pin its global hopes on cross-sector corporate transformation, but manage BPR assignments locally. Ahead of a full-scale transnational structure, these chosen services will have global resources and targets – they will, in effect, form a core of new, 'super' services. This process will clearly be linked to that of increased specialisation (discussed in Chapter 8) in that there will be a tendency for each firm to pick global specialisations which differentiate it from its competitors. Over time, as these new services grow and acquire an established reputation, the overall positioning of consulting firms will become more differentiated, reducing the high level of generic competition which bedevils the industry at present.

A further effect is likely to be the emergence of a division between global and national services. Global services will inevitably be the areas of high market profile and strong investment; they will attract and retain the best people. From feeling slightly neglected in the first instance, national services will begin to be marginalised. Success will feed success, and failure, failure. As the global services recruit better people, they will deliver better assignments and attract more clients; this will in turn boost recruitment, and the virtuous circle will continue. By contrast, national services will be pulled into a downward spiral, as they continually lose their best people to their global counterparts. Internal conflict is likely to grow, at least until the inevitable is recognised – that the global and national services constitute two separate firms, the former focused on international clients in a limited range of sectors, the latter offering much more generic services to a domestic market, concentrating on clients with no or little international aspirations.

In this environment, it is likely that the characteristic of being 'global' may be more important than the precise nature of the service being offered; it is the fact that one can bring together world experts and marshal international know-how and resources that will be the important factor. For the global practice areas, this will mean that they have more in common with other transnational service providers – advertising agencies, law firms, banks – than with their national consulting counterparts. Gradually, this synergy will translate into the emergence of a new type of business services firm, offering a range of purely global services, probably in a very focused sector (Figure 10.1). It will, for example, make sense

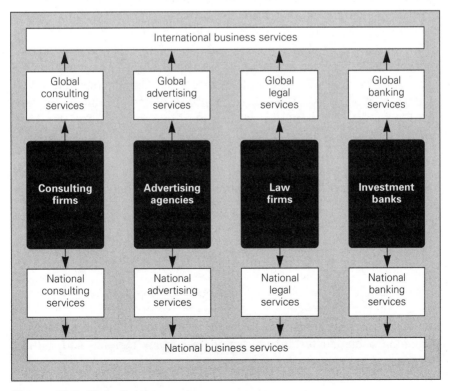

Figure 10.1 Globalisation and convergence

for the companies specialising in offering global services to the tele-communications industry to join together, rather than trying to re-create, on a global basis, the generic practice areas of national consulting firms. This movement in the transnational arena will probably be mirrored on the domestic front. As the national firms are increasingly abandoned by their more glamorous siblings, there will be a tendency for mergers and acquisitions to occur among the national firms, though perhaps retaining the generalist approach of consulting firms at present. Thus, the pattern of restructuring within the consulting industry will have changed significantly: historically, a combination of client pressures and operating requirements have meant that consulting firms have aimed at vertical integration – adding more services to its existing portfolio. In this model of the future, the emphasis will shift to cross-firm integration, where elements of existing firms come together under a new entity, rather than an extension of the old one.

This kind of restructuring will change the nature of competition, certainly for global consulting services. If having the ability to provide services which are built around an understanding of how companies operate on a transnational basis is the key to success in the global consulting market, then it will not just be consulting firms who can lay claim to that sort of ability. Traditional consulting experience will count for less than experience of managing on a global basis. The organisations most skilled in this area are clients themselves (after all, consultants have said that they are only going where clients are already leading them), and it follows that they may start to enter into competition with the consultants.

The pattern is no different to that which emerged in the IT-related consultancy market in the mid-1980s. Hardware and software companies, such as IBM and Lotus, were attracted by the high margins of the consulting industry. They launched, in response, proprietary consultancies which were designed to build on the core competencies of their individual companies (systems integration, developing software) in order to compete with existing consultancies whose skills in this area were necessarily more generic.

So far as global consulting is concerned, we should perhaps be looking to the largest transnational companies as the source of future consulting expertise, offering advice on subjects ranging from global logistics to managing a human resource function that spans national and cultural boundaries.

Notes

1. *Director*, June 1989.
2. Quoted in Charles Rassam and David Oates, *Management Consulting: The Inside Story*, London: Mercury, 1991, p. 88.
3. Christopher Bartlett and Sumantra Ghoshal, *Managing Across Borders: The Transnational Solution*, London: Century Business, 1992, p. 209.
4. Charles Hampden-Turner and Fons Trompenaars, *The Seven Cultures of Capitalism: Value Systems for Creating Wealth in the United States, Britain, Japan, Germany, France, Sweden and The Netherlands*, New York: Doubleday, 1993, p. 61.

11 The Polarisation of Consulting Styles

Seymour Tilles, the author of a 1961 article on consultancy, told clients that they should not be seeking to obtain facts from their advisers: much more of an issue was the need to convert these facts into action:

> If what the executive wants is not information but help, he must realize that 'help' is a highly personal thing, and does not come neatly bound in plastic covers.[1]

'Facts' and 'action' have often, usually unconsciously, been seen to be mutually exclusive in consultancy.

Prior to the emergence of IT-related consultancy, the role of consultants was to provide the factual analysis which fuelled management action: most consultants were not expected to take actions themselves (something which, as we have already seen, has been an increasing source of frustration to clients). Above everything else, the industry has been characterised and defined by its facts: the bottom line for consultants was that they had more facts (in the form of wider knowledge, experience, and so on) than their clients. But, in the past 20 years, the pendulum has swung much more towards action. Facts have been less important: what has mattered has been the extent to which a group of consultants can work with a team from the client's own staff in order to help make decisions and then execute them.

All consulting assignments vary in the extent to which they involve the client. On one side of the scale, we have what we could term 'fact-based' consultancy, where the consultant is effectively hired to tell the client what to do. By contrast, 'action-based' consultancy is much more process-orientated. In this case, the means by which the ends are arrived at are as important as the ends themselves; rather than wanting to be told what to do, clients in this type of assignment want to learn how to decide what to do for themselves. At its most extreme form, the consulting process shifts into a secondment in which the consultant works for the client, as part of the client's own team.

Fact versus action

The fact-based assignment model is essentially where a team of consultants is commissioned by a client to examine a particular problem and where, in resolving it, the consultants mainly rely on gathering data on the problem, analysing that data in relative isolation from the client and on a highly objective basis. To this extent, the fact-based model was the original form of consulting – this was very much the approach adopted by Frederick Taylor and the other proponents of the scientific school of management – and it continues to be a very common method of operating today. Some firms only offer this type of consulting and have constructed their differentiated brand around this style of working.

Fact-based consulting is used to resolve problems (or parts of the problem) that are:

- discrete – that is, it is possible to use data to understand the issues involved, something which might not be possible if the problem was particularly complex and open to a variety of ill-defined variables;
- strategic or logistical – because the analytic model relies on data, rather than softer issues such as the behaviour of people or the effectiveness of organisations, it tends to be used to address areas where data is both available and an accepted means of investigating the environment (market sizes, customer penetration levels, allocation of resources, optimal location of distribution channels, and so on); and
- finite – an analytic approach provides a snapshot of a particular situation, but it is less effective at addressing ongoing issues where the circumstances change almost daily.

However, the crucial factor in using the fact-based consulting model is that the problem is one to which either there is a factual answer or where factual analysis will form the basis of the decision-making process. For example, a company considering moving into a new market will want – usually – to base their decision on the available facts: the size of that market, its price sensitivity, the costs of distribution, and so on. When they commission a consulting firm to undertake this analysis, they are looking to the consultants to confirm or reject the company's proposed approach.

Clearly, this situation can sometimes be complicated by internal politics, but essentially it remains a question of fact: first, because it is possible to produce a factual answer to the issue (the precise detail of the answer may be limited, perhaps because of poor data, but the client will still pay attention to the findings); secondly, facts provide an acceptable basis on which the client can make its decision – that is, facts are seen to provide a reasonable justification for the venture whereas gut-feel does not.

This reliance on facts will vary from company to company, and is more a function of culture and management style: some are prepared to take decisions based on instinct which others would spend months and millions of dollars evaluating. Thus, the exact nature of the problems consultancies are asked to analyse varies widely.

However, the strength of this very analytical approach – its objectivity – is also its weakness. In the first place, the data-gathering and subsequent analysis often ignores information which is not easy to assimilate – in other words, there is often a risk in analytical assignments that the data which is gathered to fit an initial hypothesis can only ever prove or disprove that hypothesis and not suggest more lateral solutions. Secondly, almost all business situations are, in practice, open and complex: an analytical approach can only handle such complexity by essentially ignoring or simplifying it (thus, even a very well-prepared market valuation may prove wrong in practice). Thirdly – and most importantly – facts may not always be enough to change things in an organisation. It is possible for a consultant to write an excellent report, highlighting a clear action plan, based on an objective assessment of the facts involved, but for his or her report never to be implemented because either the facts used were not sufficient to galvanise the client's organisation or the client's organisation was motivated by other factors – the subjective vision of a small number of senior executives, for example – rather than objective data.

Action-based consulting has, in effect, been the industry's response to these issues. Over the past 20 years, the emphasis has been on process consulting, to the extent that even strategy firms have been forced to incorporate some aspects of implementation – 'doing' – into their work. As the name suggests, the emphasis in process consulting falls on the process by which the consulting is done, as much as on its output, the premise being that a client's organisation should be consulted 'with' rather than be presented with a fait accompli, as is usually the case with analytical consulting.

In a process-based assignment consultants will work with members of the client's staff to discuss, investigate and design solutions to the problems at hand: this can range from working very closely with a small number of individuals, to having to engage the collective intelligence and enthusiasm of a much larger group. A key component is that the consultant uses the relationships and trust he or she builds to obtain a more profound understanding of the issues, rather than accepting information at its face value. The process consultant will therefore look for the underlying causes of a problem, rather than the symptoms with which it manifests itself; he or she will listen as much as talk – and analytical consulting is very much about talking to clients – and will explore lateral options rather than following through a pre-specified framework.

It is an approach which is clearly suited to confused and complex situations, the nature of which cannot be captured by conventional data sources. During the course of an assignment, the process consultant is able to access more sources of data (many of which will be informal) as well as gauge the views of people within the client organisation – both of which aspects are crucial to the success of difficult assignments.

Process consulting has proved invaluable over the past decade as it has been seen as the profession's response to the frequent criticism that consultants do not engage constructively with client organisations and impose preconceived ideas on very different situations. It has also allowed consultants to deal with much more complex and lengthy assignments than pure analytical consulting would. There are, however, some significant drawbacks to this approach:

- Process consulting is highly subjective: it supplements objective data with the personal impressions of a consultant, and these may unduly influence the outcome of an assignment. Subjective input is also more difficult to defend to clients and can mean that the consultant's recommendations are dismissed.
- Some aspects of process consulting – discussing with the clients the emotions or motivation which may give rise to problems within their organisation, for example – are not dissimilar from counselling. For the untrained consultant, there is a danger that questions of these sorts may point to problems which are beyond the consultant's power to help resolve (personal problems of the client, for example): by airing such issues but leaving them unresolved, the consultant may be making an already bad situation worse.
- Clients feel – quite rightly – that they want to get value for money from consultants. Often – and this is an unfortunate repercussion – this translates into the consultant providing new information or telling an organisation to do something; it neglects the softer side of consulting

where the consultant may be working with a client's own staff to help them develop a solution which they can accept. Thus, process consulting may inadvertently expose an assignment team to the charge that they have not contributed anything tangible to the organisation.

The end of equilibrium

In the 'ideal' consulting assignment, because of the strengths and weaknesses of each model, fact- and process-based consulting would occur together in an optimum ratio – an equilibrium of the two styles that is precisely tailored to the needs of the individual problem faced. In practice, however, the proportions have varied more in line with the culture and working styles of the individual consulting firms, than as a result of a conscious analysis of client needs. While a minority of consulting firms have managed to balance the two effectively, the majority have tended to be biased towards one approach. The signs are that it will become more difficult for any firm to achieve this balance.

Why? The first reason is that action-based consulting has been gradually metamorphosing: with the drawbacks to the process model described above, the emphasis has been gradually shifting towards consulting firms 'doing' more – primarily in the form of outsourcing. This takes the 'doing' involved in process consulting to a new extreme in which the 'process' aspects of the consulting assignment are subordinated to the 'doing'. There is no need, in an outsourced arrangement, to spend time in transferring knowledge from the consultancy to the client, because the client will never be directly engaged in the process, only in its overall management. But, at the same time that this is happening, there is the trend among clients to demand more ideas more often and to see instantaneous results – a trend which will inexorably lead to analytical assignments (there will not be time for process; process does not deliver instant results). Moreover, other factors are likely to reinforce this trend, not least the greater availability of objective data (from information technology).

What we therefore have is an industry in which the pressures from clients will be pulling in two, diametrically opposed directions. One trend leads to more fact-based consultancy, the other to (a now, with the emergence of outsourcing, much more extreme model of) action-based assignments. This is a very different pattern from the one which characterised the growth of the consulting industry in the past – where the trend has been, relatively consistently, from fact-based to action-based consultancy (Figure 11.1). Conventional process consulting – effectively

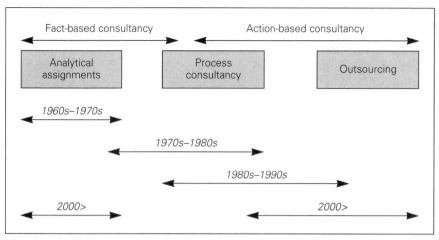

Figure 11.1 The polarisation of fact- and process-based consultancy

the bridge between the two forms which maintained the balance between them – will either disappear, as the market moves in two opposing directions, or be significantly reduced.

At a high level, the impact of this does not seem overly significant. Since the shift towards action-based consultancy occurred in the 1970s, most firms have always maintained a bias towards one side or the other. Thus, by dividing consulting work more clearly between fact-based and action-based, this trend will only be making more visible a demarcation which is already present in the industry. Strategy houses will tend to do only fact-based consultancy; firms that focus on IT-related consultancy will find it increasingly difficult to win fact-based work; clients will tend to pigeon-hole firms into one style or the other. The larger firms, in order to ensure that they continue to have access to both potentially lucrative markets, will probably try to divide their organisations into fact-based and action-based consultancies and build up separate brands.

However, look below the surface, and the implications of the disappearance of process-based consultancy are much more serious. From a commercial viewpoint, process assignments have three fundamental advantages to consulting firms:

- they provide the time and money for consulting firms to develop their intellectual capital;
- they are the single most important means by which consulting firms can build and cement the relationships they have with their clients; and
- they enable the consulting labour market to stay highly flexible.

Process consulting as investment

It is probably confirming every client's worst suspicions to say that consultants use billable work to develop services which can then be sold profitably to other clients. But, rationally, we have to accept that consultants will inevitably learn from their assignments and it would be foolish to prevent this learning being applied elsewhere. After all, we accept that a chair-maker's skill in making chairs is likely to rise with the number of chairs he has made. The issue, therefore, is one of acceptable balance: we do not want to buy a poorly made chair by an inexperienced craftsman, any more than we want to hire inexperienced consultants, but we should accept that, if we hire an experienced person (whether chair-maker or consultant), that person will gain further experience as the result of our hiring.

Process consulting plays an essential role in developing the experience of consultants. It allows them to go into an assignment with some knowledge of a generic process and apply that to a client's specific situation. As a result, the consultant gains both further knowledge about the process (particularly how it can be applied in the client's sector or in the context of certain issues) and an in-depth understanding of the client's own business and industry. Both types of knowledge can be reused with later clients. Moreover, it is comparatively rare that consulting firms decide to develop a new service on their own initiative. One of the advantages of working as closely with the market as they do is that consultants can be very quick to identify new clients as they emerge. It is often, for example, only with working with an actual client that a consulting firm realises that there is a wider need across a particular market.

But if clients are going to expect consultants to have a prepared solution (and this will be true of both fact-based consultancy and outsourcing), then the opportunity for consultancies to use assignments to create and develop intellectual capital will be very limited. On a wider scale, this will make it difficult for consultancy firms to evolve: what we are more likely to see is firms effectively getting stuck in different areas, unable to move from service to service as markets and clients develop. Like manufacturers, consultancies aim to move from product to product as each one passes through the traditional stages of a product life-cycle – early adoption, mass take-up, maturity and decline. But, in this scenario, firms will find it more difficult to abandon a product as it starts to decline and shift to another which is starting to take off.

Process consulting and client relationships

Nor is process consulting simply important from an internal perspective: it also provides perhaps the critical means by which consulting firms get to know their clients better. In both fact-based consultancy and outsourcing, the interaction between consultants and clients is minimal. In fact-based consultancy, the consultants tell their clients what to do; in outsourcing, they also do the 'doing' on their clients' behalf. In these environments, the client–consultant relationship is founded on a combination of the reputation of the firm, the extent to which the firm delivers results and the contractual framework within which the work is carried out. In essence, the relationship is very much between the client and the consulting firm as a whole. By contrast, process consulting provides consultancies with the chance to build up relationships at an individual level (because the client and consulting team work closely together). In time, these personal relationships grow, providing a bedrock of future client contacts.

Thus, without process consulting, consulting firms will rely much more on their overall reputation (or the reputation of a small number of gurus) in order to win business, and will have to look towards winning work on a proactive basis rather than relying on reacting to initiatives from existing client contacts.

The flexibility of the consulting labour market

But perhaps the most serious implication of the disappearance of process consulting will be on the way in which the labour market for consultancy operates. Process consulting is a broad church – an Anglican institution compared with the Catholicism of fact-based consultancy or low-church outsourcing. And, as befits a broad church, it involves a wide range of people with different skills and experience. Someone who has worked on corporate transformation in one industry will be able to redeploy their knowledge in another sector. Equally, someone who works effectively in involving clients in one process – say, change management – is likely to be equally effective at involving them in another process – say, business process re-engineering. Clearly, the nuances of each project will be different – there will be new tools and techniques – but the underlying principles will remain unchanged. How else, in the 1980s, could all those experts in change management have made the transition to business process re-engineering so seamlessly? Process consulting relies on a way of doing things: by contrast, fact-based consultancy involves knowing about specific factual issues; crucially, it involves having opinions which can be debated and defended. For this reason, fact-based consultants are considerably less 'portable' than process consultants. Once you have become a specialist in a particular field, it makes sense to become even more of a specialist – because clients will be prepared to pay even more for your opinions; but, once you have become a specialist, it becomes increasingly difficult to work in a different field.

Crucially, therefore, the disappearance of process consulting work, and the emergence of many more specialists (which both fact-based consulting and outsourcing will necessitate) will mean that consulting firms find it more and more difficult to move consultants around. At the moment, the predominance of process consultancy in many of the biggest firms guarantees flexibility: as markets develop and shift, people can be redirected with comparatively little disruption. But, as people become more tied to their specific areas of expertise, the structure of consulting firms will inevitably become far more rigid.

Such rigidity will cause immense problems for firms which have grown up with the idea of unending flexibility. Recruitment will need to become much more specific. Internal division between practice areas will be more marked (and there will be fewer transfers of people between them). Expansion will be much more difficult to achieve organically (because there will be less opportunity to retrain people), meaning that consultancies will look more at acquiring smaller, ready-made firms working in specific fields.

Such challenges are substantial enough. But there is a greater underlying challenge. The shrinking opportunity for working with clients in a process consulting environment and the growth of action-based consulting in particular suggest a significant change in the relationship between clients and consultants: from being advisers, consultants will become the doers. The implications of this are explored in the following chapter.

Note

1. Seymour Tilles, 'Understanding the Consultant's Role', *Harvard Business Review*, November–December, 1961, p. 89.

12

From Advising to Doing

The 'advising' to 'doing' ratio

Perhaps the most consistent criticism levelled against consultants is that they are all talk and no action. The archetypal hit-and-run approach to consulting involved writing a lengthy report on the client's desk, containing unrealistic suggestions couched in management jargon – and running before anyone actually tried to do anything.

Yet the origins of consulting lie in advice. Frederick Taylor did not use a shovel: he employed his expertise in working out how others could use the shovel more efficiently. And this remained the case, largely up until the mid-1970s. Three things then changed.

First, although firms like Andersen Consulting had been involved in IT since it began to be applied in business, this period saw the first real growth in IT-related consultancy. IT posed a challenge to consultancies. On the one hand, it was clearly forming an increasingly significant part of a client's operations and was therefore a market – in terms of both size and strategic importance – which consulting firms could hardly ignore. But, on the other hand, IT involved doing, just as much as advising. The major firms tried to square this particular circle in two ways: they developed methodologies for implementation (so that they could 'advise' clients on the 'doing') and they formed partnerships with the larger hardware and software companies (who would do the 'doing'). But it was a balance which was difficult to maintain – where does 'advising' stop and 'doing' start in this arrangement? Moreover, it became increasingly obvious that it was a balance that consultancies should not maintain: much of the revenue and profits from IT-related projects came from the implementation.

Second, as a result of the growing market for IT-related consultancy the number of consultants and consultancies grew suddenly and rapidly: in ten years, an entire industry was born which had barely existed a decade earlier. Accounting firms merged and spawned consulting practices; recruitment into the sector soared. Finally, and again as the result of these first two trends, the consulting industry began to be demystified: no longer was it a function confined to a handful of gurus, discussing strategic issues in hushed tones in the shadowier corners of board rooms. If you were not a consultant yourself, then you knew someone who was. Consultants were not special, but people like you or me.

Consultants themselves were comparatively slow in grasping the implications of these changes, and continued to stress their detachment from the doing process:

> Management consultancy work involves *working through others* to help them seize opportunities, manage conflicting forces, harness people's energy and talents, and solve problems to move the organisation in a particular direction.[1]

However, this stance has gradually become more proactive, translating into familiar phrases: 'working in partnership with clients', 'delivering results', commitment:

> The *realpolitik* of a falling market demands tangible results and quantifiability … Consulting in general is becoming market-drawn, less academic, ivory-tower … Today's nominalist consultancy catch-phrase is implementation.[2]

Several factors look set to sustain, even increase, this trend.

The first of these is the nature of consulting work itself. There appears to be no foreseeable let-up in the extent to which IT dominates the consulting industry. As in the past, this will continue to put consultants under pressure to do, rather than advise.

Nowhere will this trend be more marked than in the area of outsourcing. Confined in the early 1990s to IT, outsourcing is now occurring in a wide variety of functions – finance, internal audit, tax. Outsourcing – in the broadest sense – poses exactly the same problem for consultancies as IT did 20 years ago. Even more than systems implementation, outsourcing involves 'doing'; hence the fact that some consulting firms have consciously decided not to move into this field. Yet, simultaneously, the temptation to get involved is proving almost irresistible, mainly because of the size and duration of typical contracts.

Furthermore, the growth in fees (whether for outsourcing or for other services) presents a problem in its own right. While clients continue to pay often massive bills, questions about value for money are being asked more often and more loudly. As *Fortune* noted:

Oh, yes, we almost forgot. There's that small matter of the millions of dollars you're going to have to shell out. 'The fee?' shouts Home Depot's chief administrative officer, Ron Brill, when asked what he's paying McKinsey to add rigor to the company's cost-reduction program. 'It's totally outrageous! I'm not telling you what it is.' Like an increasing number of executives, Brill desperately wanted McKinsey to have some skin in the game. 'I would have liked for them to work on some sort of contingency-fee arrangement, where their fee would have been calculated by giving them a percentage of all the money we hope to save,' he says. 'I wanted it to be painful for them if it didn't end up working.'[3]

And because high fee rates will encourage clients to demand more tangible results, consulting firms will be forced to do: they may have devised the most efficient shovelling systems imaginable, but – to meet their clients' expectations – they will have no choice but to pick up shovels themselves. Of course, justifying large fees by acting as well as advising is a two-way process. Consultants will be forced to 'do', in order to obtain a high fee, but they will also increasingly command high fees by offering to 'do'. Of all the trends which are likely to increase the doing to advising ratio, it is this last point which is the most important. It will be in their own interests, as much as their clients', for consultants to 'do' more and 'advise' less. In an industry in which – as we have seen – investment is becoming crucial to long-term survival, the money to be gained from 'doing' may represent the difference between success and failure.

In this environment, statements about 'working in partnership' will not be enough. Instead, we should expect to see:

- the relationship between clients and consultants on individual assignments change, as the 'advising'/'doing' distinction breaks down;
- a growing number of joint ventures between consulting firms and their clients, where each side shares the 'doing' and 'advising' role; and
- consulting firms demanding premium fees for 'doing', often in the form of equity from their clients.

The changing relationship between client and consultant

Consultancy has always involved balancing two potentially conflicting sets of objectives – the client's and the consultant's. Although clients continue to be suspicious that consultants' only interest is in raising the biggest possible bill, significant problems have been avoided by recognising that both sides stand to win or lose together. As one recent study of the industry by two American academics has concluded:

> Consultants draw on their professional reputation to argue that their interests are those of the organization – that is, that they have nothing to gain from advocating a system which will cost more and possibly achieve less from the organization's perspective ... Consultants stress that their own interests in terms of securing further work are best served by working closely with the user organization ... in other words, an equivalence is posited between their own and the client's interests.[4]

'Doing' goes far beyond this type of commitment and relationship.

Let's take a hypothetical client to illustrate this. Suppose the client is a medium-sized retailer operating a large number of drugstores across the country. It is 1998 and the company has been losing market share in one of its core lines – over-the-counter healthcare products – as the supermarket chains have gradually encroached on its traditional territory and tempted loyal customers away with the discounts they can afford to give because of the economies of scale they achieve. If this company was to ask a consulting firm to work with it, the resulting assignment would look something like this. About 20 per cent of the time would be spent on market analysis, establishing the size of the healthcare market, and the opportunities and threats faced by the retailer. Probably about 40 per cent would be given over to interviews, workshops and brainstorming sessions in which the consultants bring together people with different expertise from across the client's business and facilitate a discussion between them. The aim would be for both consultants and clients to work together to develop a new approach to this particular category. Once agreement had been reached on the strategic issues, the remainder of the assignment would be given over to developing the implementation plan, identifying organisational changes or resource shortages, and other such operational areas.

Clearly, this type of assignment is vastly more hands-on than the hit-and-run tactics of which consultants are so often accused. However, it still falls short of actually 'doing' anything.

Now let's suppose that exactly the same retailer faced exactly the same problem in ten years' time. What would the consulting assignment look like then? In the first place, it is likely that the client's objectives would be stated differently: rather than asking for assistance, the company would be looking for a specific result, increasing their market share in the healthcare sector by a given percentage, for example. It would then hire a consultancy to do this. This time, only a small proportion of the assignment would be given over to the traditional consulting activities – analysis, knowledge transfer, facilitation. An approach and plan would still have to be developed, but there would be no need to ensure that the client's own staff 'owned' the process, as they would not be responsible for implementing it. Moreover, there will be a positive disincentive to including the client's staff, because they will represent an unknown quantity – a risk which could jeopardise the success of the assignment.

Most of the 'assignment' would, therefore, be given over to carrying out the actions identified. Realistically, a single consulting firm is unlikely to be able to provide all the skills and resources required. One of the key secondary implications of the growing demand from clients for 'doing' will be the need for consulting firms to form consortia bids with other companies (which in this case might include an advertising agency, a database marketing company, even a manufacturer of healthcare products). The structure of the assignment, together with contractual issues and payment terms, would therefore be significantly more complex than for its equivalent today.

Such a scenario is not far fetched. Retailers, such as Wal-Mart, are already giving over the management of entire categories to single manufacturers, in the belief that the manufacturer has more in-depth knowledge of consumer behaviour in this category than the retailer itself. This is perhaps evidence of a much more fundamental shift. For most of the twentieth century – since the rise of the ideas of scientific management – business has sought to separate knowledge from action (this, after all, is the essence of management). Principally as a result of the technology we now have at our disposal, that division is disappearing. Having access to a spreadsheet package means that managers no longer need a team of clerks or accountants under them: they no longer need to manage because they have a much more effective and efficient way of doing. Consultancy is inevitably affected by this shift: in fact the very nature of consulting means that this industry will be more affected than almost any other. How could a consulting firm still operate on the basis of a model – one that says that 'advising' and 'doing' are different activities – when it is clear that that model is becoming redundant?

Joint ventures between clients and consultancies

However, the changes which the need to 'do' will force on individual assignments pale in comparison to the possibilities that will be created across the consulting industry as a whole.

'Doing' will give consulting firms the excuse to engage in new ventures and activities. Chief among these – and it is a trend which is just starting to emerge – will be converting long-standing assignments with clients into joint ventures, where the knowledge and skills gained on both sides will be redeployed in other similar situations.

We can see how this will work by taking our hypothetical drugstore example a stage further. Suppose that the consultancy consortium has now completed the assignment successfully: the client's market share in this key category has been restored to its former dominance. Suppose also that the consortium, with some input from the client, developed a particular direct marketing tool, software which was very effective at identifying the propensity of individual consumers to buy. Rather than leaving the tool with the client (the 1998 approach), it will make much more sense in the future to try to sell the tool on to other clients. After all, the original client has already achieved its goal (increase in market share) and its own staff may have little use for the tool on an ongoing basis – assuming that the consultancy consortium continues to manage the category once the assignment proper has finished. Clearly the drugstore retailer will want to ensure that the same tool is not sold to its direct competitors, but there would be little conflict of interest in, say, amending it for the home improvement market. Thus, a new consortium may be formed, this time involving the client, to take and develop the tool for other markets.

There are only a few examples of this happening at present. Ernst & Young established a joint venture with America's largest agricultural co-operative, Farmland Industries, in 1997. Called OneSystem Group, the venture will provide IT and process-related services for Farmland and affiliated organisations. The investment from Ernst & Young was signifi–cant: 'It's more than just putting compensation at risk – it involves putting our equity at risk, too.'[5] Andersen Consulting has also started to enter into this type of relationship. Earlier in the same year, Mercedes-Benz agreed to pay the firm a form of royalty payment for each new Micro Compact Car produced; Andersen's *Via* World Network is another example. There is no doubt, however, that the trend will grow: if consultants will increasingly win work on the basis that they will act rather than advise, having a track record of 'doing' will be absolutely essential. Joint ventures will be tomorrow's equivalent of today's methodologies.

We will discuss later in this chapter the overall issues raised by the 'advising'-to-'doing' shift, but there are some – more detailed but still important – implications which arise directly from the trend towards joint ventures with clients. The first of these is that this environment will lead consultancies to favour a certain type of assignment – one where the intellectual capital gained can obviously be redeployed elsewhere. Consultancies will become more reluctant to undertake one-off assignments, such as developing a strategy for an individual company, and more interested in assignments which focus on generic, even back-room functions (and Andersen Consulting's focus on ticket processing is a good example of this).

Equally important is the length of time which may be required to set up these ventures. A methodology for corporate transformation may take months to develop (we have already noted that product development is not one of the consulting industry's stronger suits). But for a joint venture to be successful may take years. In other words, the 'doing' services of tomorrow are already being developed (consciously or otherwise) in assignments today. The firms that recognise this and start to focus time and investment on these opportunities will stand to gain massively in the next decade; those that do not will find it immensely difficult – if not impossible – to make up the lost ground.

Taking an equity stake in clients

Let's take our drugstore example one stage further again. It may be, as a result of the success of the consulting assignment and the client's burgeoning market share, that the company decides to launch a new company, perhaps specialising in the manufacture of certain types of over-the-counter healthcare products, products for which the assignment showed there was clear demand but relatively restricted supply. As a fledging business, the new manufacturer may need but be unable to afford consultancy advice. The consulting firm meanwhile sees a great opportunity about to be lost. To exploit the opportunity, the consulting firm offers to run the company in return for a portion of equity.

This is taking 'doing' to a new extreme. The consulting firm here is not simply acting on its client's behalf, but has taken over all the 'doing' and has a clear, long-term interest in ensuring that that 'doing' translates into material success.

The parallel is with venture capital firms, but where venture capitalists offer cash in exchange for shares, the consulting firm will be offering management expertise. Given the present excess of available capital over management ideas and skills, this could well prove to be a highly successful strategy.

As with joint ventures with clients, there are, however, major implications for consulting firms – the opportunity is not one of unalloyed potential. Perhaps most significant is the fact that consulting firms will have to be very astute in identifying those clients in which they wish to invest. While – like joint ventures – taking an equity stake in a company could potentially generate a much higher return than conventional time- and materials-based consulting, it also carries a far greater risk. At the moment, consultants are usually paid, whether their clients succeed or not: shareholding clearly changes that. Nor are consulting firms particularly equipped to meet this particular challenge – unlike venture capitalists. Moreover, if we cast our minds back to the level of bad debts incurred by banks (which supposedly had this expertise) in the last two recessions, when many of the small businesses to which they loaned money defaulted, the scale of the potential threat to consulting firms becomes readily apparent.

The issues raised by the shift from 'advising' to 'doing'

In addition to the individual implications of each of the three ways of 'doing' just discussed, the overall move from 'advising' to 'doing' raises other important issues for consultants and their clients alike.

The first issue raised is one of ethics: consultants are supposed to be independent outsiders, and that integrity will be compromised if they identify too closely with their clients. But a more serious concern is that as roles are reversed – as consultants become 'doers' (and, potentially, clients become 'advisers' as they relinquish 'doing' to the consultants) – responsibilities will become increasingly blurred. Assignments where responsibilities are unclear or are shared between two or more parties have always carried the highest risk. As consultants 'do' more, and as the terms which surround that 'doing' are made increasingly contingent on the 'doing' being done well, then risk and opportunity for conflict can only grow exponentially.

Contingency fees also distort the ownership of your business problem, which creates quandaries for both parties. 'If we're going to accept these fees, we have to make sure that you do what needs to be done,' says James Champy, head of strategy at Perot Systems. 'But if I was a client, I would never accept that, because you don't want a consultant running your business.' The flip side of this is the question consultants won't ask on the record: Why should they sacrifice their fee simply because you take your eye off the ball and screw it up?[6]

But perhaps the single most fundamental issue is with the ability of consulting firms to 'do'. This is not simply a matter of the adage: 'if you can't do, teach; if you can't teach, consult'. Most consultants are ill-equipped for action. Much of their work takes place in a world of 'meta-reality', a world in which everything is logical, where a plan made is as good as a plan implemented, where people and markets behave in a rational fashion. And their world has to be like this because, like economists, it would be impossible to theorise about a world which was not inherently predictable. Consultants (and, indeed, managers) exist because most working people are prepared to accept that business, unlike next summer's weather, can be forecast with a reasonable (and workable) degree of accuracy. In practice, we all know that it is guesswork – we know that a strategy, however well honed, can be swept aside overnight – but we accept that guesswork for what it is, an imperfect reflection of the real world. But conventional consultancy – 'advising' – exists in that guessed world: 'the consulting process', two American academics have argued, 'takes place within a context of perceptions, identities, accounts and representations'.[7] A recent UK study concurs:

> Consultants seek to create and sustain a reality that persuades clients of their value in the same way that actors seeks to create a 'theoretical reality'.[8]

The important question, then, is whether consultants can move from the 'fictional' to the 'real' world without ceasing to be consultants.

Notes

1. S. Kehoe, *Management Consultancy*, p. 1
2. Charles Darwent, 'Consultants After the Party', *Management Today*, January, 1988.
3. *Fortune*, 14 October 1996.
4. Brian P. Bloomfield and Ardha Daniel, 'The Role of Management Consultants in the Development of Information Technology: The Indissoluble Naute of Socio-Political Technical Skills', *Journal of Management*, 1995, p. 29.
5. Quoted in *Management Consultant International*, April, 1997.
6. *Fortune*, 14 October 1996.
7. Brian P. Bloomfield and Ardha Daniel, 'The Role of Management Consultants in the Development of Information Technology: The Indissoluble Naute of Socio-Political Technical Skills', *Journal of Management*, 1995, p. 29.
8. Timothy Clark, *Managing Consultants: Consultancy as the Management of Impressions*, Buckingham: Open University Press, 1995, p. 87.

Part II

Consultancy in 2020

The second part of this book looks into the longer-term future of the consulting industry. Rather than attempt to construct a single picture of the future, which would, almost inevitably, be proved wrong, it seemed more appropriate to present a variety of possible scenarios.

To this end, around 30 of the most senior partners in most of the world's major consulting firms were separately asked their views on what the consulting industry would look like in ten or 20 years' time. Asking people to look so far into the future is always an unfair question, but it is especially so in an industry, like consultancy, which is people and knowledge based.

Some clear themes emerge: on the types of challenges clients will face in the future; on the importance of being able to manage intellectual capital. There was almost unanimous agreement that the greatest internal problem facing the industry was the recruitment and retention of the best people (which is why an entire chapter is given over to this issue). But there was also a wide range of opinions:

- on the way in which the structure of the consulting market will develop – some people thought that new entrants will have an advantage because they will carry so little cultural baggage; others saw the barriers between new and established firms becoming steadily more difficult to cross;
- on the importance of globalisation – is it something which is still developing, or have consulting firms largely adapted to the demands being made from clients in this respect?

129

- on intellectual capital – will this be freely available in the future, or are we likely to see increasing fierce arguments over ownership? What kind of threat does the commoditisation of knowledge pose?
- on the rate at which the consulting market will continue to grow – some of those interviewed thought that the current boom was coming to an end, while others could see no change in the underlying rate of business volatility which has fuelled growth over the past few years.

This section offers no easy answers, therefore: its aim is present this diversity of opinion as it stands, in the hope of stimulating debate, both in the consulting industry and across business more widely.

13

Changes in the Business Environment and Their Impact on Clients' Use of Consultancy

Philip Evans ....

The single biggest influence on client needs in the future is likely to be the deconstruction of industries and markets to which we are accustomed. There are several implications of this trend which are particularly important in the context of consultancy.

The first is the commoditisation of the physical assets of a company. A car manufacturer would be a good illustration of this: in the past, the way in which it organised its physical processes could have been a source of competitive advantage, but, today, its competitors will have been able to replicate these. In the future, its advantage will lie, not in its physical assets, but in the knowledge it has accumulated. Similarly, for the manufacturer of computer components, its most valuable asset may be the knowledge it has about its customers, which enables it to serve those customers much more effectively than a less well-informed rival could. The precise nature of the knowledge asset, and its relative importance compared to the residual physical assets, will vary from company to company. It follows that there will be much more inter-company collaboration as organisations seek out synergies between their knowledge base and that of others.

A second implication of deconstruction is that competitive advantage will be much harder to sustain. We are already accustomed to the idea that products have a much shorter life-cycle today than they had ten years ago; in the future, we will see this trend extend to all sources of competitive advantage. Deconstruction will mean that a new entrant is able to reinvent completely the rules of your industry, and it will therefore become almost impossible to develop a long-term strategy.

These changes will be accompanied by deconstruction on a human scale, by fundamental changes in the labour market. Because the level of available information will have increased massively, parts of the labour force will be much better informed. Better information will mean that individuals will be more flexible but also much more aware of their market value.

Combine the macroeconomic and human implications of deconstruction and it becomes clear that the notion of a company itself could be endangered. We will see the emergence of hybrid organisations in which the concept of a shareholder is much less meaningful than it is at present. Power, accountability, risk and reward will all become more complex. Some of these organisations will be massive, as genuine economies of scale become achievable through globalisation, but many more traditionally scale-sensitive companies will be broken up, as knowledge – which is not scale-sensitive – becomes the predominant economic driver. In some areas, this trend will realise itself in a return to an almost pre-industrial environment, with many more, much smaller companies than we have today.

What impact will this have on the way clients use consultants? There will be much less of a need for the 'Battle of the Somme' approach to strategy: the idea of a grand, integrative plan will be thrown away in favour of much more contingent and tactical approaches. Strategic direction will be set by the equivalent of NCOs, as much as four-star generals. Execution will be critical because the price of failure will be very high – and one of the chief things that clients will be looking to their consultants for will be assistance in this area.

The logic behind having a full-service firm will be far weaker. Focusing on tactical solutions will mean that clients will tend to look for specific expertise, and some of the department store firms will either have to develop specialisations in a small number of areas or be in danger of finding themselves unbundling as a result. Specialist firms will benefit.

Brian Harrison

If there is to be any paradigm shift in the future, it will probably come from one of two sources – technology or changes in the prevalence of free market economics. It is, of course, impossible to know exactly the direction that technology will take us longer term. But, if we look around today, there are already trends – such as dis-intermediation – that are affecting the products that companies produce, the services they offer and the channels they use. A car is not just a car: it is also a platform for consumer electronics. The whole area of consumer behaviour is undergoing a radical transformation: the wider availability of knowledge is meaning that power is shifting from the seller to the buyer; it is consumers, not manufacturers, who are deciding how products and services should be bundled together. Millions of dollars' worth of car purchases are now influenced by information that consumers have gathered via the Internet. Similarly, the threat that this poses to financial service companies is tremendous. These changes in technology, together with the new markets and competitors that will undoubtedly emerge, could mean that the underlying structure of entire industries will change – in ways that we cannot even begin to imagine at the moment.

Brian O'Rorke

What kind of world will consultants and their clients be operating in, in 2020? In the first place, although the fall-out from the recent crises among the 'tiger' economies of Asia may delay the process slightly, there can be little doubt that the world of 2020 will have far fewer trade barriers. In 1960, world trade represented 10 per cent of world GNP: it has been estimated that it will be 30 per cent by 2000. In 1950, ten of the largest cities in the world were in Europe or the United States. By 2000, New York will be the only US city in the top ten. By 2015, China and India will be the world's greatest economies. Today, OECD countries account for 80 per cent of global car ownership. By 2020, this percentage will have fallen to 45 per cent.

Secondly, we should expect to see commercial organisations increasingly polarised between – on the one hand – massive global operations, and – on the other – small and medium-sized enterprises which operate on a purely national basis. At the moment, most domestic product markets are dominated by between three and seven large competitors. By 2010, the same will be true of the global product markets. As clients, we should expect to see their consulting needs being equally polarised, with the large transnational corporations demanding consulting firms that can match their geographical and cultural range, and the much smaller domestic firms, not surprisingly, having comparatively little interest in such matters.

Faced with the enormous opportunities and threats of this genuinely global economy, companies will be looking to form networks and alliances with others in order to gain access to the products/services/markets to which they need to have access in this new environment. Uncertainty will trigger a backlash against outsourcing in its current form, with companies more keen to retain, rather than disperse, their existing resources.

Finally, IT will continue to be a major influence, providing businesses with the means by which they can manage their global operations and networks of alliances. Most companies have little understanding of how technology will change their business. In 1995, $350 million of business was conducted across the Internet; by 2000, it is estimated that this will be nearer $45 billion, just in terms of the business-to-business trade. The supply chain, for example, which has barely changed since the Industrial Revolution, is going to change out of all recognition.

Orit Gadiesh

Looking particularly at strategic consultancy, it is most unlikely that clients' fundamental needs will change. The business of doing business will still be the same in 20 years' time; the way in which CEOs will want to work will still be the same; human and organisational behaviour will still be the same. It follows, therefore, that the essential business of strategy will continue to be – as it always has been – about the allocation of resources in the widest sense, making choices and trade-offs.

Success for a consulting firm in this sector will come from having a focus on results, because, without results, consultancy is in danger of being nothing more than theory (at best) or entertainment (at worst). Being able to deliver results will depend, in turn, on being able to stay ahead of clients, by sharing knowledge internally, and by anticipating changes in the business environment and adapting to them.

Particular fads will come and go; a new tool or technique may gain temporary popularity, but the underlying nature of strategic consultancy will not change. Moreover, there is little risk that strategic consultancy could ever become commoditised in the way that some other areas of consultancy have been. This is because strategic consultancy involves stepping back and really listening to your client's problem, and developing a unique solution, rather than trying to impose a pre-packaged idea. No two strategy assignments are the same, making standardisation virtually impossible.

Rafael Cerezo

It is the environment in which a client finds itself that always determines the needs it has from its consultants. This environment, in the future, is likely to be dominated by the deconstruction of conventional industry boundaries. The business environment is like a puzzle in which you shift the pieces round in order to make a picture. In the future the number of possible pictures and variations is going to increase relentlessly: we are already seeing the emergence of mega-companies, but this will be matched by a growing number of companies which manage a broad portfolio of activities. At the other end of the spectrum, we will see the emergence of nifty niche payers. The sort of people who will thrive in this environment will be different – they will be much more entrepreneurial than is the norm today, and this will be something that society fosters much more positively. These people will be jealous of their independence and more able to negotiate individual deals with their employers, balancing home and work.

These people will want consultants of the same mindset – people who are equally entrepreneurial, fast-thinkers, who are willing to work with the client side by side. Fundamentally, they will also be looking for two different types of consultant. On the one hand, they will want a long-term relationship with people whom they can trust. These are the people to whom the client will say: 'tell me what you are good at and show me that you can bring in the specialists we need in areas which you do not cover'. On the other hand there are the specialists themselves. Trust here will be based on depth of expertise. These niche payers are also likely to be global.

Paul Mitchell

Clients' predominant strategic need in the future will be to develop a sense of direction in an increasingly uncertain business environment. Some of the causes of this uncertainty will be familiar – deregulation, the emergence of new markets, technology, changes in consumer behaviour or in government policy, changes in the relationship between organisations and their employees, and the shift from shareholders to stakeholders. Others will be completely new.

As a result, clients will be looking above all else for reassurance that their chosen consulting firm knows how to deal with a particular issue. Thus, some clients will want the comfort of a tried and tested 'me-too' solution. But the majority of clients will, however, be seeking an innovative solution, one that addresses their unique circumstances. The fact is that 'me-too' solutions can only ever deliver 'me-too' results and that is unacceptable when the financial markets increasingly demand above average performance in both the short *and* long term. Clients will also recognise that the tendency for senior executives to stay in one job for perhaps just a couple of years is not conducive to long-term thinking. These companies will want the reassurance of knowing that the consultancy they have hired has the processes, experience and people to develop a fresh approach, not that it has a pre-existing solution.

Clients will become increasingly polarised between two extremes – those seeking 'me-too' and those seeking innovative solutions. The consulting market will reflect this, with a vastly different type of consultancy being undertaken by those firms that offer 'me-too' solutions compared with those that offer innovative thinking.

For many client companies, radical change will be provoked only by a crisis. One of the most likely scenarios involves a major established player in a market facing competition from a totally new and unexpected source, which cherry-picks its most valuable customers. Companies in this situation will have little alternative: staring into the abyss will provide the concentration, energy and commitment required to identify a genuine solution. In this segment of the market, consultancy work will tend to be analytical and quantitative work. There will be little need here for concensus-building skills, since the seriousness of the client's business situation will provide the motivation to act on the consultant's conclusions. The most difficult assignments will be with clients who are approaching, but not yet peering over, that abyss; clients where the rationale for change is as strong, but the commitment is significantly weaker. Many of these organisations will be populated with managers, perhaps in their late fifties, who will feel very threatened by the level of change. It may be that functions will disappear that were traditionally seen as core to the company's sense of identity. This environment will require a different type of consultancy, one which balances analytical content with a process that creates the enthusiasm, courage – even fear – required to initiate major change. The need for this is not new – in fact, it has been a growing trend over the past few years – but it will become absolutely critical to consulting in this type of environment in the future. In the past, many consultancies have seen their role in this market primarily as facilitators. Their work has essentially been low on content and high on process. However, facilitation in isolation will not generate the innovative strategies that companies need, not least because it is comparatively easy to facilitate people into a process where they do nothing. It is therefore likely that we will see analytical consultancy return to play a much more significant part in these assignments than has been the norm.

Allan Steinmetz

Client needs are already changing significantly. For the past decade, the major sources of demand have come from a desire either to increase production efficiency or to reinvent the organisation through restructuring – trends which have all manifested themselves through the popularity of methodologies such as total quality management, business process re-engineering and economic value added. The overall stress has been on cost efficiencies and long-term commercial viability. But, as a consequence, we are now in a position where business is beginning to stagnate: everyone has ended up at around the same level of efficiency, and how can you compete when you are the same as your competitors?

Growth in the future will come from a different source – innovation – and this, in turn, will become one of the most important drivers of the consulting market in the future. It is a phenomenon that is strongest in the US; although there are signs of it moving into Europe and Latin America, there is still a fair amount of scepticism in these areas, not least because they are still in the tail-end of the BPR market. Why will innovation be such an important factor? Because there is nowhere else that business can look to in order to find new sources of competitive advantage. And you will only be able to innovate if you can do two things: harness the creativity of your people and encourage them to change the rules of the game; and identify new processes or products which will themselves change the rules of any industry in which they are deployed. If we look around us even today, it is clear that the new and successful companies are those that have reinvented the rules of their particular sector.

How will consultancies adapt to this new environment? First, they will have to change their mode of operation. At the moment, the majority of consulting firms still operate in silos, with each functional group working in quasi-isolation from the others – something they have been advising clients against for years. A firm which is structured like this will find it very difficult to develop the innovative consulting skills and services required by clients who themselves want to be innovative. Innovation – whether in strategy, processes, products or change management – will always involve working across the traditional functional boundaries. A firm which cannot do this is not going to be able to help its clients succeed. Second, consulting firms will need to be much more creative. A D Little recently had a client – a manufacturing company – which had commissioned a team of consultants to carry out a strategic review of one of its core markets, a market where the company was finding it increasingly difficult to compete. The consulting team did all the things that you would expect – extensive analysis of the market, competitor analysis, and so on – and they concluded that the case was hopeless: the client should sell the relevant factories and get out of this market. We took a different approach: we looked at the products the factories were producing and identified ways to improve them. The client followed our recommendations and their re-engineered products now out-perform their rivals'. What this story illustrates is that traditional consulting, where you analyse the facts, is not going to tell you all the answers: the successful consultancies of the future will be the ones who are prepared to roll up their sleeves and work in their clients' factories, on their shop-floors. In order to innovate, you need to be able to couple things together which have always been seen as separate. Not everyone has the mindset to be able to do this – which is why this type of consultancy will involve clients and consultants working very closely in tandem.

Clearly, one of the implications of this is that clients will want their consultants to take a much more hands-on role, to become much more involved with implementation than they traditionally did. At the same time, you can go too far in this direction: you could not have the consultants taking over a company's entire product development process without running the risk of losing essential creative input from the client itself. The challenge for consultancy will therefore be to help clients create an environment in which innovation can take place; consultants will be less advisers than coaches and facilitators.

14

Segmenting the Consulting Industry of the Future

Tom Tierney ....

One of the trends we are most likely to see over the next few years is increasing segmentation of the consulting market.

An industry does not become as prosperous as consultancy has done over the past 80–90 years without being underpinned by a solid economic model. In this model, there are four principal segments, each of which has very different cultural characteristics: strategy houses; systems integrators; specialist firms, including those set up by 'client' companies in order to market their in-house expertise; and operations consultancies. Although the distribution of firms across these four segments varies by geography, operations consultancies tend to be by far the largest group, and strategy houses the smallest. Underneath these established firms, you then have a whole host of small firms, sole traders and new entrants who have not yet found any sustainable market positioning. It is a truism of the consulting world that the industry has low barriers to entry; while this is true so far as new entrants – 'first generation' firms – are concerned, there are significant barriers – for firms that are trying to evolve from being a new entrant into being a 'second generation' established player. New entrants may succeed for a short period, while the product they sell or the people they employ have a particular currency in the market, but it is extremely rare for any one of them to acquire the breadth and depth needed to be a long-term participant in this industry.

Moreover, the differences between these four primary sectors are becoming increasingly clear, helped by clients themselves, whose understanding of the industry has become much more sophisticated in recent years and who have been increasingly asking consultants from the different segments to work together.

For the firms in these segments, a key challenge in the future will be to grow without losing their focus. It is a challenge which will be most acutely felt by the type of consulting firm that is trying to be all things to all people. To do so means that these firms will not be concentrating on the firms' core competencies but will be spreading themselves across multiple departments, none of which excel at any one thing. This will probably only exacerbate the existing lack of focus.

As we look further into the future, we should expect to see the sub-segments within each of these four primary segments emerge much more clearly. These sub-segments will probably be based around client needs, the most obvious ones being the need for a holistic approach to business issues, demanded by the most senior executives of Fortune 500 companies, and the need for much more specialised functionally-based consultancy among the people who report to these executives. These two consultancy roles – the business generalist and the specialist – are likely to become increasingly polarised, as the types of skills and experience required become more clearly differentiated. Historically, clients have often purchased consultancy in order to ratify a proposal or to provide the industry-related expertise and knowledge of best practice to which an individual client does not have access. For the business generalist, the stress has always been – and will continue to be – on results: an ability that will still require industry-specific knowledge, but will, more importantly, involve an understanding of how you can change the behaviour of an organisation in order to deliver results. This is not an ability that every consultant or firm has or could have. Just as the barriers to movement between first- and second-generation consulting firms, and between the four main industry segments, will be more difficult to overcome in the future, so will the barriers between sub-segments. A firm which has focused on certain specialist skills will find it increasingly difficult to be seen as a credible player in the generalist consulting market; those firms that already have generalist positioning in clients' eyes will be able to consolidate this. Nor is this a problem which you will be able to solve through merger and acquisition: too many people leave and the intellectual capital acquired has too short a shelf-life to constitute a valuable asset on a long-term basis.

As the segmentation and sub-segmentation of the consulting market emerges more distinctly, it is almost inevitable that we will see different economic patterns emerging. Margins, price sensitivity and types of fee will all start to diverge, as the firms in each segment begin to recognise that they employ different types of people and serve different client needs – that they are not the homogeneous industry that is often claimed. It may take some time to happen, but a number of the established firms will not be able to make this transition and will fail as a result. Increased segmentation will also change the nature of competition within the industry. We should, for example, expect to see much more in the way of collaboration between consulting firms, with the firms themselves, rather than clients, taking the initiative in this matter.

Paul Mitchell

One of the most significant challenges facing consulting firms in the future will be the need to balance an empathetic process, which engages the client on an emotional level, with a high degree of analytical rigour – 'content'. It will be hard for a process-orientated company to start adding content, because its people will not have been exposed to this kind of work, and training them or acquiring new people will take too long. Similarly, it will be hard for the content-orientated company to find the people with high levels of communication and inter-personal skills they will need: such people exist, but only in very short supply, in an increasingly competitive recruitment market. The consultancies that have already recognised the importance of this mixture of skills have a head-start – and a head-start that will probably be insurmountable in the future, as their existing reputation creates a virtuous circle, attracting and retaining the best people available. Thus, while the barriers to entry in the consulting market will remain very low, the barriers *between* segments of the market will become much higher.

But this does not mean, however, that the market will become completely static. The more flexible consulting firms – whose skills and culture are focused on creative problem-solving rather than a specialist area – will find themselves collaborating much more with other, complementary firms. The best analogy is perhaps with architectural firms, who combine their own specialist field of expertise with an ability to manage a whole host of other specialists on their clients' behalf. But it should be stressed that you can only work like this if your client trusts you – trusts you not to shape the requirements for your own gain and to stay within the limits of your own capabilities. Trust – belief in your integrity as a consultancy – creates the opportunity for flexibility.

How will consulting firms go about generating trust, especially given that consultancy does not have a particularly good reputation? If you look at surveys of industry leaders, the common complaints are: consultants are too often brash young things, straight out of business school; they don't say anything new; they cost too much; and their process is too disruptive. Yet, at the same time, organisations continue to buy consultancy. It is therefore important to recognise that some of the criticisms levelled at the profession come from individuals, rather than from organisations: in any period of upheaval, there are bound to be people who are made to feel acutely uncomfortable by the level of the change, and these criticisms are often a symptom of their underlying resistance. Trust, therefore, will be something which needs to operate above the level of the individual, perhaps at organisational level.

When clients buy consultancy, they are buying two things: first, the brand of the consulting firm; second, the individuals who embody this brand. When a client is looking for specialist help, meeting the individuals is often enough, as the primary concern is to check that the latter have the skills required. But as the range of support being sought by a client widens, the relative importance of brand grows. Clients in this segment are still buying individuals, but they are also looking for reassurance that those individuals are backed by collective experience of the firm as a whole. Similarly, the importance of brand grows in proportion to the level of change facing the client because brand generates trust at an organisational, not individual level. Brand is essentially the promise made by the consulting firm: it is what it stands for.

Alan Buckle

The consultancy market at the moment is still a very immature and unfriendly one, with individual firms appearing and disappearing relatively quickly. However, the next 20 years are likely to see its maturation: the market will be increasingly dominated by a small number of firms, supported by a wide range of specialist players; the middle-sized firms will be squeezed out. In fact, the largest firms may not be 'firms' as we think of them today, but rather complex networks of alliances and joint ventures, probably focused around different aspects of the supply chain. We may, for example, see a consulting firm forging an alliance with Microsoft in order to serve a particular type of client, or see more Big Five firms establishing formal links with strategy houses (alliances which may be much more important than the links with audit are in today's market). We are already seeing joint ventures between rival consulting firms, and between consultancies and other professional consulting firms (notably corporate finance houses) to bid for specific assignments, and this type of activity is likely to increase in the future. In 20 years' time, we will find a whole host of different, even unexpected, services being housed under the same roof.

These structural changes will happen partly as a result of the increasingly uncertain environment in which both clients and consultants will be operating, but they will also be a reflection of changes to particular segments within the consulting industry. Take technology as an example:

it may be a big issue at the moment, but by 2020 it will largely have gone away. Clearly, we will probably all have video-conferencing facilities on our desks – even hand-held video-conferencing tools; but where else can you go after this? There will come a point where technological progress ceases to be the enabler of business, and may even have become a hindrance. As a result, the IT practices of many of the larger consultancies will have shrunk: they may even have ceased to exist. Something will probably have emerged that will fill this gap, although it is clearly impossible to predict what that might be.

Brian O'Rorke

It used to be possible to segment consulting firms into categories: strategy houses, systems houses, and so on, but the late 1980s saw firms moving into each others' territories. Today, that rectangle has become a rainbow (Figure 14.1) with the two ends having little in common except the brand name of management consultancy. The leaders of the 1980s – the international practices – will have difficulty, in my view, in retaining their pre-eminent position, for accounting partnerships are not leaders in investing in the future, certainly not at the levels I envisage being required. Accordingly, we are seeing new leading players, who are those not only with greater capital resources but technical support as well. This group will come from the right end of my spectrum who have weight to undertake research and the money to throw at problems.

The future market is likely to be structured around the relative cost

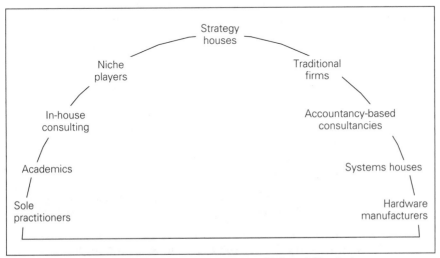

Figure 14.1 The 'spectrum' of consultancy (Brian O'Rorke)

positions of consulting firms, and two main functional distinctions: organisational and operational consulting (Figure 14.2).

But what about outsourcing? Will this still be playing such a major role within the consulting industry in 20 years' time? Outsourcing has been the banker of consulting firms over the past decade, providing them with a hugely important stream of long-term income, which has, in turn, enabled companies to make the type of large-scale investment which has not been possible under the traditional, cash-rich partnership structure. A typical consulting firm is lucky if it can predict its income six weeks in advance: outsourcing has allowed companies to look ahead for six years. But, while outsourcing provides a valuable revenue flow for consultants, for clients, the pendulum of opinion may be swinging back against outsourcing. To resolve the tension here, it is likely that the nature of outsourcing will change. Perhaps rather than being a black and white arrangement – a department is either part of an organisation or outsourced – what we will see emerge is a range of greys, with the emphasis falling much more on finding collaborative structures, alliances and networks, some of which may involve outsiders, such as consulting firms, others of which may be internal.

To meet the needs of this rather more flexible and unstructured environment, it is possible that there will be some fragmentation within consulting firms. The outsourcing divisions may themselves be outsourced, giving the core firms the opportunity to create new entities in response to specific client needs.

This type of restructuring will also clear the way for new models of ownership – an area where we are likely to see considerable change over the next 20 years. A few consulting firms already have links with banks

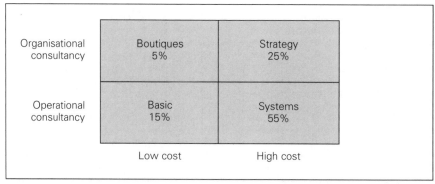

Figure 14.2 Segmenting the consultancy market of the future
(Brian O'Rorke)

– Roland Berger with Deutsche Bank, Sema with Bank Paribas, for example. When you stop to think about it, there are many similarities between the client–bank relationship and the client–consultant relationship. It will make good commercial sense for these companies to combine their client bases in order to offer an integrated set of services which provides investment in terms of both finance and know-how. At the moment, it is US anti-trust laws which are holding back this kind of development, but this is already being challenged. Looking forward to 2020, it would not be surprising to discover that the world's major consulting firms – separated from their outsourcing divisions and their national, generalist consulting wings – had been bought out by Japanese banks.

Consultancy will have reinvented itself in response to changing client demands, much as it did in the 1960s when the accountancy-based firms entered the market, and in the 1980s with the emergence of technology and globalisation as the driving forces in business. Management consulting will always be a viable and a growing industry because it is, by its very nature, a dynamic service which changes to meet the needs of its market-place. It thrives on change and discontinuity, but not on uncertainty.

Eddie Oliver

The consulting industry is in its late teens – quite a young profession compared to many others – and its history has been characterised by huge fads – 'this year's wonder technique'. Despite its relative immaturity, the industry has provided some really valuable advice to its clients, but its mistake has been to focus on one area of their business at a time: a consulting firm may have helped to take one function forward, while other parts of the business either could not keep up or actually deteriorated. The overall net benefit to clients has therefore been less than it could have been. As much as anything, this illustrates how much we are still in the early days of formulating the 'science of consulting'. Over the next two decades, we will see this science – which will take a far more holistic approach to business – emerge much more clearly. The development of this shared understanding will allow further consolidation across the industry, so that we should expect to see it dominated by 3–4 firms at most, competing across all markets: all the other firms will be confined to specific markets or services.

Although the small number of dominant firms will probably distinguish themselves from their rivals by focusing on different parts of the value chain, this much more concentrated market poses a particular threat for the strategy houses, not least because the distinction between formulating a strategy and implementing it will be much more blurred. Strategic consultancies will be seen to be too rational: the key to a successful strategy is not its clever formulation, but the extent to which it can mobilise an organisation. It is this mobilisation of all parts of a client's value chain in support of a strategy that will be the key to success in the future: the consulting company that develops an effective way of doing this will dominate the market. What stops us doing this at the moment is that we tend to be quite territorial – we want to 'own' our specialist area of the value chain and we tend to be reluctant to involve others. If we, either as an individual firm or as an industry, are to develop a much more integrated approach to the value chain, we are going to have to work much more closely with individuals and organisations involved in the value chain. From the perspective of the strategic consultancy, this will mean working with a business integration firm, and vice versa. Doing this will involve jettisoning some of our most cherished beliefs – that a single firm in isolation is capable of adding maximum value to a client. Consultants, just as much as clients, are trapped in our existing paradigms: we are afraid of moving too far from the business model we know and understand, afraid that we will not be able to make the cultural shift on which future success will depend.

Steve Beck

The consulting market at present can be divided into four segments:

- *Studies* – the most detached client–consultant relationship, where the consulting firm prepares a report which helps to frame a client's thinking.
- *Issues* – where a client is concerned with a major issue or is focused on achieving a specific result; here, consultancy is aimed at resolving the problem – making a supply chain more efficient would be a good example.
- *Transformation* – consultancy in this area is more of a partnership with a client, focused on realising strategic goals. Unlike issues-related consultancy, where each 'issue' is comparatively discrete, 'transformation' consultancy operates on more parts of the organisation, and it means that consultants have to 'roll up their sleeves' and become much more involved in the client's business. This is the segment of the market in which Gemini sees its focus.
- *Mega-deals* – these are the long-term agreements where the consultancy takes over the running of part of a client's business – outsourcing is the prime example, where the management of the outsourced function is

often linked to the provision of more conventional consultancy services. The difference between this and 'transformation' consulting is partly one of scale, but also of risk. Consultancies entering into 'mega-deals' with clients are doing far more than working in partnership with them: they are sharing the clients' risks.

What we are seeing at the moment is that the lines between these segments are becoming blurred, as consulting firms try to expand into the adjoining areas. Thus, 'issues' consultancies are moving into 'transformation' work; and 'transformation' consultancies – Gemini among them – are expanding into 'issues' and 'mega-deal' work – trends which are visible in the way in which firms' average fee income is changing.

But this convergence by the consulting firms is not being matched on the clients' side. Clients look for specialist advice and expertise, rather than generalist services. Ten years ago, Gemini Consulting lost a bid to re-engineer the back office processes of a US bank; although it had a track record in carrying out this type of work, it was beaten by a niche consultancy who had carried out similar assignments maybe 25 times and who hired specialist banking staff, rather than MBAs. As the traditional value chain decouples, we should expect to see clients developing even more specialised demands in the future. At the moment, most consulting firms are expanding by widening the scope of the service they provide. But, in the future, the consultancies that succeed will be those that can marshal specialised resources more effectively and leverage their skills more efficiently than their competitors. This means that consulting firms will need to make many more conscious choices about the markets in which they intend to operate.

But, while clients will be more sophisticated in their choice of consultants, they will also be much more demanding in the way of tangible results – real implementations – where the risks and rewards of the assignment are shared, and where the client and consultant have to be joined at the hip because clients have staked their career on the programme. Outsourcing is therefore here to stay: it is not just a 1990s phenomenon. But many firms don't understand the 'results business' – they still tend to work in a purely advisory role – and the shift to delivering results will be something that they will find difficult to adapt to – some firms will fail to adapt.

Robin Buchanan ....
I recently picked up a business book which was published in 1880. The points it made – the importance of taking care of your customers and

employees – were a salutary reminder of how little the fundamentals of business change. Everyone gets swept along by the excitement of a new idea, but more often than not it is simply an old idea that has been relabelled.

Similarly, it is tempting to think of consultancy in terms of its 'products', but underneath the fashionable labels we use, what is important – certainly so far as strategic consulting is concerned – are the capabilities that we have which mean that we can help clients address a problem more quickly, effectively and lastingly than most clients could do independently. Thus, while the fundamental objective of the consulting process has not changed, the means by which it is carried out is very different. Fifteen years ago, a typical strategy assignment might have taken the best part of a year; today, we are considerably more efficient at gathering and analysing information, and – crucially – at avoiding 'yield loss' in the transfer of knowledge from the consultant to the client.

One of the challenges of the future will be to continue to improve this process.

Where will improvements come from? First, technology will clearly continue to play an important role, especially in providing training and facilitating a knowledge-sharing culture. In the past, a senior consultant would have spent time coaching more junior staff in basic skills: today, these can be learnt via computer-based training. Technology will also play an important role in minimising 'yield loss' by ensuring that knowledge can be transferred both from consultant to client and consultant to consultant increasingly effectively. A second factor will be clients themselves, who will continue to become smarter and smarter in the way they hire and use consultants – something that will, in turn, create a virtuous circle in which consultants produce higher quality work in the face of stiffer challenges. Being able to identify the people that we want will also be crucial.

But all these improvements will be redundant if we cannot also do more to ensure that clients follow through on the suggestions made by their consultants. This is not a question of carrying out better analysis or writing better reports: it means being able to excite the management team by designing strategies that are implementable and by generating buy-in to execute the implementation plan and so make results happen. It is critical that the passion felt by the team, both inside the organisation and out, is translated into the whole organisation.

Crawford Gillies

It is important in the consultancy market to distinguish between the needs of strategy clients, and the needs of IT/operational consultancy clients. The needs of the first group will not fundamentally change: CEOs will still be interested, as they are today, in results and competitive advantage. Faced with increasing competition, clients will be looking for an increasing number of innovative ideas. This is a change we have already seen happen in the financial services sector: five years ago, there seemed to be little appetite for creative thinking or new approaches; today, it has become difficult to keep up with the level of demand. The pressure to perform is likewise growing: there is a new generation of CEOs appearing, who face increased pressure from the capital markets to deliver results, which in turn will depend on differentiated strategies. By contrast, clients that are seeking for operational IT solutions will want lower and lower cost solutions; they will want standardisation, rather than innovation.

That being said, the 'how' of consulting is likely to change in both areas of the market. Fifteen years ago, before the personal computer was widely available, strategy consultants spent much of their time gathering data. Today, the value (again in a strategy assignment) comes from synthesising complex sources of information, and it is the value of this process that will increase in the future, as the sheer volume of information increases exponentially. New techniques for carrying out this synthesis will undoubtedly emerge, although it is impossible – at this stage – to predict what they will look like.

The process of synthesis, and the development of new tools to support it, will be one of the key ways in which strategic consultancies will mark themselves out from other types of consulting firms. Elsewhere in the consulting market, knowledge life-cycles will be shortening (they are in every other industry, and why should consultancy be any different?). There will also be pressure from some segments of the market to commoditise consultancy services by developing inferior, derivative services – much as we saw happening with business process re-engineering in the early 1990s. The division, therefore, between the consulting companies that help their clients create genuine competitive advantage and those that help them simply copy the competitive advantage of others, will become much wider.

Similarly, there will be an increasing gulf between the top and middle-tier firms, as the entry barriers between tiers become more difficult to overcome. Scale will be a major factor here. Historically, most costs in the consulting industry have not been scale-dependent, and a firm's size therefore had little impact on its performance. This is likely to change in the future, as investment in knowledge-sharing technologies and global reach become much more influential factors. As scale becomes more important, we should expect to see an increasing number of mergers (despite the difficulty of realising these successfully in a people-based business).

Bruce Petter

While it is never easy to generalise about the trends in any industry, there is one factor in the consulting industry which is likely to have a major impact over the next 20 years – the increasing sophistication of clients' purchasing skills.

One of the effects of this will be that, as client staff acquire the skills and qualifications of consultants, consultancies themselves will find it increasingly difficult to maintain their traditional mystique and will be forced into being considerably more transparent in terms of their services and market positioning. This pressure from clients for greater clarity will change the structure of the market itself, making it more polarised as the middle tier of firms are threatened by, on the one hand, a large number of niche consulting firms and, on the other, a very small group of genuinely global consultancies. More explicit positioning will also make partnerships and alliances, especially between niche consulting firms, much more common.

The watchword will be 'focus': focus on specific markets, clients, services. And focus will be especially important because it is difficult to believe that the consulting market can carry on growing at its current rate. Current growth is being driven by merger activity and specific IT issues, both of which are unlikely to be sustained, so we should expect to see a period of, at least, flattening in parts of the industry. Looking longer term, however, it is clear that consultancy has become an indispensable function of business: client companies are not going to revert to trying to do everything in-house. Within reasonable parameters, therefore, the industry will continue to grow over the next two decades, but what we should not expect to see are the stunning growth rates of the past few years continuing indefinitely.

With fewer 'bad' clients around, with more transparent positioning and with lower levels of growth, consultants will have to put much more effort into constructing their fee arrangements. At the moment, many firms are shifting from time-based billing to fixed fees and/or payment by results. While the theory behind this shift is right – clients should be paying consultancies by what they deliver, not what they recommend – the practice is still far from perfect. If you are a consultancy outlining a number of options to a client, there is always the temptation to recommend that option which will earn your firm the most money. You can carry on doing this for a few years, but it is, ultimately, not a sustainable way of doing business. Consultants will therefore need to look at much more flexible fee arrangements which genuinely reflect the impact of their work – changes in share price, for example – and it will probably be inevitable that consulting firms will start to take equity stakes in their clients. What would be wrong with paying consultants on a commission basis, with proportions of their fees being wholly based on the delivery of certain aspects of an assignment? Commissions – or whatever you want to call this type of arrangement – are a way of life in other industries: consultancy should not be any different.

But, although this trend is driven by client demand far more than by the consulting industry itself, it is one which poses significant challenges for the future. What, for example, will be the impact on competition law? In particular, the practice of taking an equity stake in clients could be judged to be anti-competitive, especially where it is part of an attempt by consulting firms to tie their clients in for long periods. As the distinction between client and consulting organisations becomes less distinct, the need for regulation is likely to grow. In the future, being a consultant may be much more like being a chartered accountant or engineer: in addition to having what will become 'standard' qualifications (an MBA, for instance, or a degree from a specialist consulting business school), practitioners will also require a licence of some sort. We will end up with a two-tier market of accredited and unaccredited consultants, of regulated and unregulated firms.

Glen Peters

Management consultancy tends to be all things to all people – the term embraces activities as disparate as major systems implementations and facilitated change management. In the future, we are likely to see two types of consultancy – two distinct market segments – emerge much more clearly.

The first of these will be process outsourcing. Why do most consultancies only implement systems? It would be much more logical for them to manage the transition to the new systems and the ongoing operation of those systems. This logic makes it almost inevitable that, over the next few years, consultancies will move further and further along the continuum from implementation into post-implementation management. In fact, this is already the pattern in emerging markets, such as Eastern Europe, where consultancies often end up running complete parts of a client's business, simply because the skilled resources required are not available internally and would take time to develop. In the future, this trend will extend to the more mature consulting markets: clients will be less interested in reshaping an existing process and more prepared to hand over responsibility for it to a new team of future managers; change management will evolve into 'transition management'. Consultancies and clients will both become parts of virtual organisations – joint ventures, partnerships, stock-sharing arrangements – much as manufacturers and suppliers have tended to over the past few years.

The other style of consultancy will, in effect, be the mirror image of the first. For those processes which clients believe are core to their businesses, the role of consultancy will not be to outsource them, but to help clients manage them much more effectively themselves. A key part of this process will be access to intellectual capital: clients will want their consultants to bring them new ideas at an ever-increasing rate and this will, in turn, force the consultancies themselves to become much more innovative. Large companies have always found it difficult to get to the place where they want to be: they lack the flexibility and fleetness-of-foot of their smaller rivals. As intellectual capital becomes more widely recognised as a tradable – indeed, purchasable – commodity, these companies will be less concerned to innovate internally, and more interested in buying the new intellectual capital they need and then integrating it into their existing organisations. At the other end of the spectrum, it is clearly also going to be intellectual capital – not conventional financial capital – which allows start-up companies to grow immensely quickly, operating with just a handful of individuals and without the logistical infrastructure we associate with conventional business.

Consultancies will be one of the main intermediaries in this process. For larger clients, they will be acting as the brokers, seeking out the intellectual capital required for a particular venture or change of direction. For smaller clients, their role will be more one of helping them translate highly intellectual-capital-dependent business models into long-term, profitable businesses. In both instances, the ability to manage and transfer knowledge will be fundamental. This changing role will inevitably place strains on the way in which consulting firms are managed. Access to new intellectual capital, for example, demands new people with fresh ideas: consulting firms of the future may be recruiting social scientists and anthropologists, rather than business school graduates. To be effective in this context, firms will have to be much more tolerant of diversity than many are at present: they will need to be able to ensure that an SAP specialist does not feel threatened by, say, a psychologist, and vice versa.

For all the talk about being 'people-based businesses', most consulting firms still treat their staff very poorly. We have a high level of credibility in the recruitment market, invest massively in training – but then make people work ridiculous hours and do not even provide them with desks. If we are serious about trying to attract and retain the kind of high-quality, diversely talented staff our clients are likely to demand, then this model will have to change.

David Harding ....

One of the essential problems facing the strategy consultant in particular is dealing with general managers in client companies who have had, of necessity, to simplify their thinking because they cannot handle the number of variables in today's business environment. Thus, what may start off as a complex problem is ultimately resolved in a 'standardised' way. A recent client illustrated this. It was faced with a competitor which was behaving, to all intents and purposes, quite irrationally. The senior management team was at a loss as to what to do: they simply did not understand what was going on. The issue here was that the management team's perspective was too narrow and too deeply ingrained for them to consider any other possibilities. But what they saw as 'irrational' behaviour was, in fact, rational behaviour – but rational according to a different frame of reference. Working in a complex and shifting environment, they had found it impossible to hold all the potential variables in their heads: as a result, their conclusions came down to the level of the lowest common denominator.

The key challenge for consultants in the future will be to give companies like this the ability to see the facts from different perspectives, to make them see hidden links, but without overwhelming them with information.

Bain, for example, has invested in a 'strategic visualisation' tool. Based on a collaboration between consultants and academics, this is a software tool that can be used interactively with clients to capture the factors that are shaping their industry, and identify links between different factors and weight their relative importance. All of this can be built up by clients – and displayed back to them in graphics – in an interactive workshop, allowing the consultancy team to build consensus and commitment, as well as articulate a complex set of issues.

Having access to tools like this will be vital in the future, as the volatility of the business environment continues to increase. But, although we should expect to see such software becoming a much more common feature of consultancy, including strategic consultancy, this does not mean that the assignment process will itself become commoditised. The value here will lie not in the package, but in the way in which the different inputs are translated into a picture which is complex yet clear in its meaning, and which the client organisation has helped to create and thus subscribes to.

James Hall ....

If we look back across the past ten years at the factors which have dictated the business environment in which consultants work, and then extrapolate these trends into the future, we would see that change has happened across two dimensions.

In the first place, clients have increasingly wanted consultancies to be implementers of change: no one is really interested any more in the consultant who writes a report and runs away. Business process management – outsourcing – is simply the logical extension of this trend, and we should expect to see it continue into the future. In the US, outsourcing has always tended to be driven by IT and, to some extent, it was originally driven by a rather negative mindset: 'take this problem off our hands' was what clients were effectively saying. That view has changed, and the reasons for outsourcing have latterly become much more positive: 'we have a lot to do and outsourcing this process will allow us to focus on more important things'. In Europe, outsourcing has extended well beyond IT, into accounting, human resource management, logistics and call centres, and it seems likely that this trend will continue over the next few years.

Secondly, consulting firms have gone from being single discipline entities to being multi-disciplinary. Ten years ago, for example, Andersen Consulting was dominated by IT implementation work. But what we started to realise was that, although we could win specific battles, we could not win the war: in order to be able to deliver results to clients we needed to be able to put other processes around IT – change management, business strategy, analysis of core competencies, and so on – something which today we call business integration. For us to continue delivering results in the future, we are going to have to add a whole series of additional processes: corporate finance, financial engineering, brand management and product design and development.

Product design and development will be particularly important because, when companies reinvent themselves today, they almost always build their new business around a new product or service. IT will permeate these new products in the future: cars and home appliances will, for instance, become nodes on our domestic intranets. Many financial service products are already completely 'virtual'. So does this mean that consultants will be developing products on behalf of clients in the future? In fact, what we will probably see will be a much closer working relationship between client and consultant in this area. The best relationships have always been founded on the sharing of ideas, and this is not going to change. Very few new products are developed from entirely blank pieces of paper: what matters are the collaborative, innovative processes which take the germs of ideas and convert them into perhaps very different end products – and it will be these processes which clients will be more and more looking to consultants to provide.

Technology will clearly play a fundamental role in all areas of business – in fact, the technology revolution, as we have so far seen it, has barely begun. At the moment, a degree of technology 'fatigue' has crept in, partly as a result of the Year 2000 issue but, once this is out of the way, we should expect to see the pace of change rapidly accelerate, changing entire industry structures in the process. We have to remember that, today, we are only just beginning to get a generation of people into the workforce who are truly technologically literate: the real sea-change in the use of technology will come when we have people who have grown up with technology being an integral part of their lives.

However, one of the challenges of the future will be for the multi-disciplinary firm to avoid being a department store for consultancy. There will be no point in building up a whole series of boutique franchises, each selling something slightly different, all on different floors. The key will be integration, so that you can, say, take a marketing idea and see how this can be realised through IT and other business processes. The whole firm will be much richer than the sum of its individual business units.

How far will this process go? Where will the boundaries of integration stop? In theory, there is no reason why consultancies should not expand into architectural or interior design firms. It may happen in the future, although, for the moment, there would appear to be little practical logic in it.

David Maister

One of the key questions consulting firms should be asking themselves is: when will IT-related consultancy dry up? Although the consulting industry has always been fad-driven, IT has been one of its more 'reality-based' and therefore longer-lasting services, but this does not mean that the market will go on for ever. The historical growth of IT-related consultancy was largely driven by hardware developments, but these are pretty much over. Future growth will be dependent on software innovation – and software does not obey Moore's law: once everyone has been SAP-ed, what more can the software makers offer?

Mick James

While we clearly cannot predict precisely what the consulting market in 2020 will look like, there are trends in today's market which may well have run their course by then.

First, we should expect the current pace of IT development to have tailed off. Technically, we may be able to achieve continual reductions in the power/cost ratio of computing, but these improvements will become less and less relevant to business. There will, in effect, be a backlash against today's rapid obsolescence of – for example – personal computers: people will be looking to buy them for their durability, rather than their increased processing power. Product lifetimes will lengthen, to a point that businesses will expect their computers to last as long as their air-conditioning systems. IT will simply not be as crucial as it is today.

Second, by 2020, many more of the tasks which are still carried out by people at the moment will have been converted into software. Equipment will install and configure itself without the need for human intervention; smaller businesses especially will be able to buy complete technology packs; and, rather than call in a consultant to help install it, they will be able to just plug it in; even non-technology processes, such as some aspects of marketing, will have been automated. The process of automation will extend into the footholds of what we think of as consultancy: clients will not be buying consultants, they will be buying software. In fact, much of the software available may have been developed by consultancies, as a response to the cannibalisation of some of their core markets. Equally, we may well find software companies moving into the consulting arena. Microsoft is already offering 'solutions' for businesses: how long will it be before this extends to consultancy? A few years ago, many people thought that the process of commoditisation would stop with computer hardware, but the process has continued into the software market: there is no reason why it should stop before it reaches consultancy.

The types of changes outlined above will have most impact on small consulting firms and on freelance consultants, for whom such work is the staple of their income. At the other end of the scale, we are likely to see global client organisations which will want to deal with only the number one or number two consultancy in the world. The consulting market will consolidate even more than at present, with one firm emerging as the biggest by far, perhaps followed some way behind by one other very large firm, but with the gap between these two dominant firms and the remainder being much wider than at present.

But the fact that IT has ceased to be the key leverage point for business (and, therefore, for consultancy) will still have a significant impact on the larger consultancies. These firms will find themselves looking for alternative points of leverage – and the one they are most likely to focus on will be capital. There has, after all, always been a thin and artificial dividing line between providing clients with advice and money: both are mechanisms by which the supplier helps its client progress to the next stage of its development. People talk about 'sharing risk' at the moment, but this is a highly misleading term: at worst, what a consulting firm may be risking is the opportunity costs of having its consultants employed on a more profitable assignment; for the client, the risk is that the assignment – and possibly even their business – fails. The future version of this – 'reward pricing', where the consultancy fees are paid out of the successes achieved for the client – will involve a much higher level of risks for the consulting firms. Indeed, the risk may have to be shared across several assignments, so that one success brings in sufficient fees to offset a number of failures. There are two implications to this. First, sharing rewards rather than risks will encourage consulting firms to make recommendations to their clients which offer short-term rewards. Second, consultancies will need to become much more sophisticated in the way they measure and manage risk. These are skills which consulting firms do not necessarily have: they are, however, much more a part of the core competencies of venture capital and actuarial firms, and it may be easier for these types of institutions to acquire consulting skills than it is for the consulting firms to acquire capital and risk management skills. As the advice/money distinction collapses, we should therefore expect to see investment banks and venture capitalists entering the consulting market.

David Ogram

To understand where technology may be in 20 years' time, we really need to cast our minds back 20 years, in order to appreciate the leap that has already taken place – and may well take place again in the future.

Twenty years ago, the first programmable PCs had only just appeared. The really powerful computers had 30 Mb of disk space, but the majority had just 8 Mb. There were relatively few on-line systems; leased lines ran at a maximum of 2400 bits per second; telex and teletext machines were dominant, not VDUs; there were Gestetner machines, not photocopiers. Many people thought that the pace of development and the cost/performance ratio would level out, but it never has – and it is unlikely to do so now.

What will that mean in the future?

It means that we will be transferring vast quantities of information for almost insignificant costs. It means that storage will be so cheap that we may never have to throw anything away. It means that all information will be available in an electronic form – at least in the developed Western economies: newspapers, books, magazines may not exist. It means that there will be little need for fixed wire devices: we will be living in a world in which technology and information are completely mobile.

The result is that we will have constant access to an almost infinite amount of information at almost no cost. A key problem will be information overload – you may already spend most of your work time trying to keep up to date with all the information you are sent, especially in an environment where everyone (colleagues, clients, sub-contractors, suppliers) uses email. Moreover, you tend to look at informaton that is 'pushed' at you – emails and so forth – rather than 'pulling' out the information from a database that might be of real use. In the future, the challenge will be identifying the information you actually need. Undoubtedly someone will solve this: much more sophisticated search engines will be designed that will enable people to sort the important information from the unimportant.

If we look at what this will mean for business, it is likely that we will see a massive change in the way in which organisations are structured, staffed and managed. Telephony companies have already given us a taste of this future. Ten years ago, they may have had between 60 and 70 per cent of their staff involved in the maintenance and support of the network, 20 per cent would have worked in the back office, leaving around just 20 per cent dealing with customers. Today, we are undergoing a complete shift, both in the absolute numbers employed, which may have fallen by as much as a third, and in the distribution of the people employed. Since monitoring and supporting the network is now largely an automated activity, the proportion of staff absorbed by this area has shrunk to perhaps 30 per cent of this total. Around 30 per cent are involved in interacting directly with customers, but this proportion will sink significantly as touch tone dialling and other access media such as the Internet give customers direct access to the facilities they need: there cannot be a role for people in this area in the longer term. All this means that the remaining staff – approximately half of the total – are occupied with back-room, primarily IT-related activities.

If we extrapolate this experience in the macroeconomic context, then we will see a very significant proportion of the population being employed in IT-related areas. But, with fewer people employed in a conventional corporate setting than before, we will also see far more people than at present being employed by the service sector.

Twenty years ago, the labour market was a pyramid. As we stripped out the layers of middle management and empowered the remaining people at the top and bottom of our organisations we ended up today with a labour market more like an hour-glass, with people employed either towards the top in senior management and supporting positions, or at the bottom in the rapidly increasing service sector, with a small middle-management layer. In 20 years' time, we should expect that the people employed by large organisations, other than their senior management, will be almost wholly occupied with IT-related work and that the overall number and proportion of people at the bottom end of the labour market will have increased markedly (see Figure 14.3).

In the economy overall, around 10 per cent may be employed in agriculture and manufacturing, 60 per cent in the service industries, with the remaining third working in IT-related areas. Unlike other areas of work, technology – especially software programming – will always need some human input: you can automate the generation of code, but you cannot fully automate the process by which business requirements are translated into the functional or technical specification of a system.

In terms of how this translates into consultancy needs, it is obvious that clients will be wanting even more IT-related consultancy than they do at present. However, at the moment, this type of work is pretty much split between ongoing, regular support and specific work for discrete projects. In the future, we should expect the ongoing support to decline, primarily because more and more of its functions will have been automated, but we should expect the project-related work to increase. With the routine IT-related tasks automated, clients' IT demands will be much more volatile: they will probably have fewer people in-house (because the underlying level of continual work will be lower than at present) but will (because of their ever-increasing dependence on technology) be faced with sudden,

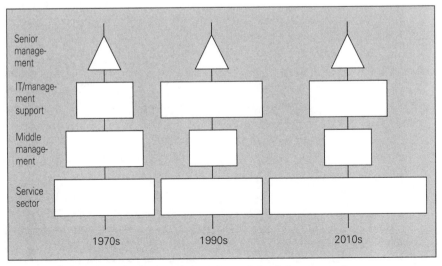

Figure 14.3 The changing distribution of the labour market (David Ogram)

much higher peaks of activity. This will mean that a client may well meet between 80 and 90 per cent of its IT needs from external sources.

One implication of this is that the service providers – consultancies, systems integrators and outsourcers – will be some of the biggest employers in the economy. Clients will be completely reliant on them and will therefore demand a much more stable relationship with them than at present. This, in turn, will lead to the market for these types of services being concentrated in a shrinking number of very large firms – the business integrators – who will provide the core services that clients require in long-term contracts, supplemented by a large number of small but highly specialised companies, focusing on niche areas of the market. Part of the role of the largest firms will be to act as intermediaries for these small, niche players.

15 The Future Nature of Consulting Services

John Everett

One of the most important attributes of a consultancy in the future will be its ability to integrate different skills. Today's consulting market is characterised by its focus on 'thought-ware', but it is just these types of analytical methodologies that are likely to become semi-commoditised in the future and which consultants will be expected to leave behind with their clients. However, the ability to orchestrate such methodologies and marshal specialist skills will be increasingly sought-after, and, because it is a skill which will be difficult to transfer to clients, it will be hugely valuable to the consulting firms. It is a trend which will take consulting away from its core, analytical way of working into the less rational sides of a client's business – helping them grasp and respond to complex issues.

But this opportunity poses several potential challenges. First is the issue that this kind of work is not especially time-intensive: typically, today it absorbs between 5 and 10 per cent of the total time on an assignment, but between 20 and 25 per cent of its costs – an imbalance that will need to be corrected via alternative pricing mechanisms. Second will be the need for consulting firms to bring non-traditional thinking to bear on their clients' problems: dealing with complex, emerging issues will require new intellectual capital, and we may therefore see consulting firms forming alliances that would seem strange in today's market – with engineering firms, say – which will bring a different approach to problem solving. Third, some of the highly focused skills which will be required in this environment may not necessarily thrive in a large consulting practice. At the moment, consultants tend to become less specialised and more generalist as they are promoted, and one of the fundamental challenges in the future will be to try to create an environment which recognises and nurtures individual differences and skills.

161

Keith Ferrazzi

Over the past 20 years or so, the consulting industry has had two very clear approaches to the market. For strategy houses it has been: 'we're the brightest and can tell you what you need to know'; for the IT-related consultancies it has been: 'technology is the critical driver of your business'. In the future – and this is Deloitte & Touche's positioning – the approach will be more along the lines of: 'change won't happen until your people and processes change' – the emphasis will be on making ideas work in practice.

A good example of this will be the 'second wave' of IT-related consultancy. At the moment, much consultancy in this area is being driven by the Year 2000 problem and the implementation of large-scale software packages, notably SAP. But in the second wave, we should expect to see this move more towards providing a set of services which assimilate such packages into the organisation more effectively – a recognition that the process has to change in order for the system to add maximum value. The 'third wave' will perhaps be the use of the Internet, which will allow companies to integrate or merge in order to exploit their individual competence in a core process. Thus a firm that has a particular strength in sales order processing takes on the sales order processing of other companies, all facilitated by an instantaneous and low-cost interface across the Internet. What this will do, is force companies to identify their core competencies much more explicitly than at present – to know where their roots are. Both these factors – the need to assimilate technology much more effectively into an organisation and the importance of recognising and exploiting an organisation's strength in a specific process – will raise demand for consultancy in these areas.

Outsourcing will continue to be a growth market for consultants – and one which is hugely attractive internally because of the injections of capital that accompany it. What is difficult to foresee is the extent to which clients will start to pigeon-hole consultancies into outsourcing and non-outsourcing firms, making it more difficult for the firms themselves to balance the two aspects of their business. For consultancies that rely heavily on outsourcing revenues, this could be a real threat.

Globalisation will also continue to be important, but perhaps more as a 'given' rather than a significant issue in its own right. Already a minority of business leaders say that globalisation is top of their agenda. A consulting firm will still need to be able to understand the overall issues involved, but it will be specific services, such as supply chain management and product development, that take on a more global shape.

Mick James

There is a lot of talk about knowledge at the moment, much of which sounds very scientific, but there is not much in the way of real method underpinning it. But, over the next 20 years, we should expect to see new sciences of organisations emerging, which bridge the gap between consultancy and sociology, and where the focus is people, not information technology. Developing these sciences poses an enormous challenge. Consultants have tended to view themselves as 'right wing', sociologists as 'left wing', but these new organisational sciences will only emerge if consultants and academics work together to develop them: neither side will be able to do so independently. The consultant of the future will be better off reading Tolstoy than Michael Hammer.

Moreover, as these new sciences emerge, they will lead to whole areas of today's homogeneous consulting market breaking off to form distinct markets of their own. Change management, for example, may become a market in its own right, rather than being – as it is today – a sub-set of the wider consulting market. The relationship between 'management consulting' and 'change management' will be analogous to that between philosophy and natural science: as philosophical thought develops over time, specific ideas crystallise into new sciences. This same process of 'Balkanisation' will occur in consulting, particularly in relation to the 'softer' people issues. These new markets present a tremendous opportunity for consulting firms: there are many real issues in organisational terms where consultants have barely scratched the surface.

But these new organisational sciences are probably just one aspect of the more conceptual services we will see emerging in the consulting market. Complexity theory is another example. At the moment, it is very much an emergent phenomenon and very little work has been done on its application to business, but it is also very much the kind of intellectual high ground that the successful consulting firms of the future will seek to occupy.

Such services also represent a shift away from reacting to client needs to anticipating them. Building on the example of the new organisational sciences, we may see consultancies creating, not so much new markets, as entire new industries, facilitated by new organisational models and global infrastructures. To an extent, this is what companies like IBM have been doing for decades – staking out new areas of business by creating new information technology architectures. Consultancies may play the same role in the future.

Geoffrey Cullinan

For the past couple of years, Bain & Company has been working with private equity houses to provide advice on transactions before and after their completion. This is very different to conventional consulting. Unlike typical corporate clients, private equity houses are culturally akin to consulting firms; they typically comprise a small group of people whose skills lie in bringing investment and ideas together and who leave once the deal has been completed. This is also an industry which is itself undergoing significant change: the huge amount of money available for investment has had the effect of pushing prices up and this has, in turn, forced the private equity house to bring added value to the transaction. As the background of most of the people working in the industry tends to be in banking and law, turning to a consultancy firm to provide additional value in the form of management advice is a logical step. And, because the cultures and skills of the two kinds of firm are complementary, we end up working much more on a partnership basis than we ever would with a corporate client.

But it is not just the client–consulting relationship that is different: we have had to redefine the whole consulting process in order to match the much shorter time horizons of this type of work. Of course, there is no question of needing to win commitment from the client's organisation here – it does not exist yet: the end product might be a conversation rather than a report. The focus, therefore, is on being able to marshal the relevant facts and develop recommendations in a very short space of time. It is important to be able to identify the most important issues and focus on them almost instantly, as these are not particularly patient clients. Equally, because there will not be time to take them through all of the detailed thinking which has led to your conclusions, they have to be able to trust you to get it right. All of this requires energy as much as good ideas and industry-related expertise.

This way of working is now starting to have knock-on effects on the firm's mainstream consulting practice, and we expect it to have an even more significant impact in the future. Externally, it will reinforce the importance of being able to deliver results to consulting clients as a whole, but, even more important internally, it provides a fresh perspective with which to view other clients' issues. We can think with a different – private equity – hat on as a means of being able to stimulate debate about strategic options with corporate clients. This type of work is also forcing us to use our own resources much more effectively and to be more flexible: it is an environment in which being able to come up with the right insight or the pertinent piece of information is essential to success.

The skills and ways of working that we are acquiring via private equity work are ones which it will be essential for any strategy firm to have in the future in order to succeed. Focus of resources will be key in an increasingly segmented consultancy market, where clients have become much smarter and are interested in addressing those most critical strategic issues affecting their future success.

Steve Beck

The shift away from the driven, ambitious, '1980s' person to the '1990s' person who wants to balance work and home, and is motivated by more than money, suggests that, as consultants, we will need to pay more attention to the irrational side of organisations in the future. We will need to engage the hearts and minds of the organisation, not simply present our findings. Consultancies have not done that in the past: they are quintessential – even hyper – rational organisations. But this is going to be less and less true going forward.

One aspect is that consultants will need to change the way in which they communicate with clients. Rather than going over the results of our analysis, we will be telling a story – about how a problem can be solved, or how a new strategy can be implemented. This does not happen at the moment because most CEOs – like most consultants – are rationalists. But as the post-modernists replace the modernists, one of the consultant's key roles will be as a story-teller.

Tom Tierney

So far as strategy consulting is concerned, it is the client who, at the end of the day, implements whatever decision is taken. However, this does not mean that the strategy consultant has no role to play at this stage. Indeed, building consensus within an organisation so that a decision is acted upon and acting as a catalyst for change are both increasingly important aspects of this type of consultancy. Underpinning this, there may also be consultancy work to help an organisation find the resources it needs to carry out its decision, perhaps through taking costs out of another part of the business or to modify asset allocation within a portfolio of businesses.

Although, as a consultant, you recognise that the prime responsibility for implementation lies with the client, you also know that your job is not done – or not done properly – until you have helped the client achieve real results. Often, this means that you have to change the behaviours within the organisation – and this can be the hardest part of consultancy. Some companies – especially successful ones – will not want to change; others, whatever their recent performance, will simply lack the 'change gene'. It is incumbent on the consultant to understand what an organisation's fundamental values are and to use this understanding to develop and disseminate strategic ideas in such a customised way that they appeal to these core values and are therefore readily adopted.

Vince Tobkin

How will technology change the way in which consultants operate? If we look back across the past 20 years, it is clear that technology has had a major impact on what consultants do on a day-to-day basis, but it has not changed the end result of strategic consultancy – delivering results. Technology has, however, had a significant impact on the structure of the consulting market as a whole. Two decades ago, IT-related consultancy was a very small sector: today it is huge, fuelled by advances in the hardware and software available, by business drivers such as globalisation and deregulation, and latterly by enterprise integration packages like SAP. Technology today is now so pervasive and so fundamental to the operations of a business that it has made it on to the CEO's agenda, but for most companies it remains a way of catching up with their competitors, rather than achieving a sustainable competitive advantage. This may be one of the reasons why the big computing firms that have tried to enter the consulting market have largely failed to move out of IT-related areas. Another reason may be that CEOs see them as too specialised and less proficient at being able to take the more holistic view that a generalist consultant can take – and this is symptomatic of the increasing barriers between generalist and specialist consultancy across the industry as a whole.

One of the changes we are likely to see in the future is that the more informed CEOs will be starting to look to IT to bring them a genuine competitive advantage, rather than simply to enable them to catch up with their competitors. There are signs of this today: PC manufacturers, for instance, who email customers at their next potential purchase points; or the development of much more sophisticated computer models for tracking and projecting industry dynamics – the company 'dashboards' of the future. But it is probable that this trend will be accompanied by a growing rejection of standard software packages, and we will witness a return to much more in-house IT work (something we are already beginning to see, in fact, if we look at telecommunications or Web-based technologies). This will be accompanied by the growing prominence of a very different type of IT-related consultancy, one that brings analysis and creativity together to develop innovative solutions.

IT therefore represents a new opportunity – at least for strategy consultancies. But does it pose any kind of threat? Will we, for instance, see our intellectual capital being packaged for sale across the Internet? To an extent this threat is not a new one, and it is not specifically related to the Internet. Twenty years ago, the Economist Intelligence Unit was producing briefing packs on key issues for CEOs. Nowadays, most CEOs have their own teams of people to do this for them, because information is much more readily available than it used to be. The real value in consultancy will continue to lie in creative thinking and problem solving, and this is a process which technology may help to facilitate, but will never replace.

Keith Ferrazzi

Consultancy has always had to deal with a market of one – having the flexibility to develop solutions which meet the needs of individual clients and the ability to respond instantly. This is not going to change. However, the business environment of the future will pose a real challenge to this way of working. As the pace of change continues to accelerate, clients will be changing their infrastructures even while they are still implementing them. In this kind of world, the emphasis will shift from developing and applying a solution, to finding ways of working even more closely with clients than at present, and to providing them with the opportunity to focus on their core competency by fielding specialists to handle their non-core areas.

16

Client–Consultant Relations

Brian O'Rorke

In this world where the pace of change will be fast, businesses and their advisers will have to remain cohesive: if they are not, they will be thrown off the spinning wheel of survival, as if by a centrifugal force. It will be a world where courage, creativity, confidence and competence provide the path not only to being at the leading edge, but to survival itself.

It is already apparent that clients want their 'advisers' to take a much more hands-on role; strategy firms, for example, are constantly exposed over their perceived reluctance to be involved in the implementation of their recommendations. In 2020, the pressure from clients will be significantly greater: to survive, consultants will have had to adopt a significantly more proactive approach. This will mean greater investment in their clients' affairs, perhaps in the form of purchasing shares, but also by entering into much deeper partnerships with them, where reward and risk are more equally shared. It will also mean that the relationship between clients and consultants becomes more like that between clients and auditors, or clients and legal advisers. In other words, consultancies will be working for their clients much more positively: they will be buying in, in moral terms, to their clients' goals and objectives.

All this envisages a considerable mutual exchange of information between company and management consultant. Indeed, a much closer partnership will have to be built than exists at present, and this will imply greater loyalty on both sides. Rather than independence, the foundation of the client–consultant relationship, as well as the reputation of individual firms, will be integrity.

This will be especially true of the largest, global clients. But smaller, domestic companies will perhaps be looking more towards networking with complementary organisations, even moving back towards vertical integration. While global companies will be seeking out consulting firms that are able to provide highly specialised advice, their smaller, domestic counterparts will be more interested in firms which can offer a broad range of advice. Thus, the polarisation – which is already apparent in today's market – between firms that provide specialist consultants and those whose people are more generalist will become exacerbated in the future.

Eddie Oliver

Although the focus of consulting work may change, the essential nature of a client's business will not. If we look, for example, at technology, we can expect to see quite staggering changes in the mechanics of how businesses work. But these will not alter the underlying paradigms – the decision-making processes and the way in which people interact and relate to each other – which are the core areas in which consultants operate. In fact, the consultants of the future will probably be moving even further up the emotional value chain, and their great successes will lie in managing the emotional side of their clients' businesses. It is a change that will mean that consultants are likely to be operating closer and closer to the heart of client organisations, engaging with the latter's aspirations, emotions and politics. 'Partnership' is a fashionable word, but consulting firms have hardly started to explore the possibilities entailed.

Interestingly, as consultants start to develop much closer working relationships with clients, we may find that distinct differences emerge between private and public sector consulting. Some of these differences are already discernible in today's market. It is always dangerous to generalise, but the private sector tends to bring consultants in earlier in their decision-making process. They may, for example, want to think through the issues with consultants before they identify a possible solution. As a result, the distinction between clients and consultants is becoming less clear, less formally defined. The idea of allocating responsibilities to each side is becoming less relevant: both sides stand or fall together. By contrast, in the public sector, some consultants are finding that they are being pushed further and further down the decision chain, and are being asked to quote for providing a pre-defined solution. This trend is neither universal (there are examples of enlightened public sector purchases of consulting) nor inevitable. However, an increasing formalisation and precision of demand is, in fact, to the long-term detriment of the public sector itself. It will mean that introducing new ideas and fresh approaches will be more difficult: consultancy will be a commodity activity – a cost rather than added value to the client.

Glen Peters

The world is already a complex place, but the chief executive of the future is going to have deal with far more, and far more complex, issues than we can envisage at present. As companies and industries converge to form virtual business entities, the absolute number of people operating in the chief executive role may be fewer: they will, however, need to maintain a holistic view of a much more sophisticated and diverse organisation. Consultancies will need to deal with these people as equals, especially where they (the consultants) are actively engaged in managing some of the organisation's processes, where they are business partners, rather than advisers. And to be able to deal with them, you will need to be able to field people of equal calibre – business people with a comparable range of experience, rather than consultants of the conventional, 'home-grown' mould. Few consultants, brought up in an environment which promotes and rewards specialisation, will naturally develop the type of people skills required to manage relationships at the CEO level. Few, for example, will have the capacity to understand genuinely the nature of global businesses; most, when faced with a problem, will come up with a solution based around a specific (and, to them, familiar) skill, rather than a more holistic approach. From this perspective, the CEO will be the better 'consultant', because he or she will be able to see the connections between parts of the business which are likely to elude the more narrowly focused consultant. With the necessary relationship management skills difficult to nurture internally, consultancies will probably need to start recruiting much more senior people (perhaps retired CEOs) in order to work with their largest and most sophisticated clients.

Recruiting people who speak to CEOs on their own terms will also be one way in which a more value-based relationship is created between clients and their consultants. At present – especially among the largest consulting firms – the idea of 'value' is based purely on fees; in the future, we will need to define what that 'value' is and know who is responsible for providing it much more precisely, and for each assignment individually. This will allow firms to move to much more credible methods of value-based charging.

Alan Buckle

Consultancy has always been a flexible industry, and on that basis has been able to move from issue to issue – from cost-cutting to revenue generation – as the economic conditions change. Historically, consultants have thrived on change: the industry's best clients have been those companies that are in a state of almost continuous flux. But we also need to recognise that there is a danger of change fatigue where clients become much more interested in implementing changes – seeing them through and making them work – rather than in taking decisions that will initiate yet more change. Faced with growing resistance to change further, the traditional desire by consultants to encourage clients to change may well lead to tensions in the client–consultant relationship.

The continuously growing pressure from clients to implement, rather than simply advise, has several major implications for consultants. Implementation will test the mettle of a consultancy in a way that writing a report never did: there is, for example, a huge difference between recommending and even putting in a system, and actually running it. Implementation will also highlight the core skills of a consulting firm: you cannot implement on hype; it may also push firms more and more into outsourcing although the difference here will be that, as both clients and consultants build networked organisations, the distinction between in-sourcing and outsourcing will be much less clear.

James Hall

The combined effect of client-led demand for implementation and the emergence of genuinely multi-disciplined consulting firms will mean that client–consultant relationships in the future are likely to be much closer, much more interconnected and longer-lasting. Rather than being a relationship between client and supplier, it will be one based on the co-operation of equals. Such closer interaction will not, however, mean that the contractual side of the relationship becomes redundant. Indeed, as clients ask consultants to undertake increasingly important and investment-intensive change programmes, having a tight legal framework will be essential. Everyone at the moment is talking a lot about 'partner relationships', but more often than not, the practice can be confusing.

At the moment, consulting firms are still exploring what we think will be the appropriate model: it is likely that there will be no single solution to this. Some firms, for example, will probably opt for value-based arrangements – where payment is based on results – but this type of relationship will only work effectively in certain circumstances, where 'value' can be clearly defined. The Private Finance Initiative, launched by the UK government, is one way in which the client side is attempting to find a solution – by drawing up contracts which try to encourage the right kind of behaviour and which protect the public interest, rather than relying solely on output-based measurements. While it is not yet clear what the dominant economic models of the future will be, we can be reasonably sure that it will not be the time-based or fixed fee arrangements that have characterised consultancy over the past decade.

Jean-Pierre Le Calvez

Much consulting work has focused on process efficiency, with little consideration being given to the human aspects involved. We are all guilty of having tried to apply precisely the same technique in two different situations, only to be surprised that the outcome is not what we expected. What some consultants have neglected is the fact that people – at whatever level in an organisation – become resistant to change where they do not understand what is happening. And this is a problem which, as companies become increasingly internationalised, is only going to get much worse, as cultural diversity creates new barriers.

To deal with this issue, consultants are going to have to listen to what clients have to say, as much as tell them what to do. This is something that most consultants pay lip-service to at the moment, but it is going to be immensely important in the future to be able to do it effectively and to work much more closely with clients. But this shift, in itself, will pose a challenge for consultants. Clients buy consultancy because they need access to an objective perspective, to fresh ideas, but a consultant who works very closely with his or her client is in constant danger of losing this. Similarly, some advertising agencies tend to say 'we' when they talk about themselves and their clients: their identification with their clients can become so strong that their ability to add value through new ideas is ultimately compromised; they start thinking too much like their clients. The challenge for consultancies will be to manage the inevitable tension. In order to help their clients develop and implement their strategies, consultants will need to work with them, side by side, but, at the same time, they will need to preserve their distance if they are to continue to play the role for which the client has hired them. Resolving this issue is not impossible – even today there are a few examples of consulting firms that are very deeply involved with their clients' businesses and that still manage to maintain their objectivity – but for most firms, accustomed to having a more distant relationship with their clients, keeping a balance will be very difficult. There is a real risk that consultants will become too much like their clients and unable to add value as a result.

Richard Measelle

Clients in the future will want what they have always wanted from consultants – the ability to provide an external, objective view. In fact, as the world becomes a more complex and volatile place, as the scrutiny by external analysts and stakeholders becomes more intense, companies are going to become increasingly reluctant to take decisions without outside help. Involving consultants represents a type of insurance policy and one for which demand can only increase as the pace of change accelerates.

In the case of accounting firms, this objectivity reflects the fact that much consulting work today originally developed out of firms' audit relationships. In spite of this, the link between auditing and consultancy has always been under attack; the nature of these attacks has not changed much over the years, but they have grown louder. But the criticisms that people make, when a professional service firm provides a client with both auditing and consultancy advice, miss the fundamental point: each is providing the client with a different, but complementary service. Auditing is not unlike the physical examination one receives when applying for a life insurance policy: the aim is to establish whether or not you are a good risk for the insurance company. But consultancy is more like a visit to your internist/doctor, where you have the opportunity to discuss how you feel and to look at what you might do to improve or maintain your overall level of health. No one would think of saying that you could not visit the same person for both a physical examination (diagnostic) and specific recommendations for improving one's state of health (prescriptive) and yet, at the same time, some people think that auditors should not provide their clients with consulting services.

A new threat to this objectivity in the future are the different types of billing arrangements with which some firms are experimenting. There are some good reasons for doing this. If we look at, say, lobbying firms in Washington, who bill on the value of their connections and ability to achieve results based on those connections, then it is clear that the traditional time-based fees of consulting will be much less dominant in the future, as firms attempt to exploit the value of what they deliver. Moving towards gain-sharing arrangements or long-standing retainers will be essential to levelling out the increasing volatility of consulting income. There is always a danger that these types of arrangements may reduce the fundamental objectivity of the client–consultant relationship, but the rotation of management staff in client companies tends to militate against this.

John Everett

The blurring of boundaries between consultants and clients poses a major threat in the future. As clients increasingly contract out their peripheral activities, the remaining 'centre' of the organisation will have two key functions: the management of the organisation's intellectual capital and the facilitation of change (making things happen, in other words). The implication of this is that both clients and consultants will be in the 'thought-ware' business, with clients selling intellectual capital to consultants as much as vice versa. This closer type of relationship is already making itself apparent in the type of partnering arrangements between clients and consultants which are becoming more common. One of the problems here is that what involves sharing of risk and rewards in today's market may extend, in the future, into consultants taking an equity stake in their clients on a widespread basis – a scenario in which consulting firms would evolve into managers of share portfolios. One of the core characteristics of consultancy would be diluted as a result: consultants should be providing ideas and independent thought, not finance.

The fact that consultancies and their clients will be competing for the same recruits could also be a source of friction. From a consultancy's point of view, there will be a huge competitive advantage in attracting better people than its rivals, but it will generate resentment among clients at the same time.

Do these two threats mean that the client–consultant relationship will, in fact, change significantly? Probably not, because the underlying relationship will continue to be, essentially, a symbiotic one. The foundation of this relationship is trust: although one side may become the dominant partner in a particular field at some stage, the advantage will be a temporary one. Trust will be maintained, providing that consulting companies continue to recognise that people and intellectual capital are their core business – not taking an equity stake in their clients – and providing that they are able to manage these two core assets effectively.

17

Critical Success Factors

Brian Harrison

There will be three determinants of success in the future – relationships, expertise and value – all of which are interrelated.

So far as client–consultant relationships are concerned, there is already a definite trend – certainly in the US, but perhaps to a lesser extent in Europe – towards consultants having longer and stronger relationships with their clients. Consultancy used to be a project-based profession: it is now much more of a relationship-based one. Why? Because clients are looking for change to be implemented, not simply recommended, and because the changes they are looking to implement are often on a much larger scale. Not surprisingly, there is a greater appetite among clients for risk-sharing arrangements – what they are trying to buy is sustained performance improvement, not just one-off gains, and this is not going to change in the future. Although large client organisations will probably always have relationships with multiple consultancies, we are likely to see a shift from the position where the client takes responsibility for integrating those relationships to where a consulting firm plays that role and orchestrates the variety of skills and expertise which the client needs.

Relationships will also play an important role in the management of intellectual capital in the future. New ideas come from client engagements. You can look back over the history of the industry to see examples of consulting firms which expanded based on a highly successful assignment for one client, which was then applied to similar clients in similar situations. By contrast, it is hard to think of a single example of where the consultancy has thought up an effective idea in isolation. This is unlikely to change in the future, but what will certainly be different will be the ability of the consulting company to collate and then disseminate intellectual capital electronically. Consultancies will be able to share information – internally and externally – much more

175

quickly than at present. Where an assignment is in a strategically important area for a client and has delivered a significant competitive advantage, we may therefore expect clients to become more restrictive about the consulting company redeploying the same idea elsewhere. This is not an issue which will be resolved by signing more restrictive contracts: it will only be managed through a strong relationship between the client and consultant.

Moving on to expertise, there are essentially three types of skill within the consulting profession: analytical expertise (the raw brainpower often supplied by the strategy houses), experience (the track record of having done whatever it is that the client wants) and process-based expertise (in other words, the skill to bring about change in a client's business – which may range from a simple ability to facilitate management teams to be able to facilitate large-scale change). In the past, consultancy has tended to rely on uni-dimensional people – people who had enormous depth in a single specialist area – but the key attribute for the future will be multi-dimensionality. The only people capable of facilitating large-scale change will be those who can bring together all three types of expertise and who can ensure that the specialists in each area – many of whom will be client staff – can work together in a high-performance team. This integration with the client will be especially important: some consultancies have a very élitist outlook, believing themselves to be superior to their clients, and this culture is going to make it very difficult for them to make effective use of client skills. In large-scale transformation, the consulting team has to be able to integrate itself organically into the heart of the client organisation.

The final critical success factor will be value. The exact definition of value will vary from client to client, reflecting what each one most wants to achieve, but the underlying value of consultancy comes from helping the client organisation to perform better. For example, over the past few years, A T Kearney has helped many clients develop more effective sourcing strategies. Most companies spend between 30 and 50 per cent of their revenue on externally purchased goods and services, and we developed a service to reduce significantly these costs. The value to clients has been very tangible and very measurable, and it has only been possible to deliver it because, as consultants, we were able to make different parts of the client organisation work together. Sourcing is a function which runs across traditional departmental boundaries: to be able to change it, you need to be able to get the buy-in of these different groups, each of whom has their own perspectives and agendas.

Of course, services like this – which look for tangible results in a specific area – are not new to consultancy. They are, however, likely to be a much more common model in the future, as the pressure from clients to be able to define and deliver 'value' continues to increase.

Allan Steinmetz

A major success factor in the future has to be the speed with which consultancy assignments can be delivered. Clients are becoming increasingly accustomed to instant gratification in other areas of their lives, and there is no reason to suppose that consultancy should be immune from this trend. It cannot be long before we have clients calling up and demanding, for example, 'innovation on demand', where you do not get paid if you cannot provide an answer in a couple of hours. Moreover, it is unlikely that this trend will be confined to taking ideas to clients: we should expect to see every aspect of consulting – including systems integration, change management and implementation – all affected by the need for greater precision, speed and accuracy.

Technology will undoubtedly play a fundamental role in making this possible – in ways that we can scarcely begin to imagine today. Perhaps we will have virtual consultancies or time-sharing on assignments. Longer-term, we should not be surprised to see the electronic equivalent of newspaper advice columns, available on a subscription basis, become much more a part of the accepted norm.

James Hall

One of the most important success factors of the future will be the nature of the consulting organisation itself.

Many of the largest firms at the moment work in what could best be described as 'federal organisations', combining a wide range of loosely linked, but semi-autonomous business units. Being successful in the future is going to require considerably greater integration, so that specialist skills can be combined to provide uniquely powerful solutions for clients. But achieving this integration poses a major challenge. A command and control culture is not the solution: you cannot simply say to people: 'become integrated'. Clearly, finding effective organisational structures, capable of creating a common strategic mindset – an operating framework, in effect – within which business units can respond to changing client needs and market conditions, will be fundamentally important. But so too will be the people recruited into that organisational structure. No consulting firm can ever be better than the people it hires and retains. One of the challenges in the future will be recruiting the best people at a time when their aspirations, ambitions and motivations are all changing rapidly.

A third feature of the successful consulting organisation in the future will be its ability to acquire and disseminate knowledge. At the moment, we think it is enough to be able to field the best ten people on a given subject from anywhere in the world; in the future, we are going to have to be twice as good as this. Whatever systems we currently have are going to be inadequate faced with the increasingly complex nature of client demands and the speed with which we will be expected to produce a result. Developing the new systems that we will need will perhaps be the most capital-intensive part of consultancy in the future.

Philip Evans

Consultancies of the future will have two potential sources of competitive advantage. First, there will be the quality of the client relationships a firm has and its coverage in a given organisation. The CEO may be the key person to whom all consultancies aim to sell, but having contacts in functional areas or at a divisional level enables a firm to be able to cross-sell its services much more effectively. The second source of competitive advantage will come from having consultancy expertise or products in a specific domain: the impact of *cumulative* knowledge and experience will prove to be fundamental in securing a firm's credibility and reputation. All consulting firms will need to look at themselves in this regard, to understand where their own core strength lies and maximise it, thus making themselves attractive to potential partners who are equally strong, but along the opposite dimension.

Jean-Pierre Le Calvez

Consultancy has always been event-driven, but it will appear to be even more so in the future as the 'events' themselves become much more visible – globalisation, the dissemination of information, political and economic change in Europe. The fact that these events will seem more prominent is a reflection of the extent to which consultancies will be focusing more of their time on identifying client opportunities and needs before or as they emerge, rather than waiting to react to them once they have emerged. Getting to the market at the right time will be fundamental to success – but this will not always mean being first to market. More crucial will be being able both to identify long- and short-term trends and to distinguish those which will be especially influential and understand why this is.

Keith Ferrazzi

There are four key factors that will distinguish the winning firms of the future from the losing ones. First, the successful consultancy will have a clearly differentiated brand and market positioning – one that reflects its increasingly sophisticated clients. Second, no consulting practice will survive without an effective knowledge database. Third will be having access to the right kind of people – something that will mean investing heavily in achieving the right balance between work and home for employees. Most people recognise these priorities, but a fourth and equally important factor will be the corporatisation of the consulting firm, where the partners and owners are forced to compromise their individual agendas, where the values of the organisation are made very explicit, where there is a recognition that people should play different roles – not every one can hunt, fish, skin and eat. In consulting terms, this means recognising that practitioners do not always make greater sales people and that we need to provide alternative career paths and reward structures.

But, if this is such an important issue, why not go the whole way? Why not go public? Because the partnership model still works better overall. When you are a partner, you are also a shareholder. What reason is there for sharing your rewards with outside shareholders, when it is the high earnings that ensure that consulting firms can recruit the most talented people? What is important in the future, though, is being able to balance this underlying model with a much more corporate, 'business-like' operating structure.

Michael de Kare-Silver

One of the most important trends in the industry today – and one which will have a significant impact in the future – is consolidation.

This takes three forms. First, we have inter-firm consolidation – the growing prevalence for mergers and alliances in all areas of consultancy. Although there is no sign of this activity abating, one has to question whether it will be possible for the 'mega-firms' that will emerge to capture the anticipated synergies and economies of scale.

Second, there is the consolidation of consultancy services. IT-related consultancy is a good example of a service which is expanding into other types of implementation work, but the trend holds for almost all segments of the consulting industry. Like the merger and acquisition activity, this consolidation is driven partly out of a desire to achieve economies of scale, but it is equally true that consultancy is becoming more issue-driven. Look, for instance, at the number of firms that have published brochures on European Monetary Union, which bring together a host of disparate services in order to address an important issue for clients.

Finally, consolidation is also happening at the human level: consultants, like the firms for which they work, need to be more multi-dimensional. It is not enough, these days, simply to be an IT specialist: you need to know how to advise on a broad range of business issues.

Consolidation – in all its forms – is the sign of a maturing industry. It reflects the fact that product life-cycles are becoming shorter because they are being copied more quickly by competitors. It reflects the fact that niche consultancies, which grow up around a single idea, are finding it much more difficult to break into the mainstream consulting market than it would have been even ten years ago. It reflects the fact that clients continue to find most consulting firms undifferentiated. And the implication of this – as you would expect in a mature industry – is that consulting firms are going to have to look for new sources of competitive advantage in the future. In doing so, they have only a limited number of options from which to choose. They could compete on price – and the current experimentation with contingency and other success-related fees are all symptomatic of this. Alternatively, they could try to build up a strong brand identity or differentiate themselves through the quality of their client service (global reach being one example of this). They could develop new products or services – typically the source of competitive advantage in other industries – but, with shortening life-cycles, this strategy is unlikely to result in a sustainable benefit. You only have to draw an analogy with the financial services market to know that any consultancy that believes it can win and keep competitive advantage through a specific product is simply kidding itself.

Competitive advantage in the future will, instead, come from having a much improved understanding of who your target customers are and from being able to build lasting relationships with them. Different firms may cut the market very differently – by size of client, geography, specialist needs, attitude to risk, level of business change: success will depend, not on your definition, but on the fact that you have a definition. Segmentation is the first step in building an understanding of what your clients really want from you, and, once you build this understanding, it is clearly easier to answer the question: 'how can I differentiate myself?' Look at Intel: its competitive advantage does not lie so much in its actual product, as in the fact that it has developed an expert understanding of the sector it serves and it keeps its customers by staying leading-edge and innovative with them. Similarly, we should expect to see the successful consulting firms of the future developing very strong ties with a small number of core clients, where the client–consultant relationship is as much based on accumulated and in-depth knowledge as it is on the consulting firm's ability to field specific expertise. To do this, firms will become more willing to invest in clients – seconding people to them for free, using people in an account management role, and so on – and it will make economic sense to do this because the expectation will be that the relationship will last 3–5 years, rather than just a few months, as you often see today.

Steve Beck

Successful consultancy is all about getting a share of mind – particularly the Chief Executive's mind: it is about understanding the critical issues with which the board of a company is grappling and being able to field the appropriate response. At the moment CEOs go to different places, depending on the advice they are looking for. They will go to an investment banker for advice on acquisitions/disposals, and other more general portfolio management expertise. They will go to a PR firm when they are worried about investor relations, or an advertising agency about their corporate brand. They will go to a head-hunting firm when they want to recruit non-executive directors. They come to management consultancies when they are considering major initiatives which will have a strategic impact: this is the traditional heartland of the management consultant. In the past, these areas were very clearly demarcated: a minority of advisory firms tried to do everything, but most have accepted their pigeon-holing. In the future, the challenge will be to move into new areas – to retain and expand your share of mind.

To be successful in this environment, consulting firms will need to be able to bring together specialist services, to integrate specific ideas into a synergistic whole, but without losing their specialist focus. This will be difficult to achieve through organic growth alone. We should expect to see further mergers and acquisitions as consulting firms look to access new ideas, and more collaborative working between consultancies. This latter process has already started – in response to increasingly complex client demands – but it is still one that most consultancies find very uncomfortable.

Bruce Petter

At the moment, there is no way to penalise a firm or individual consultant who has performed poorly: unlike in regulated industries, they cannot be struck off. We would not consider allowing the healthcare or financial services sector to work like this: how much longer are we going to tolerate it among consultants? Clients may be becoming much more sophisticated in the way they purchase consultancy, but few recognise just how much the industry has changed, even over the past few years. This emerging, more complex industry is likely to require a new approach to maintaining standards in order to preserve its long-term reputation. Regulation will be one key to ensuring that it continues to be well regarded among clients. Another will be for consultancies themselves to invest more time and money obtaining feedback from clients. This is something that is happening more and more, especially in the largest consultancies, but the industry still has a long way to go before it starts to treat clients like customers. Conversely, *not* demonstrating that they are willing to be regulated poses a considerable threat to consulting firms: consultants have to show that they are serious about delivering value to their clients and providing an acceptable rate of return on consulting assignments. Without this, the industry will be in danger of being tarred with the brush of a minority of poor performers.

Robin Buchanan

As the consultancy market becomes more segmented and as clients increasingly use this segmentation to inform their purchasing decisions, an important determinant of success will be the extent to which consulting firms recognise their segment. Being an innovative strategy house, or being a firm that relies on having an established track record in a given area, are both perfectly viable approaches: the key will be not to confuse the two – to try to be what you are not.

Alan Buckle

Size will be an immensely important factor, because it gives a consulting firm global reach and access to capabilities both internally and externally because of its negotiating power: and these provide operational flexibility.

But size brings with it challenges: the ability to manage cultural diversity (how are we going to be able to work with Chinese clients?); the need to share knowledge effectively and to make it relevant to a given situation (anyone will be able to transmit information around an organisation, but how can we make sure that it gets used?); the ability to manage the expectations and aspirations of individuals (how are we going to accommodate the portfolio careerists of the future?).

18

Key Threats and Challenges

Brian Harrison

The biggest single threat to the industry has to be that it ceases to grow. The internal systems and organisational structures of almost every firm are predicated on continuous growth. Career development is a good example: how can we sustain the apprenticeship model if we cannot move people up through the firm, and how can we move people up through the firm if we are not expanding?

But there is a threat too, in continued growth. This is an industry in which no firm can afford to rest on the laurels of past or even present successes. Consultancies have to continue to innovate and find new ways to add value to clients' businesses. We cannot stop changing, because our clients' industries have not stopped changing. It is the process of continually adapting to client needs which will keep a consulting firm successful in the future, not its past reputation.

Michael Younger

The key questions for consulting firms are whether they can continue growing at the current rate of 20–25 per cent per annum and, if they cannot do this, what the consequences will be.

The consulting industry is made up of three primary markets – 'classical' management consultancy, IT-related consultancy and outsourcing – each of which is at a different stage of development. In practice, the growth of the past few years has been fuelled by one area – outsourcing – something which has concealed the relative maturity of the two other markets. But outsourcing has its limits and it cannot be long before companies begin to question the process, before they find that they have lost control of the costs of core areas of their business. It therefore seems probable that the outsourcing market will mature over the next few years.

The impact on firms such as Arthur D Little – which have focused on the 'classical' consulting market, which may recommend outsourcing as an option but do not offer it as a service themselves – will be slight. But for consultancies that are highly dependent on a constant stream of income from outsourcing, the maturation of this particular market poses a threat. These organisations are accustomed to operating in a growth environment: how will they manage a market which is no longer expanding?

This is not to suggest that the 'classical' consultancies will not be facing challenges of their own – after all, this type of consultancy is simply another, much older, form of outsourcing in which the client 'outsources' its strategy function to an external supplier much in the same way that they are currently outsourcing their IT function. This market is already a more mature one, but its ability to expand will be further threatened in the future by clients' increasing ability to access information. In the past, clients used consultants as a means of obtaining information to which they would not otherwise have had access. But, today, there are so many more sources of information to which the client has direct access, that the role of the consultant as 'information provider' will be limited. Instead, the focus of consultancy will be on helping clients find ways to apply and exploit that information – a shift which threatens companies that specialise in market research and competitor analysis. Although these trends are already well under way, we can be sure that they have a very long way still to go – and that some consulting firms have barely started to grapple with their implications.

Techniques of strategic planning, performance improvement and so on are also much better understood and leave fewer opportunities for imaginative repackaging under new names. In future, consulting companies will certainly have to pay much more attention to the softer sides of their profession – change management, knowledge transfer and the building of learning organisations. Consultants have always claimed that they can help clients implement. In certain cases they have taken on direct responsibility, often with unfortunate results. In other cases they have not been good at skill transfer. As a consequence, the clients are no better equipped to stand on their own feet at the end of the assignment than they were at the beginning.

How else will the 'classical' market respond to an increasingly mature industry? It is likely that many of the medium-sized consulting firms will be squeezed between the largest firms and a large number of highly specialised niche players, but the fundamental structure of the industry will not change. We should expect the number of large and medium-sized firms to reduce – but not drastically – and these will continue to be balanced by a large number of very small consultancies. Similarly, while clients are likely to demand increasingly specialised services, consultancies will always need to maintain a certain level of multi-disciplinary skills. The exact composition of this minimum portfolio of functional know-how will vary over time – we have already seen how the need for organisational consultancy has superseded specific functional skills (such as marketing) which had previously replaced generic processes (such as cost-cutting) – but the underlying portfolio structure will remain.

What will change will be the ability that consulting firms have to respond to changes in the environment. As the consulting market matures, the decisions they take will be irreversible. As the industry structure solidifies, the consulting world will be a much less forgiving place in which to operate. The strategic decisions consultancies make will be harder to change. If the growth rate goes out of the sector, consultancies will not know how to react – as organisations, they have never been particularly strong at making good, long-term and proactive strategic choices. In the past, the levels of growth enjoyed by the industry have meant that firms have escaped the consequences of poor decisions. In the future, they will not be able to hide these so effectively.

Moreover, in 20 years' time, the American-liberal-capitalist economic model which dominates our markets today may have been superseded by a model which is altogether different. The regional economic balance of the world may also have changed. In theory, such developments are a matter for clients more than consultants, because management consultancy has always been able to redefine itself to meet shifting market conditions and changing client needs. But a market that is no longer growing at the rate to which consultants are accustomed will mean that their ability to reinvent themselves is reduced. Without room to find external solutions – new markets, new services – consulting firms will have to turn to internal solutions, reinventing their internal organisation and processes in order to maintain profits.

At the same time that they are grappling with more difficult choices and greater constraints, consulting firms will inevitably be – in this mature market – facing greater pressure from clients to perform, as the latter exploit their increasingly strong negotiating position. The consulting industry has had a very good run for the past 25 years, with growth rates of more than 10 per cent: it should assume that the next 25 cannot be as good. Before this recent boom – before 1975 – the consulting industry was growing at about 5 per cent per year. While we should not expect it to shrink in real terms in the future, it seems likely that the levels of growth will return to their pre-1975 levels. This is the kind of growth that other sectors experience: why should consultancy be any different?

Crawford Gillies

There is always a danger in any thriving industry of being complacent. We cannot, for example, be sure of the impact the current series of crises in Asian economies will have over the long term. At the moment, business in this area continues to be very robust: some companies may be looking to pull out of the region, but many others are now looking for opportunities to move in, while the costs of doing so are relatively low. We tend to be optimistic about the future of consultancy because the industry has always managed to adapt to change and the Far East is a good illustration of this. The key threat we face, therefore, is the loss for whatever reason of this core flexibility. As long as the industry remains flexible, its survival is almost guaranteed.

Peter Davis

Perhaps the big unknown is how big clients' organisations are going to be. Will the largest companies get still larger, or will there be a backlash against the current round of 'mega-mergers'? Will markets fragment? Will middle-sized companies be squeezed by increasing polarisation between very large and very small organisations? Growth in the consultancy industry has been fuelled by the demands of the largest, transnational clients: could the industry survive in a highly fragmented environment?

James Hall

Leaving aside the possible macroeconomic risks – a significant downturn in the world economy, for example – the most important microeconomic risk that consultancies face may be the increasingly litigious nature of society. People assume that litigation will have the effect of correcting whatever is wrong, but there is no evidence that this is the case. The effect that it may have will be to force consulting firms to direct considerable time and resources to preventing court cases – dealing with the symptoms rather than whatever the underlying causes may be. The risk here is not that litigation will bankrupt consulting firms, but that the threat of it will make them unable to serve their clients effectively because they become far too cautious.

Paul Mitchell

The first – and almost overwhelming – challenge faced by the consulting industry is the need to recruit and retain the best people. But the importance of this issue should not blind us to other threats. For the consulting market as a whole, one of the key threats has to be related to risk. Litigation is already becoming much more common in the US; in

Europe it is mostly confined to audits, but this may change. At the moment, also, litigation tends to be confined to the parts of the consulting market where it is comparatively easy to trace a connection between a consulting assignment and a poor result – systems implementation is a good illustration. But it is not impossible to see this changing, so that clients become more willing to blame their strategic consultants for poor performance, even though there may be many other factors – the implementation of the strategy, for instance – which could be implicated.

Another threat, and one which relates particularly to strategy consultancies, could arise if a firm develops a new way of selling strategy consulting – bundling it in free with a massive systems integration assignment perhaps. Although many clients – especially the largest ones, which are more accustomed to segmenting their use of consultants – will be very resistant to this notion, there could be a significant area of the market which is attracted to the idea.

Michael de Kare-Silver

Many consulting firms underestimate the extent to which a new entrant or a new channel could radically change this industry. Computer hardware and software manufacturers are already trying to enter the consulting market; companies like AT&T are starting to set up their own specialist firms. Given that the sector has enjoyed almost continuous growth for the past decade and a half, the time seems ripe for a wave of new firms. The last time we were in a similar position, it was the big accountancy firms that moved in; perhaps this time it will be companies like Microsoft or Intel, or investment banks.

Clearly, such new entrants pose a potential threat to the incumbent firms, but, while they continue to compete within the existing business model for consultancy, they are unlikely to have a significant impact by themselves. The real change could come when a firm – new or established – develops a different set of rules. And, if we look across other industries, the new models which are emerging revolve around electronic commerce. It cannot be long before someone launches a 'virtual consulting service', starting off as a source of advice on a specific issue – the Year 2000 problem or European Monetary Union, but rapidly expanding into other areas. Perhaps it could take the form of a directory, telling clients who to phone in which firm in order to get help on a particular matter, where contact details are only listed for a fee. Perhaps it will begin as an interactive chat-room, or a virtual 'surgery' where people can email named experts at specific times. Whatever the form it takes, 'virtual consulting' will succeed if it creates a more powerful relationship between itself and potential clients than the traditional consulting firms themselves can maintain and if it can make genuine intellectual capital accessible to its subscribers in a way in which consulting firms have historically been unwilling to do.

Robin Buchanan

One of the most fundamental threats to the industry is that change will stop. It has happened before: during the Gulf War, the majority of companies simply sat on their hands because they were totally unsure about what would happen next.

We can comfort ourselves that such a scenario, although not impossible, remains unlikely. Change – from a consultancy perspective – is driven by three primary factors. First, there is technology in the broadest sense. Change here looks set to continue, as technology continues to enable companies to globalise their operations and, simultaneously, to balance this with micro-marketing which addresses the needs of individual customers, wherever they are. Second, there are changes in corporate strategy. Currently, we are going through a phase in which the big and simple corporate ideal seems very attractive: companies are unbundling their services – but at the same time, the pressures towards convergence means that re-bundling is happening in new ways. Both these apparently contradictory trends offer a major opportunity for consultancies. Finally, there is the human side to all of this – the fact that individual employment patterns and the way in which companies are organised are both starting to change significantly.

David Maister

The central problem facing the consulting industry is not so much forecasting what will happen in the future, but adapting to the trends we already know about. For the past decade, consulting firms have largely chosen to ignore a whole series of operational issues which reduce their profitability. Most, for example, continue to use antiquated accounting systems which make it difficult, if not impossible, to analyse the profitability and efficiency of individual assignments. This has affected their ability to allocate resources wisely. Simply put, they don't know where they make their money and where they do not. Most firms are not particularly good at people development, still relying heavily on a sink-or-swim approach to people management. Firms also under-invest in important areas such as quality improvement. They are so busy getting the product out of the door, they take little time to ask if there are better ways of doing what they do. They have been able to get away with this situation because it is rarely visible to the external world: some firms, for example, have been able to claim to be world-class when there is little internally to prove that this is the case. Irrespective of what actually happens in the future, it will be increasingly difficult for consulting firms to have their cake and eat it in this respect: they will not be able to claim one thing in the market without being able to back it up internally.

The most significant barrier to making the internal changes needed is a lack of management courage. The industry has tended to be tolerant of what is simply satisfactory and has been unwilling to make the type of hard choices required in order to progress from 'satisfactory' to 'excellent'. Suppose you are a partner: your workload is already full, but someone offers you another assignment. You know that you will only have time to do a competent job for this new client, although you profess to deliver excellent results. What will your senior partners want you to do? In nine out of ten cases, they will want you to put income above strategy and take the extra work. The real issue here is hypocrisy – the fact that firms do not have the courage to stick to their own strategies. If you as an individual, and you as a collective organisation, are refusing to acknowledge the fact that you accept competent, rather than world-class work, then you are nowhere near being able to resolve it: your hypocrisy will prevent you from becoming what you claim to be.

The same is true of people development. You will probably have established an internal appraisal system; the chances are that it will involve upward as well as downward feedback. You will have explained the process to your staff, and everyone will have agreed that it is the right thing to do. So why is it that you continue to find people who treat their staff poorly? It is because your organisation is always too busy – too busy working on an assignment, too busy trying to sell the next piece of work. For all the talk, your organisation believes that people development is secondary to profit enhancement.

And it is important to recognise that consulting firms do not – and will not – become excellent simply by increasing their profits. It takes much more than money to create and continue a great organisation: the secret of great consulting work is making sure your people are excited, and excitement comes from setting audacious goals, from having a strong set of values and from having fun. Achieving this will mean being able to balance the short and long term; it will also mean creating a culture which provides genuine motivation for the people who work within it. An organisation with a strong set of values has the courage of its convictions: it will say no to that extra piece of work which would compromise its standards of excellence. Without values, you have expediency: your standards are eroded because you give way to the temptation of earning some money in the short term, rather than more money in the long term. Moreover, it is not enough to articulate a set of values or to write an aspirational mission statement: you have to be prepared to live and die by them. 'Values' are not what you aspire to; they are what you are prepared to enforce. Excellence, therefore, will come about by having values that are both backed up by and support managerial courage (see Figure 18.1).

We should not underestimate the challenge that this will pose the majority of consulting firms. For a firm to have a strong set of values, it will need to make choices and take risks. It will need to exert authority, often in an environment where decentralised power (and autonomy) is the norm. It will need to penalise, instead of tolerate, the people that do not live by the values set. New entrants will have the edge, because changing existing cultures is almost always a long and difficult process. Consultancy – known for its consensus management – will need some great leaders, leaders who can inspire organisations rather than compel them.

But if 'competent' firms have thrived in the past, why should the future be any different? The answer lies in the state of the market, at both the macro and micro levels.

On the macro level, if the market continues to grow – as it pretty much has done for the past 15 years – then your competence will be sufficient to allow you to sustain your market share and positioning. But if the market slows, or even ceases to grow, then competence will not be enough.

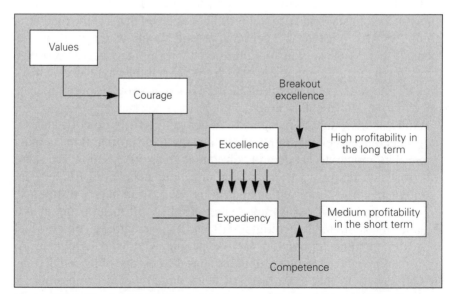

Figure 18.1 The obstacles to achieving excellence in consulting firms

To survive – let alone thrive – in this environment, you will need to be excellent, in internal action as much as external perception.

On the micro level, clients are not stupid: in fact, we all recognise that they are becoming increasingly sophisticated in the way they buy consultancy. Clients can distinguish, for instance, between the firms that genuinely operate on a global basis, and those that just claim to do so. Growing client perceptiveness, therefore, is likely to force many consulting firms to start actually living up to the image they project, in order to protect their brand – many people think that branding is the same as marketing but, especially for professional service firms, it is a much more operational issue.

Of course, ensuring that your actions live up to your image is about more than effective branding: it goes straight to the heart of the client–consultant relationship. Clients buy consultancy on trust: they trust you to be sufficiently professional to deliver a good piece of work and not to try to over-charge for it. The more a client trusts you, the more they will buy from you. In recognition of this, many consulting firms have invested heavily in sales training – which teaches their consultants how to look as though they care, even when they do not. Again, clients are unlikely to be convinced by this in the future, but will be looking to employ firms which genuinely care and which are prepared to work much more closely with them than the majority of consultants do today. This will probably mean that we see much more use of different types of fee arrangements, but these will not be the end in themselves. They will be means by which consulting companies are trying to gain and prove the trust of their clients.

Eddie Oliver

At the moment, clients want two things which often seem incompatible: they want *process* – the seamless integration of global resources by the consulting firm – but they also want *content*; one of the major criticisms levelled at consultants is that they are insufficiently innovative – 'you didn't surprise us' runs the complaint. Being able to deliver both aspects is very difficult: developing a 'one-firm' culture should not stifle creativity in theory, but it often tends to produce standardised content in practice. Over the next 10–20 years, the consulting industry will need to distinguish between process and content more clearly and manage them both more effectively: clients will always want both, not one or the other. Process may be better managed from a centralised perspective, but content may become more and more the preserve of local, distributed teams.

The danger of not balancing process and content is that organisations will become much more process-driven – that they focus too much on the way they work and not enough on the intellectual input to an assignment. There are three reasons why consulting organisations are often stronger on process than content, each of which poses a challenge for the future.

In the first place, many firms struggle to produce innovative content, especially Big Five firms, where the culture and history have tended to be conformist and risk averse. But why spend so much time trying to innovate? The consultancy industry as a whole has been much more successful at identifying and recycling good ideas, rather than necessarily being the originators of them. People – clients and consultants – under-value this process, although it is, effectively, what good consultants do with their clients: they listen to the evidence, sift through all the available options or ideas, and focus on the most relevant. Success in the future will come, not so much from internal innovation, but from being able to access a wide range of external ideas and identify the minority that are likely to be of interest to clients.

A second issue – again relating to the way in which consultancies manage the content of an assignment – is that many firms are finding it very difficult to marshal their intellectual capital effectively. Consultants, as individuals, are usually very effective at acquiring and deploying knowledge, but consultancies, as organisations, are poor at corporate learning. Information may be shared effectively within small teams of people but, once it is shared more broadly – institutionalised, in effect – it ceases to be meaningful to most people and becomes yet more of the apparently irrelevant data which fills formal knowledge libraries. Today's obsession with knowledge databases and the accompanying technology is therefore contributing to the problem, not to the solution. Databases do not increase knowledge: they tend to make more data available to people who do not want it. A major challenge in the future will be to manage this issue, so that information is accessible to those who genuinely need it, so that the value of intellectual capital does not deteriorate as it is shared across the organisation.

Third and finally, there are recruitment issues. As the consultancy market matures, it will become harder for people to enter it at a senior level. Firms will also be recruiting from a narrower and narrower pool, as many younger people, faced with the often totally unreasonable pressure under which consultants are put and the lifestyle that accompanies that pressure, choose alternative careers. In a few years' time, consultancies could be trying to appeal to a very small group of people, all of whom pretty much fit the same mould, to work in an industry where variety and flexibility are essential. One of the implications of this is that firms will be generating even less new content internally: the organisational structure will be much more dependent on standardised ways of doing things.

Glen Peters

The biggest threat to consulting firms in the future will be reputation. People used to tell stories about how consultants will take all your money without adding anything new, or make passing comments on its lack of ethics. But today that whole attitude has become much more endemic within business – you only have to read Scott Adam's Dilbert to see this. After all, what kind of moral positioning does a firm have which is rewarded on the basis of its ability to downsize companies? Consultants used to have a reputation for being scientific and analytical: they are now in danger of being seen as cowboys.

The companies that succeed in the future will have been able to survive this, to recognise that, when we talk about reputation, we do not simply mean the quality of service a firm gives, but the way in which it handles its wider responsibilities – to clients, employees, suppliers and other stakeholders. In an industry in which the barriers to entry are declining overall, having a good reputation will be perhaps the single most important way in which an established firm will be able to differentiate itself from its emerging rivals. Reputation will also be a key driving force in the way consultancies evolve: a reputable firm will attract the best people with the best ideas, creating a virtuous circle against which the less reputable firms will find it difficult to compete.

Alan Buckle

We have to ask ourselves what the business culture of the future will be like. At the moment, it is US-dominated, and this is a model into which consultancy fits very well. We are expecting the US business culture to become dominant in continental Europe, but will this really be the case? It is certainly possible that, sometime over the next 20 years, a different culture emerges in which consultancy is far less acceptable.

In theory, consultancy as a client service is highly flexible and responsive to changing needs. It should, therefore, be able to adapt to changing business cultures. But, in the future, we may find it much harder to change, and this will leave firms particularly exposed to wholesale changes of this order. Every consultancy likes to think that it runs a flexible organisation, but it can be as difficult, in practice, to retune an organisation as change the machinery in a factory. People are not as easy to change as we like to think. Moreover, effecting change involves having a very clear vision and purpose and some consulting firms may find it hard to articulate these. Everyone may be talking about the importance of these things at the moment, but most of the output remains vague.

Keith Ferrazzi

It is frustrating that people often tend to see the consulting industry as homogeneous, when in practice you could segment it into four main areas of consultancy: technology, strategy, process and operations, and human resources (the latter being subdivided into benefits/actuarial consultancy and change management/organisational redesign). Convergence between these segments – 'one-stop-shopping', for example, the strategy houses moving into more operational work – is driven less by client needs than it is by the consulting firms themselves. Clients will continue to want specialised services: the challenge for consulting firms in the future will be to be able to integrate specialist skills and people required into a single operational entity, without losing the distinctness of the original specialisms. If we look around at firms that have tried and failed to move into new segments, it is clear that success or otherwise was determined by the extent to which they could integrate a diverse set of skills and ideas. Putting your IT practice on another floor, well away from your 'core' consultants, is never going to result in an integrated service offering.

Although internal reorganisation can go some way to answering this problem, the key will be to focus the consulting organisation around clients or groups of clients, rather than any internal definitions. Ensuring that individual consultants are measured against client-based success criteria – and Deloitte & Touche is unique in doing this – is an essential step to breaking down the consulting industry's traditional boundaries.

A second, equally important step will be for consulting firms to move away from the highly fragmented partnership structure – where there is a great deal of autonomy across the partner-focused business units – to a more corporate structure in which it is not possible to differentiate between individual partners. Consultancies need to run themselves more as businesses, with much more collective responsibility than the conventional partnership structure could muster. For some firms, particularly those with a very strong cultural heritage, this process of corporatisation will be a difficult one.

Richard Measelle

One of the key problems facing privately owned consulting firms is how to pass on the value of the firm to owners when they leave. Exit payments are calculated based on a notional value for the firm that in no way reflects its true value, so that the owners of a large firm might be sitting on billions of dollars of value to which they have no access. Clearly, they get paid substantial salaries while they are active, but, if you look at the very wealthy people in the world today, the source of their wealth is capital, not income. Money is an irresistible force for almost all people, and, in these circumstances, you would have to be a saint not to want to try to change the ownership structure so that you can access this capital, as Goldman Sachs is in the process of doing. If we put this together with the fact that some niche consultancies are currently growing very rapidly through acquisition – having converted the value of their firm into stock – then we can expect to see many more publicly owned consultancies in the future.

An alternative to acquisition will be alliances. Competing firms are already working together on very large-scale projects – if it takes you between six and 12 months and $1 million even to propose for this kind of work, then being able to share that level of risk between several firms becomes very important. At the same time, alliances can be difficult arrangements to manage: which party, for example, is ultimately responsible for the decisions taken? Clients will want one firm to take on the role of prime contractor, but the complexity and geographical reach of many assignments make it inevitable that projects will need to be resourced by multiple firms. This is something the industry just did not see five years ago, and is likely to be a significant trend in the future.

Eddie Oliver

The role of outsourcing in the consultancy market is – potentially – a significant threat. Some consulting firms – KPMG included – have given a great deal of thought to whether they should be offering their clients this kind of service and decided against it because they think that outsourcing is a very different business from consultancy. It may also be just a temporary trend – management fashions do change over time.

But we could all be wrong: outsourcing could represent a major and permanent shift in the way in which companies operate; it could be a trend to which, ultimately, we have to respond. For typical consulting services, this would not present a problem – consulting firms are nothing if not adaptable; but outsourcing – especially IT outsourcing – requires a very high level of prior investment in the supporting infrastructure. Because of the lead time involved in such investment, late entrants will find it difficult to catch up with the established players, except, perhaps, through acquisition.

David Ogram

From the perspective of IT-related consultancy, one of the key threats will be staying profitable in an environment where clients have become much more demanding – even than they are at present – in terms of results. This will be a market where one poorly delivered project could not only affect a firm's reputation, but where it may become increasingly difficult for a single consulting firm to control its exposure. As consultancies – especially the largest – take on the role of business integrators in the widest sense, and as they become responsible, in the client's eyes, for delivering a comprehensive solution, they will not be able to avoid becoming more and more dependent on a multiplicity of sub-contractors, each of whom will supply just one piece of the whole puzzle. If a sub-contractor fails to deliver their – critical – part of the project, their liability may be only $1 million; but if the consulting firm, as the prime contractor, is responsible for the project in its entirety, then its liability may be $10 million. How do you cover for this type of shortfall? The difficulty of controlling the division of responsibilities and assigning accountability in large and complex integration projects is already a major problem. Unless clients and consultants can together come up with a legal structure which manages risks of this nature, the issue could become a barrier to future growth.

19

Globalisation

Jean-Pierre Le Calvez

From the consultant's point of view, a particularly important feature of the globalisation of business is the trend towards more homogeneity. At the moment, the levels of use and degree of maturity in the European consulting market vary quite widely, with the UK and Germany being more mature markets, and Italy and France (for example) developing at an increasing pace. One of the effects of the globalisation of clients' businesses will be that discrepancies such as these will tend to disappear: consultants, in meeting their clients' needs, will themselves become more homogeneous. But homogeneity will bring its own opportunities. We are already working with clients to establish multinational, multi-skilled – even multi-company – teams, because only through these combinations of perspectives and skills will they be able to take advantage of the borderless opportunities of a world in which industries are converging and geographical boundaries disappearing. The challenge for consulting firms, therefore, will be to maintain pools of specialised, often local knowledge in an environment where homogeneity is becoming the norm; it will be to be able to integrate very different sets of cultural values without losing their essential variety.

John Everett

By 2020, business will be taking globalisation for granted – it will simply be part of the operating environment. That being said, clients and consultants alike will be faced with tremendous challenges, a key one being how to manage change in a genuinely multi-cultural environment – just because a company is global will not make it culturally homogeneous. You only need to think about the number of misunderstandings that can occur between native and non-native English speakers to appreciate how difficult it will be to operate in this kind of complex environment. Global companies today are essentially

197

international organisations, which link together different national organisational paradigms, rather than offer any new, truly multinational paradigm. In the effort to improve reach and integration, these companies recruit from different countries, but their recruits, through their national education systems, have already acquired the cultural models which make it hard for them to work together as a team of people from the same company. If we add to this the fact that advances in technology over the next two decades will mean that people have to be physically together much less than at present, and that the levels and quality of interaction we have with others will fall as a result, then it is easy to appreciate the barriers to making anything happen in the future – including change.

Solving this issue will therefore need to start early in people's lives: companies will need to set the educational agenda to ensure that it produces the type of recruits they need. It may become standard practice, for example, for an MBA to be split across two institutions in two different countries.

Michael Younger

Globalisation as a trend is clearly set to continue, but we should be sceptical about the extent to which clients genuinely need global consulting services, or, indeed, will want to 'one-stop-shop' with a single professional services firm. Consulting firms will certainly need a global 'presence', but this is not the same as having a global operation providing, for example, assignment teams staffed from different countries; rather, it suggests that consulting firms will need to look at a client's issues and develop solutions for them from a global perspective. Most of the larger firms already have adequate global presence and, to this extent, the pressure towards globalisation is something that has pretty much run its course; it is not clear what additional advantages there will be for clients in taking the process further. It is the consulting firms themselves that stand to benefit more now: globalisation provides a mechanism for growing market share.

Mick James

What we may also see is the rise of the 'winner takes all' environment at both the corporate and individual level. The impact of global clients wanting to be served by global consultancies may make the consulting industry more look more like the music industry, with pulling power concentrated in the hands of a very few firms – the Elton Johns of the consulting world. Clients will think of consultancies in the same way that consumers think about CDs: 'Why should we buy the music of a local band, when, just as easily, we can buy the CD of an international star?'

Peter Davis ....

Business is already aware that globalisation is a major driving force in the world today. But the term 'globalisation' does not adequately summarise the depth and scope of the change we will see over the next 20 years: perhaps we need a different term – 'intergalactic globalisation' perhaps!

What will this new scale of change involve? In the first place, there will no national, regulatory boundaries: transnational corporations will operate seamlessly from a host of locations. It will also be a world in which Asia-Pacific countries have become hugely significant world-players, in which Eastern European countries have been subsumed into a genuine European Union, in which the United States contributes less than one-third of the world's GDP. Management will have become a truly international activity. Even time zones – like national sovereignty – may be a thing of the past.

Change will be fuelled by a generation of people who will have grown up in a global world. These children will have none of our prejudices: unlike their parents, they will be comfortable communicating in different languages and dealing with different cultures. They will have travelled more by the time they start going to school than most of our generation will have done by the time we retire. They will also be enormously technology-literate, having grown up in a world where every home has a personal computer and where shopping is no longer done at the hyper-market but via the Internet. It is these qualities – this multi-culturalism and familiarity with sophisticated technology – that will make the truly global business a reality.

Globalisation will create intense pressure on CEOs. We should expect to see their role shift away from day-to-day, even strategic, management towards providing leadership and shared values. They will be travelling round the world to find out what is going on, to look for fresh ideas. As the industry sectors of today will long since have converged and then exploded, CEOs will be operating in a quite alien environment, one in which strange bedfellows have come together to form new industries. Entire domestic industries will have been wiped out, as global companies select single suppliers across the world.

From the consultancy perspective, one of the key demands of such clients will be more information: they will want to share information with complementary companies, or to benchmark themselves against their competitors. They will be looking for world-class expertise and solutions, and they will not be satisfied with having the leading specialist from, say, France, or the best solution that, say, a UK firm can provide. They will want to be certain that they are working with a consulting firm with global reach. Globalisation will be *the* major source of consultancy growth over the next two decades – and we should expect that growth to be in the region of 15 per cent per year.

Consultancies do not just depend on the pace of change, they also need to be able to add real value to their clients. In a world dominated by the kind of 'second generation' globalisation envisaged here, an increasing pace of change is a given. Much more challenging will be being able to deliver tangible benefits in this environment. Clients will want to use consultants and firms who have a proven track record. But, from the consultants' perspective, it is going to be increasingly difficult to develop that track record in a world where the rules – and clients – are in a constant state of flux. Clearly, much will depend on the consulting industry's ability to use technology and to leverage knowledge more effectively than ever. But the sheer scale of the change that is possible will mean that consulting firms have to – will even be under an obligation to their clients to – explore new ways of working.

One aspect of this is that 'mega-mergers' between consulting firms, like that between Price Waterhouse and Coopers & Lybrand, are not the end-game, but simply staging posts on a journey which will see more restructuring before it comes to an end. Another will be the need to have a truly integrated global management structure. The size and global reach of a minority of consulting firms will mean that niche competitors are squeezed out of the marketplace – they simply will not make it to the bid list. The serious competition will be between 3–4 massive, truly trans-national consultancies.

Steve Beck

Consulting firms should be cautious about the globalisation bandwagon. It is true that global clients will expect a global consultancy provider, and the size and reach of the consulting firms that operate in this sector will clearly be a major determinant of success. But, while some sectors are rapidly being 'globalised', it remains the case that these sectors account for only a minority of consulting assignments at present.

By contrast, the issue of integrating strategy with technology, and vice versa, will be the single most important business phenomenon in the next five years.

Eddie Oliver

The trend towards globalisation has been remorseless and has had a huge impact on the consulting industry, primarily because it polarises it. On one side of the spectrum, the industry has had to invest massively in the kind of infrastructure and organisation which will allow it to service multinational clients effectively. But, on the other side, there are still clients who only need advice on a local scale – who have no interest in global services and are unwilling to pay the higher fee rates which the global firms have to charge in order to recoup their costs. The inevitable consequence of this is that the large consulting firms will move out of many of the smaller and less profitable niche markets in which they currently operate, to focus almost exclusively on those compamies that need and are prepared to pay for what these firms alone can offer – brand, a wide range of expertise, the processes in which they have invested, corporate knowledge, as well as global reach. Of course, firms claim to do this at the moment, but practice is very different – many continue to work in niche markets with small as well as large clients. However, over the next 20 years, this incipient shift will become a reality.

20 Recruiting and Retaining People

John Clarkeson

Human input will always be expensive: to clients in terms of fees and to consultancies in terms of the cost of recruitment and retention. But, while the competition for the best people is particularly intense, simply offering people more and more money is not the solution. To attract good people, we need to ensure that consultancy continues to be an intellectually challenging profession, one where people can have breakthrough ideas and develop a sense that they are making a significant contribution in whatever field they are working.

Strategy consulting has an advantage here in that it gives its people much greater scope to be creative, to make a real difference. What kind of long-term satisfaction does a consultant get who simply helps a client downsize, compared to one who helps create jobs by opening new frontiers for growth?

Rafael Cerezo

Responsiveness has to be one of the attributes of a successful consulting firm in the future. But 'responsiveness' in this context will not simply mean being able to react quickly to a client request; rather, it will be the ability to consider multiple inputs and outputs, to deal with the ambiguity that will be the order of the day rather than try to simplify it, and to network internally and externally in order to bring together the people needed to solve an unfamiliar and complex problem.

The partnership model provides a good structure for this process, because it is a networked organisation in which many individuals can have a personal stake, but much will also depend on the characteristics and quality of the people that populate that structure. Being able to grow, while also maintaining the core values of a firm like the Boston Consulting

Group, is one of the key challenges we face over the next few years. It is already clear that the model with which we are familiar – recruiting people from a small number of business schools, for example – is not sustainable in its current form. In fact, this is a good thing, because it will force us to break the mould and consider new models, rather than to eke out an existing one.

In creating a new model for the future, access to new intellectual capital will have to be a prioity. Hiring people who know what everybody else knows – except in specialist fields where depth of knowledge remains important – will not be enough. Whether they are sociologists or nuclear physicists, we will need to attract people who can bring a new perspective and fresh way of thinking. Nor will it be enough just to recruit them: we will also need to put in place the kinds of processes that retain, rather than blur, the differences between people. Similarly, we will need to ensure that, as we acquire knowledge from these people, we do not standardise it in order to accommodate it into our existing frames of reference. Being able to hold a variety of ways of thinking and a range of possible, sometimes contradictory meanings – ambiguity, once again – will be essential.

David Ogram

The current education system is failing business – especially knowledge-based business – and there is no reason to suppose that this will change in the future. It is therefore inevitable that companies, such as consult-ancies, will have to take a much more proactive role, if they are to have the pool of trained people they need to survive. One possibility is that companies will offer students on-the-job training as part of their degrees. Whatever the approach, it is essential that a solution is found: in order to be able to handle the wealth of information which will, in the future, be instantly accessible, we are going to need a much higher level of intellectual training than is available today.

John Everett

Developing a new organisational model will be one of the fundamental challenges of consultancy in the future. The models and structures in place today are unlikely to survive the next six to seven years, because they will not reflect the changing aspirations of the people that work in them. Deep down, people want to relate and contribute to an organisation – this is a basic human need which means that organisations will continue to have people at their core. But, in line with Maslow's hierarchy of needs, the consultants of the future will be much more concerned with lifestyle issues and with ensuring that the firms for which they work are making a positive impact on the community. Like their clients, consultancies will be responding to a host of complex changes in their operating environment, and will need a new – leading-edge – organisational structure to survive.

If we look across the consulting market today, different firms are experimenting with different ad-hoc models, but no one really understands what does and does not work in this context. We are also not being very imaginative in the range of options we consider. In the future, the issue is going to have to be considered on a much more systematic basis.

One approach will be to look at consulting firms as self-organising entities, sufficiently fluid to adapt to changes as they emerge with minimal central direction or control. The role of the centre will be to provide overall direction and leadership, while the structure itself evolves by allowing individuals to gravitate towards the areas that interest them and gradually coalesce into teams. At the moment, this is all theory and it is difficult to think of any company – even high-tech ones – who are engaged in this type of organic development process. It is relatively easy to see how this could work with new companies, but it is much harder to see how you could take existing structures and turn them into self-adapting organisms. The firms that succeed will enjoy a massive competitive advantage.

Philip Evans

Remaining innovative, at the high-value end of this process, will be immensely important in the future. Equally so will be the need to integrate new and different skills. All organisations – and consulting firms are not exceptions to this – tend to reject people or products that do not fit their existing mindset, but, in the future, it will become important to be much more inclusive. But, at the same time, integrating these different people and ways of working will be very difficult: there will be real tension between the various cultures that consulting firms will need to bring together. Being able to present a broadly based firm externally will be very important, but this will only be achieved at the cost of internal coherence. It is a trade-off with which every consulting firm will have to struggle: market share versus internal manageability. Some firms will merge, despite the internal chaos which almost always accompanies such a move; others will prefer to specialise.

Michael Younger

People are already a big issue for Arthur D Little, as they are for every other consultancy. How do you attract the best people? How do you provide them with an intellectually stimulating environment, but balance the freedom that that involves with a corporate need for control? Some degree of control is a necessity – if only to bring 3000–4000 people together under the same roof effectively, but doing this when you also have to give people the opportunity to follow their intellectual instincts will be an enormous challenge. 'Classical' management consultancies – as opposed to IT-related consultants and outsourcing companies – will have the advantage here: it is considerably easier to bring together 5–10 people on an assignment and still allow them to work creatively, than it is to find the same balance where the assignment team may be 100 people strong. Undoubtedly one mechanism for achieving a balance will be for firms to rely on freelance consultants more – and being self-employed is becoming an increasingly acceptable career option. However, that brings its own quality control challenges which may necessitate new approaches.

A real problem here is turnover. It is already so high across the industry that it is difficult to see it getting worse – if only because it would become impossible to hold together a corporate entity where the staff – even senior people – stayed no longer than a handful of years. Uncontrolled, this has a damaging impact on a company's style, ethos and standards.

But new solutions will evolve; a new paradigm for people management will emerge which manages to balance the growing tension in the consulting organisation between central control and individual freedom.

Mick James
The existing consulting model may be more resilient than we give it credit for. After all, consulting firms are the last refuge of corporate man, where it is possible to have a career structure of the sort rarely available elsewhere in the private sector. If we step back, it is clear, for example, that consulting organisations offer individuals something that they would find difficult to do for themselves – systematic, formal training. The wide experience such training gives will be even more essential in the future than it is today. Trends like increased outsourcing will mean that we may see a resurgence in the role of the general business manager and consulting firms will need to respond by fielding consultants with a breadth as well as depth of experience. This is equally something that small consultancies or sole practitioners will find very difficult to do and it will be one of the areas in which the differences between the big and small consultancies are particularly exacerbated.

While these changes tend to favour the existing model, there will still be pressures against it. One of the problems with the conventional partnership structure, for example, is that the partners themselves often end up becoming unhappy with their own organisation: they are expected to keep the consultants underneath them occupied, when they could be leading less stressful, better rewarded lives if they worked either by themselves or in very small partnerships.

To reconcile these conflicting demands, we may see a more flexible structure emerging in which people regularly move in and out of the consulting profession. Recruiting consultants in their early thirties, as firms tend to at the moment, has two drawbacks: first, it can be difficult to integrate these people into the firm (many do not find the transition from client to consultant an easy one to make); second, once they have joined the firm, their knowledge and skills acquired from industry are frozen. In future, rather than being a consultant or a client, people may have a 'business career' in which they move between formal study, consultancy and industry. Of course, this raises problems over who funds the training and the development of such people, as no one organisation may employ someone long enough to justify this kind of development. To resolve this issue, rather than writing off their investment when someone leaves, consulting firms may levy a type of tax – equivalent to a student loan – through which the individual employee reimburses the company for the intellectual capital he or she has acquired at its expense. This, in turn, will mean that consulting firms will need both a much more rigorous approach to valuing intellectual capital and its transfer to individuals, and accounting systems that can handle this kind of transaction.

Peter Davis

But perhaps the most important issue to be addressed will be the education and development of the consultants who will work in a highly globalised world. These people will need many more skills – technological literacy and comfort with extensive travel being just two of the more obvious ones. At the same time, these are also likely to be people who are looking for more balanced lifestyles, who may be put off by the consulting industry's reputation for long hours. The result will be a tension between the corporate needs of consulting firms and increased individualism among those people they are seeking to recruit. Why should these people join? Why, once they have joined, should they stay? The whole work/reward structure will need to be revisited.

Moreover, no one should underestimate the time it will take for a generation of people to emerge who will be able to work effectively in this environment. Our thinking on human resources is already 30 years behind where it should be – the people side of the consulting industry is horribly out of balance with the way in which the market is developing. How are we going to adapt to a world where there is genuine freedom in the movement of labour, where an employee transfer that used to take six months will happen in a matter of seconds? Ally this to an educational system that is already failing to deliver the calibre of people we need at the moment, and it becomes clear that consulting firms will have to take an increasingly proactive and radical stance. This is therefore not just a question of providing sensible developmental programmes: so much is already happening. In the future, you could foresee consulting firms sponsoring – even running – their own specialist universities aimed at providing a constant stream of the kind of people they need: professional capital for the global economy.

Richard Measelle
There will always be specialists and generalists in the industry, but having access to a consultant who has in-depth experience of a particular field, who has a track record, is something that is becoming increasingly attractive to clients. Even in remote areas of the US, people who used to go and see their general medical practitioner are now much more likely to go direct to a specialist – and the same is true of consultancy clients. If you know that you have a specific problem, why go through a generalist? The exception to this has to be strategy consulting, which requires – and will continue to require – the skills of the generalist to analyse and resolve complex problems. What this means is that the division between specialist and generalist consulting services is likely to be much more distinct in the future. Ideally, a consultant develops from being a specialist to generalist during the course of his or her career. But as it becomes clearer that each area requires a different type of skill, we may find that it becomes much harder for people to move from one area to another. We may also find that, in order to overcome this problem, firms develop distinct management structures for each part of their business.

This poses a challenge for consulting firms: what happens to specialists when they become older? No consultancy service goes on forever. What, for example, will happen to all today's SAP consultants, once that market starts to contract? Moreover, consultancy is dependent on being constantly refreshed by new recruits who are in touch with what is happening in the marketplace. But if it becomes more difficult to promote specialists into a generalist role, firms run the risk of not being able to bring in the new ideas they need. There is a trend at the moment – and one that is likely to become even more marked in the future – for consultants to work for multiple employers, but, once they hit 40–50, it is questionable how much value many of them will be adding. Whose responsibility is it to ensure that people like this can continue to add value? Is it the firm's or the individual's? The key in the future will be on sharing that responsibility.

In the 1980s, companies discovered that they have customers – a recognition which has led to dramatic changes in the way in which they design and market products, even in their overall business strategies. The comparable discovery in the 1990s is that companies have employees, and that employees who feel empowered and motivated can add tremendous value. Shared responsibility for career development comes from idea that, if a firm feels it has an obligation to develop an employee, then the employee will feel that he or she has to match that sense of duty. Such a sense of responsibility translates directly into client work: consultants who are prepared to take ownership of their careers are also likely to take ownership of clients' problems – something which has a very powerful impact. Enlightened companies will understand that the motivation that comes from this sense of shared responsibility could be a source of immense competitive advantage, and will invest heavily in the human resources side of their business – much more so than at present. Human resource consulting, particularly in the areas of leadership and employee motivation, will undergo tremendous growth over the next decade.

Consulting firms will also need to create much longer-term relationships with their employees. A firm that lays off consultants one year, and tries to recruit again the following year, is not going to be able to attract the people it needs. While the markets for specific services across the industry may be quite volatile, it is in the firms' interests for them to maintain relationships with their employees and to help them move from area to area.

Steve Beck

The industry cannot continue to grow at more than 15 per cent without quality suffering as a result. A good consultant has had the opportunity to watch how the senior partner works: you cannot expect new MBAs to gain the respect of a board of directors. What a client company has always looked for, and will continue to look for, is someone – the consultant – who can make its staff do things differently. The more 'mission critical' the consulting assignment is, the more important the role played by personal relationships. When marketing documents talk about 'working with you', this is what they really mean.

In the 'cookie-cutter' approach to people management, you can grow very quickly but you will clearly be growing people who are very similar, whereas the challenge of the future is about being able to field individuals who can bring their specialist perspective to the board room table. Cookie-cutting your consultants also fails to meet the need to provide them with a higher set of values and aspirations. The consultants of the future will want to feel that they are actually doing something, making a real difference to their clients. They may also be much less interested in the conventional rewards of consulting: they may not want to be partners of their firms. Much more important to them may be things like job-sharing and project working. This is a 'post-modernist' view of people: in the 1980s, people were ambitious, hard-working, very driven: in the future we might expect to see them taking a job which is beneath their capability, just to allow them more time with their families. For them, the human cost of the long hours, high stress levels and constant travelling may be too great.

We should expect to see many more freelance consultants, who work with the consulting firms on a strictly project basis. Consulting firms may end up with a small core of permanent employees and a much wider network of part-time and freelance staff – effectively a huge shift from fixed to variable costs. Clearly such a change would help firms bring together highly specialised expertise as required, but it will also put pressure on the firm to prove its worth as a collective entity. What is the rationale for its existence if it does not own its core asset of people? Why should the client not perform the role of integrator? What we might see is greater emphasis on brand, reputation and quality control: in other words, on focusing on all those aspects of a service that only a corporate entity can provide – and which differentiate the consultancy from its client.

Technology may provide part of the solution here. It will provide the ability to pull together 'virtual' teams for short, intense assignments where the solution for the client – taking them from the 'as is' to the 'to be' – is developed at an accelerated pace, so much so that we might see three-month assignments coming down to three days, or six-month assignments coming down to six days.

Of course, this raises issues about how you charge for this kind of work – conventional time and materials will clearly not be a profitable basis. You might have to charge for the information or intellectual capital, or simply have a very high per minute fee rate – much as investment banks and venture capitalists do at present. It is a trend which poses the greatest threat to consultancies who focus on carrying out analytical studies for clients.

Tom Tierney ....

We estimate that, because search companies are now using their databases very effectively combined with demand for Bain people in the market-place, our consultants receive a job enquiry approximately every 3–6 months. The only way in which we are able to hold on to people is by effectively developing customised value propositions for each one of them, where we recognise their goals alongside our own and where we provide the opportunity to work with us on a different basis – to rotate responsibilities or work part-time. For example: in general we strive to create career flexibility over years and decades for each of our people. Strategy consulting does not leave any room for mistakes – and this applies as much to the way in which we treat our own people as to the way we work with clients.

Brian Harrison

It is dangerous to think of the consulting market – even at present – as a homogeneous entity, as it is already highly segmented, especially if we think of it in terms of the value added per consultant. A top-end strategy house can earn around $400 000 to $500 000 per year per consultant, compared to around $100 000 at an IT implementation company. For the past 20 years, IT has provided much of the growth in the consulting industry, fuelled latterly by specific issues such as the Year 2000 problem and the introduction of the Euro. But we often ignore the fact that strategy consulting has also been expanding very rapidly, and it is strategy that is more likely to continue to expand in the future, as the importance of these immediate IT issues declines.

Strategy and IT consultancies recruit very different people, and one aspect of the continued growth of strategy consulting is that we are going to encounter a constraint in what is perhaps *the* core supply of the industry – people. Management consultancy has been very successful in the past in attracting and retaining top people. But the sources of brainpower on which the profession has relied – such as business schools – are not going to be able to meet future demand; you only have to compare the planned output of the business schools against the forecast requirements of the consulting industry to appreciate how significant the shortfall is likely to be. Unlike the consulting industry, business schools are simply not planning to grow at 15 to 20 per cent per year. The industry is already on the verge of being supply constrained – something that will push up fee rates and intensify the competition for new recruits.

There is a parallel here with investment banking, which grew very dramatically in the 1980s because of the high level of merger and acquisition activity. The banks became almost desperate to expand and began to offer incredibly high salaries in an attempt to secure the best recruits. It was not a sustainable situation – the market became destabilised – and it is possible to see the same thing happening in the consultancy market.

Another factor will be the consultancy life-cycle itself.

Consultancy has always been a rapidly changing profession. In the 1960s, consulting firms were offering services in scheduling large capital investment projects, but it would be pretty difficult for a firm to offer this type of service today, essentially because the underlying expertise has been absorbed by clients. It is part of the consultancy life-cycle that expertise is gradually transferred from consultant to client. Business process re-engineering is a good example: consulting firms expanded based on their expertise in this area, only to see the market decline over time as clients absorbed the necessary skills. Clearly, it is in clients' interest to absorb new skills they need but do not have as quickly as possible. They are therefore going to become much more proficient in the future at acquiring knowledge from the consultants who work with them, and we should expect to see the life-cycle of consulting skills shorten as a result. It is clients, not consultants, who control the length of this life-cycle: the challenge for consulting firms will be to manage in an environment where the cycle is constantly shrinking.

21 Intellectual Capital

John Clarkeson

To understand how the consulting industry of the future is likely to develop, we need first to look at the two factors which have driven its growth in the immediate past.

One of the essential – and unchanging – reasons why clients buy consultancy is to acquire knowledge they do not have. A new idea is hard to standardise and can be very valuable, but gradually, over time, standard operating procedures develop and the idea becomes a commodity available to all. This commoditisation of knowledge such as engineering has benefited the larger, generalist consulting firms and helped them to expand very rapidly by packaging what has been learned in one company and taking it to others. The second is the outsourcing phenomenon. Outsourcing may be the logical answer for any organisation that is asking the question: 'How can we manage our processes most intelligently?'. It represents one approach to dealing with the complexity of a given business situation – different processes frequently require different technologies, different people and have a different working culture. In this sense, outsourcing is no different to, say, finding an alternative sales and distribution channel, and whether it should be classified as Consulting is an open question.

Strategy consulting is different. Ideas here are much less susceptible to commoditisation because they are inherently more complex, because they are cross-functional and because they have to be heavily tailored towards the needs of individual clients. Strategic consultants usually work in an environment where there is no standard solution, simply because the problems that they and their clients are facing are often unique. Second, it is difficult to outsource because it must be part of the fabric of an organisation to work. Thus, strategic consulting, although it represents only a small proportion of work compared to IT and more standardised

212

consulting, is still the most profitable. It is also an area that is likely to become more important in the future as the use of consultancy will be being driven much more by clients' strategic agendas, rather than as the tactical response to a specific problem. It may be that, as a result, the strategic consultant takes on the role of the intermediary, co-ordinating consulting activity on the client's behalf.

Extrapolating these trends into the future would suggest that the consultancy market will keep growing. 'Knowledge gap' and IT consulting will continue to benefit from the commoditisation of knowledge, as this process will, if anything, speed up. The main threat here will come from software companies taking over the role of the providers of commoditised knowledge and trying to use this position to move up the value chain.

Strategy consulting will also grow, but precisely because its intellectual capital cannot be commoditised in the same way. We should also expect to see consultancies working in more areas and with more institutions where neither conventional public nor private sector paradigms are proving adequate. The Boston Consulting Group's work in disease management, where we are seeking to re-engineer the doctor–patient relationship, is a good example of how this is already starting to happen.

Growth in all areas of consultancy means that size will not be an issue: the demise of the middle-sized firm has been predicted for many years, but there is no reason to suppose that an innovative firm of this size is any less viable in economic terms than any other. Success – viability, even – in the future will be determined by the extent to which a firm can focus its activities on what it believes to be key markets and services where it can maintain a unique or superior offering. The firms that survive and expand will do so because they are able to remain focused and to switch the subject of their focus as markets evolve and emerge.

New thinking in the consulting industry is about identifying emerging patterns: it is the process of interpretation and analysis that consultants perform on the available data that matters, not the raw data itself. The onus on the strategy consultant is to look at the information on the client's business, markets, etc. from a new perspective, in order to create new solutions. If strategy consultants are not creative, then their role is no different to that of the operational or process improvement consultants, who are simply plugging known gaps in their clients' knowledge base.

The issues being dealt with in strategy consulting are so complex that it is highly unlikely that anyone looking at the same set of data would reach the same conclusions. What matters here, therefore, is the process through which the interpretation takes place and the people who carry it out. It takes a team of very gifted consultants to look at a set of information and see something new in it. You can teach parts of this process, but too much relies on the individuals for the process ever to be routinised. Much also depends on having the type of culture which nurtures and sustains creativity. Consulting firms are currently investing a great deal of money in formal training, and in research and development, but the key ingredient is a team of people who combine practical sense with the courage to transcend conventional wisdom.

Rafael Cerezo

After building client relationships, and recruiting and retaining the best people, the next most serious operational issue facing consulting firms is knowledge management.

Clearly, the sheer availability of knowledge has massively increased over the past few years, but there is still much that remains comparatively difficult to access. In 20 years' time, there will be virtually no information that cannot be accessed anywhere in the world at any time. In consulting assignments, this will result in much more time being spent sharing and analysing existing knowledge in order to create a fresh perspective. Most knowledge will have little commercial value, as clients will recognise that they gain far more by sharing, rather than hiding, the bulk of the information they have accumulated. Moreover, information sources will have become so intermixed that it will become impossible to say where an idea originated from. Although there will be a small core of knowledge that will be enormously valuable to an organisation, much of the wrangling over intellectual property rights that we see at the moment will have disappeared.

The role of consultancies will change to reflect this. The process of information-gathering will be almost wholly redundant; consultants will instead find themselves having to focus on much more complex problems and working with clients to convert existing knowledge into new knowledge. Being able to create a new insight into a given situation or to take an unconventional approach to familiar data will therefore become two of the most valued and valuable areas of consultancy. The challenge will be to remain creative in an environment where you are almost overwhelmed by information. Fifteen years ago, when PCs first began to be introduced into business on a wide scale, people relaxed: something like building a financial model, which might have taken them days or weeks, could be done in a matter of hours. They let the computers do the work for them, and began to forget the basic economic relationships which underpinned the models they produced – they ceased to be able to tell you how their organisation made money. PCs effectively stifled creativity. The same is true today, as companies try to build their knowledge bases. We are in danger of running the same risk, of relying too much on the mechanism for gathering knowledge, at the expense of the creative interpretation.

David Maister

Much of what happens in consultancy is good at an intellectual level, but it does not help clients *do* anything. In the past, consulting firms earned their income from knowledge – you were telling clients something they did not know. Today, clients already have that knowledge, and it follows that the value of consultancy in the future will be in the skills, not knowledge, of the consultant, not in the fact that he or she has access to a specialist piece of intellectual capital. Of these skills, the most valuable will be an ability to facilitate change – and this is a skill which some individuals and some organisations have, while others do not. You will not be able to teach someone how to do this in the same way that you can give them a new piece of knowledge.

Jean-Pierre Le Calvez

The key challenge of the future, so far as intellectual capital is concerned, will not be generating new knowledge, but managing knowledge and providing insight. There can be no doubt that advances in technology will mean that communicating ideas and information will be even cheaper and easier than it is today. Our ability to extract knowledge from this wealth of data is already improving, but this soon will not be enough – we will need to be able to extract *relevant* knowledge. No organisation – client or consultant – will be able to be all things to all people in this environment: we will all have to focus on our areas of core competence and build up our knowledge bases in these areas, rather than acquiring a general knowledge of many things. An important role, therefore, for the consultant of the future, will be to help clients access this specialised knowledge more effectively – something that no one really knows how to do at the moment, and somewhere where we should expect to see consulting firms investing in the next few years. Consulting firms are becoming strategic partners in decision-making, as clients increasingly outsource to them the process of assimilating and interpreting what is happening in their external, and sometimes, internal environments. Consultancies live and die by how much they know and the extent they are able to communicate it internally and externally.

But consulting firms will only be able to play this role if they remain very close to the markets in which they are operating. Conventional strategic consulting has focused on the highest levels within organisations. Helping clients to manage their knowledge more effectively – helping them make sense of the information at their disposal – will only be achieved if we, as consultants, can work not only at the top of the organisation but with all parts of it and work even more collaboratively than at present, transferring not only information but relevant knowledge. At one client, with whom A T Kearney is currently working, we have established a centre of excellence for the organisation as a whole, which brings together client staff and consultants from both AT Kearney and EDS, in order to generate new ideas and explore new opportunities which each side, independently, would not be capable of producing. You cannot generate the type of ideas that clients need in a vacuum, because their practical application will be limited: you can only generate really valuable intellectual capital by working closely with clients – so closely, in fact, that the client–consultant distinction may start to blur.

Does this mean that the role of the consultant will extend from interpreting events as they happen, to making events happen? From identifying embryonic markets, to creating new markets? If we think back to a product like the Sony Walkman: did Sony simply tap into latent demand at just the right moment, or did the company genuinely create a new market? Whatever the precise source of the original idea, it is likely that consultancy in the future will be taking an increasingly early and formative role in identifying and helping clients develop new market and product opportunities.

Philip Evans

Over the past few years, the competition for recruits has already become very intense. Faced with a growing shortage of the kind of people they want, it becomes almost inevitable that consulting firms will have to investigate, not only more effective means of managing knowledge, but also alternative-electronic-delivery channels. Business-related chat-rooms on the Internet are already starting to take on an intermediary role, between clients and consultants, as the former have the opportunity to discuss a firm's credentials in a specific area. At the same time, there are continual downward pressures on the price of intellectual capital, partly as a result of its free availability.

The overall propensity of the world has been towards openness: even if it were possible to enforce legally, the concept of ownership would be meaningless given this predominant culture. More than almost anything else, intellectual capital is subject to the market forces of the economy: if an idea is worthless it is abandoned almost overnight; if it is valuable, it gradually becomes absorbed by the organisations that value it.

Another factor is the proliferation of knowledge-intensive sectors of the economy – sectors that are often characterised by the presence of numerous small firms, and where collaboration rather than competition is the norm. In this environment, the boundaries of the traditional consulting firm are going to become much harder to distinguish: they are already becoming confused. This will mean that in the future, the definition of a consulting team is not exclusive: it may well involve people from other knowledge-based companies on an equal basis to the conventional employees.

John Everett

The speed with which a consulting company has to get its ideas to market will be a crucial issue in the future. The speed itself will be determined by the rate at which intellectual capital is commoditised in the economy – that is, the rate at which specialist ideas and tools become widely available 'best practice'. If consulting firms do not respond to the increasing rate of commoditisation which we are already witnessing – if they do not take a lead in rebuilding their intellectual capital more effectively than at present – then we run the danger of practising 'ideas-free' consultancy. At the moment, we have the luxury of being able to develop intellectual capital as we go – a member firm in one country has the opportunity to plug into the thinking of its partner firms elsewhere. But, in the future, when being first to market is fundamental to success, there may be no time to do this: consulting firms will have to take better decisions at an earlier stage – identifying winning ideas in advance and channelling investment into them, rather than backing a wide range of potential services. Similarly, firms may need to distinguish more effectively between their 'real' ideas and the enabling tools and methodologies they have developed, so that ownership of their core intellectual capital can be established and defended.

Consultancies will also need to manage, more effectively than at present, the creative tension within their organisations: they need to create an environment in which new ideas are produced, but they need to balance this by ensuring that the ideas generated have a clear practical application. Bringing these two aspects together has always been problematic for consulting firms: 'blue sky' ideas are thrown across the organisational wall to the practising consultants who struggle to make them useful. You only need to think about the proportion of ideas which consulting firms generate internally but which never get to market, to see how serious a problem this is. Ideas and their application need to evolve together, and we will therefore need to nurture ideas in a much more practical environment than at present – where work is actually taking place and where clients can be much more closely involved in the processes.

David Ogram

The ownership of intellectual capital poses a major threat to consultancy, and to IT-related consultancy in particular. Until recently, the way that you protected your proprietary software was to copyright the completed code, but now companies are having to patent their software. This has massive implications for IT-related consultancy, because patents are much more wide ranging and can take years to challenge. Moreover, while copyrighting happens in retrospect, it is possible to take out patents on work in progress areas, effectively preventing your competitors from working in a similar area. Alternatively, you could use the patent as a bargaining chip, demanding a fee for giving a rival access to a specific area.

Clearly, it is comparatively uncharted legal territory and it is unclear how it will develop in the future. One thing we can be sure about, however, is that consultancies will be spending much more time and money in the future trying to protect their intellectual assets. Perhaps we will even reach the situation where the legal costs are comparable to the development costs.

But the risks surrounding intellectual capital do not apply solely to patenting software; for any knowledge-based business, one of the key issues will be who owns the intellectual capital of their employees – is it the consultancy or is it the employees themselves? At the moment, you can't patent an idea, but the time will surely come when this will change. In consultancies today, it is probably a condition of employment for all staff that the inventions they create, during their period of employment with the company, belong to that company, even if their inventions are not directly connected to their work. Some people, especially the more creative ones, find this uncomfortable, but how else can an organisation realistically protect itself? If it is the content of people's heads which is important to the organisation – as much as their physical presence during working hours – then it is inevitable that organisations in the future are going to takes steps to control this content in the same way that they try to regulate their employees. To survive, organisations will need to own people in a way they never have before. The implications for employment law, for the underlying employer–employee relationship, are immense.

Mick James ....

People assume that the future is going to be one of increased openness and exchange of ideas, but this may not necessarily be the case. Already we can see signs of the Internet starting to close up, with organisations either restricting access to their sites or charging visitors. Perhaps the future will be a world in which consulting firms own the intellectual capital – maybe even the brains – of their employees, a world in which no one will be able to talk without authorisation. Giving your employer rights over parts of your brain may well be the kind of price consultants of the future will have to pay for receiving training. When you move on to a new company, it may also be that your former employer retains those rights after you have left, potentially for the rest of your life. Perhaps you just will not be allowed to move and we will see a return to a much more corporatist world.

Unless the issues surrounding intellectual property and its ownership are resolved, the twenty-first century could be a second 'dark age', where consultancies, as the guardians of knowledge, become the modern equivalent of medieval monasteries.

Take language, for example. English, especially among multinational companies, is already the language of business, but it is almost running out of control at present with new management jargon constantly appearing. This poses a real threat to consultancy – especially as it tries to take the intellectual high ground in business – because its new services will constantly be at risk of being dismissed as consultancy-speak. Moreover, at the moment, you can develop a very successful concept but then lose control of its name as competitors imitate and often dilute it (business process re-engineering – which came to be applied to a wide range of conventional cost-reduction services – being a good illustration of this). To protect their investment, consulting firms may start to assert their ownership of certain words; perhaps they will even become the major creators of words in the future.

This potential closing down of the intellectual capital market would clearly have significant implications for client–consultant relations. Clients will continue to want what they have always wanted from consultants – to acquire their intellectual capital on a permanent basis for their own organisations, knowledge transfer in other words. But if intellectual capital is the only thing of real value in this market, then consulting firms may be unwilling to give it to clients in the way that they do at present. And if that is the case, you have to ask how long such a position will be sustainable. Take, for example, recruitment. In the past, consultancies and their clients did not compete for the same people; each was, in effect, offering different ways of working which appealed to different mentalities. But, as business has become more like consultancy – more task and project orientated – it follows that companies and consultancies have been increasingly competing for the same people. How long will business be prepared to put up with losing a recruit to a consulting firm for a relatively small difference in salary, only to end up hiring him or her as a consultant at a much higher rate? The analogy here is with satellite television which, in addition to the subscription fee, asks audiences to pay more for specific, usually sporting, occasions. This approach may work, if you limit the time you do this, but if you broadcast more and more programmes on a fee-paying basis, at some point you will inevitably push your audience beyond the limits of their tolerance. And this is what could happen in consulting: clients will simply refuse to pay the premium for acquiring intellectual capital indirectly.

Darrell Rigby

Managers the world over are facing increasing pressure to deliver results. Not surprisingly, they are asking themselves: 'What can I do?'. And they are looking around their markets and competitors and seeing a whole host of management tools which may help them to respond to the issues they face. Often these are tools which are taken from company to company by consultants or academics.

But it is important to remember that transferring intellectual capital in this way has its drawbacks. First, many of these tools were developed with a specific client in mind: they may be much less successful when applied in a different environment. Second, such tools will never be a source of competitive advantage, because they will always have been applied at another company first. Such issues may not concern a client: there are many companies that are essentially followers, that tend to react to something only when they have heard that their competitors have already adopted it, and that generally want to follow a tried and tested approach. But there are other companies, that are already leading-edge and determined to continue to be so, for whom this approach will never be an acceptable option.

Bain has therefore carried out a survey for the past few years which tracks the performance of the most commonly used management tools. Companies are asked to fill in a survey, indicating the extent to which they use a given tool and their rating of it. One of the key messages that emerges is that problems come, not from the idea itself, but from the misapplication of that idea in a particular environment. Choosing the right tool, therefore, has become a major challenge for today's managers and an even greater challenge for their successors in the future. Why? Because clients continually absorb intellectual capital from consultancies and other external firms. The skills that a consultant brings to a client today will have been assimilated into that organisation tomorrow. The pressure on consulting firms – especially the leading-edge ones – to continue to be innovative will be immense. The gap between clients and consultants will remain, but consultants will have to work much harder to maintain it. As other consultancies imitate these new approaches, the number of management tools available will proliferate. Deciding which tools will be appropriate for a client should be a joint client–consultant process, as it is in the latter's long-term interest to ensure that the correct tool is selected. Yet the decision-making process has been hampered on both sides by the absence of information on the tools themselves (hence part of the motivation behind the Bain survey). Although consulting firms would ultimately benefit from it, they still have a long way to go in terms of making this kind of information easily accessible.

Yet it is important to stress that success in consulting terms will not be based on tools: no CEO is going to base his or her strategy around the output from a set of tools. Tools tend to encourage you to think in discrete, often quite static, building blocks, rather than seeing the business as a dynamic whole. Strategies are developed around themes or ideas, and the successful consultancies of the future – at least so far as the strategy segment of the market is concerned – will focus on the process by which a creative, holistic approach is developed. The key 'tools' here will be those which facilitate the visioning process, not which transfer intellectual capital from one company to another.

22

Branding

Allan Steinmetz
Growing sophistication on the clients' part and a more complex, challenging business environment make it highly likely that the consulting firms of the future will have to develop deeper and deeper specialisms in order to succeed. This will make it increasingly difficult for consulting firms to establish and maintain a brand identity. There are two aspects to this. First, while some firms will find themes around which they can cluster their specialist areas – business integration or innovation are good examples – for the majority, the pressure towards specialisation will create a vicious circle in which they have less and less money and resources available to try to project a more holistic image. The smaller companies will stay small (some may even shrink), and the larger companies will get larger. Second, while the large companies may be able to afford sizeable marketing budgets, with which they can run above-the-line advertising campaigns, the trend towards specialisation will make those campaigns – which are inherently generic – much less credible. You will continually be running the risk of commoditising your intellectual capital in order to gain the attention of a wider market. Internally, as well as externally, firms will have to position themselves as being specialists because 'generalist' work will not be sufficiently differentiated to have anything other than a commodity value.

To do this, many consulting firms are going to have to reinvent themselves. And the key to doing this will be the relationships they are able to build with the senior executives in their client organisations. It is only at the individual level that it becomes possible to build up a brand which balances an overall image with highly specialist knowledge – the consulting equivalent of relationship or one-to-one marketing, in contrast to mass-marketing.

But these executives are not just important because they provide the most effective channel through which a consulting firm can promote its services, but also because they are becoming the core of the organisational decision-making process. More and more companies, in North America especially, are being run by a small number of people in whom power is concentrated: consensus management is in decline. In an internal environment in which there are few peers to consult, future clients will be increasingly looking to obtain advice externally. Of course, this mindset will mean that they will be much more open minded about where they look for this advice: they may turn to academics, investment banks, advertising agencies or systems integration houses as much as to consultancies. Once again, it will be important for consultancies to use the relationships they have to build a brand which differentiates themselves from such competitors.

External branding will need to be reinforced by internal branding, and creating a 'one-firm' environment with consistent training and methodologies will be important. But the pressure towards standardisation and centralisation which this implies will need to be balanced with the need to nurture individual creativity. This means that, while you will want consistent methodologies, you will not want all your thinking to be codified in this way; and that, while you want integration of your different specialisations, you do not want a Tower of Babel-type culture.

Michael Younger

As the consultancy industry matures, branding will become a key competitive weapon – so much so that advertising, which only a few years ago was an anathema to most firms, becomes the norm. However, the fundamental role of the consulting firm is to provide a high-quality and desirable service to clients, where 'high quality' could be defined as good work carried out for a reasonable price. Branding ought to be unnecessary if firms stick to this role.

Keith Ferrazzi

The successful consultancy of the future will need to build its brand on delivering 'real' results. This could partly take the form of focusing on knowledge transfer, but much more effective will be to be able to offer clients some sort of blanket guarantee that the consulting assignment will deliver measurable benefits, in the form either of increased sales or profits, or of increased satisfaction among the client's own customers. When Deloitte & Touche helps a client upgrade its call centre, for instance, it puts in place process measures which will track the way in which increased customer satisfaction flows through to the bottom line.

Clearly, this kind of positioning could be backed up by much greater and more visible risk-sharing between consultant and client. There is some evidence that consulting firms are already taking equity stakes in some clients, but their ability to do this on a larger scale is limited by regulation. This could, in any case, be the start of a slippery slope, because not everything a consultancy does will have an impact on shareholder value – organisational redesign is a good example. Furthermore, a single consulting team will not always be in the position to control the outcome: they may be dependent on other consulting teams and they will always be dependent on the client acting on their recommendations. At the end of the day, consultants will still always be consultants: they will not make the decisions and they cannot prevent a client from making the wrong choice.

Brand awareness will have to be built through advertising. At the moment, brand recognition is very high for Andersen Consulting and McKinsey & Co. and very low for almost all the other consulting firms. In six months of advertising, Deloitte & Touche has been able to improve its unaided brand awareness rate very significantly, and this is undoubtedly the way forward for the future. In Deloitte & Touche's case, the advertising will continue to stress the firm's focus on helping companies realise their strategy and exploit their technology through more effective processes; it will also emphasise the firm's corporate – as opposed to partnership – style. But, more generally, we should also expect the style of advertising to become more aggressive: at the moment, it is rare for a consultancy to criticise a rival, but 'knocking copy' – even in the consulting industry – will become much more accepted.

Crawford Gillies

Consulting is still about people, and how you recruit, retain and develop your people will clearly continue to be one of the fundamental drivers of success or failure in this industry. But, at the same time, it is important to recognise that even the best people have to be supported by: an infra-structure which enables them to share knowledge effectively; an organisation which has no internal geographical boundaries; and a brand image which differentiates the organisation from its rivals.

Of these, branding remains an especially difficult area, so far as consulting firms are concerned. Many smaller consultancies do not need to develop a brand: their specialist expertise and focus is sufficient to differentiate them. And there are comparatively few large service firms that have managed to create a strong brand. A consulting firm may have strong and substantial values – Bain's emphasis on results, not reports, is a good illustration – but, when these are translated into a conventional corporate brochure, they often lose much of their individuated power. You need to be able to communicate the genes of the organisation – the things that make it tick and its people come alive – and this is something you can only do effectively if you can demonstrate the substance behind the image. To do this, it is important to build and maintain a network of deep relationships with individual clients – all of whom know your organisation through the value it has delivered in an actual assignment, rather than its brochures.

Appendix

Contributors

Steve Beck
Steve Beck is the Vice President of Gemini Consulting, responsible for Gemini's consulting practice in the UK, Scandinavia, Benelux and South Africa. Prior to this, he was head of the Financial Services Practice in Northern Europe. Mr Beck has over 12 years of consulting experience in the USA and Europe, where his particular areas of focus have been retail banking, private banking and securities, and asset management.

Robin Buchanan
Robin Buchanan is the Senior Partner of Bain & Company's London office. He joined the firm in 1982 and was a member of the management buy-out team that acquired Bain in 1991. His consulting experience includes transformation, turnaround and expansion strategies, acquisitions, alliances and divestitures, performance improvement and organisational change. He is also a Director of Liberty International plc.

Alan Buckle
Alan Buckle is the Chief Operating Officer responsible for running KPMG Management Consulting in the UK. He joined the firm in 1981, initially in the audit practice, before moving into Corporate Finance. Subsequently, he was responsible for training in the UK firm and then took over responsibility for Financial Management Consulting. He studied at Durham University and the Kellogg School of Management.

Rafael Cerezo
Rafael Cerezo is a senior vice president with The Boston Consulting Group. Based in Madrid, he is chairman of BCG's European region. Prior to joining BCG, Mr Cerezo worked with various private companies as well

as for the Commission of the European Communities in Brussels and the Representation of the Council of Spanish Chambers of Commerce for the EEC in Brussels. He is a graduate of the London School of Economics and holds an MBA from Columbia University.

John Clarkeson

John Clarkeson became Chairman of The Boston Consulting Group in 1998, having been Chief Executive Officer for 12 years. Based in Boston, he has worked extensively in Europe. He chairs the US National Advisory Council, INSEAD. A former Harvard National Scholar, Mr Clarkeson holds an MBA from Harvard Business School and has served in the United States Army Reserve.

Geoffrey Cullinan

Geoffrey Cullinan leads Bain & Company's Private Equity Practice for Europe, with special responsibility for developing entrepreneurial companies, as well as focusing on mergers and acquisitions and the creation of shareholder value. He has over 25 years' general management, strategy consulting and investment experience in a wide range of consumer products, retail, automotive, chemicals, engineering and financial services. Prior to joining Bain, he was the CEO of Hamleys plc and the founder and Managing Director of OC&C Strategy Consultants.

Peter Davis

Peter Davis was appointed Deputy Global Leader of the management consulting practice of PricewaterhouseCoopers, following the merger of Price Waterhouse and Coopers & Lybrand on 1 July 1998. He is a member of the management consulting global Leadership Team and has oversight responsibility for the integration of the two firms in Europe, internal knowledge sharing and human resources. Prior to this, Peter was Director of the European practice of Price Waterhouse Management Consulting. Peter has over 20 years' experience of management consultancy, with an emphasis on strategic management, financial planning and control systems and international change programmes. This experience has spanned a wide range of sectors, both public and private, and has included extensive work on behalf of multinational organisations.

Philip Evans

Philip Evans is a senior vice president with The Boston Consulting Group and leads the firm's thinking on the new economics of information. Based in Boston, he holds an MA from Cambridge University and an MBA from

Harvard Business School. Prior to joining BCG, Mr Evans taught for the Foreign Ministry of Japan in Tokyo.

John Everett

John Everett is an economist and accountant by training. He spent the first ten years of his career working for blue chip companies in finance and strategy. His last position before joining Deloitte Consulting was as Strategic Planning Manager for the Rover Group. Since joining Deloitte, he has worked extensively in the manufacturing and energy sectors leading major assignments in strategy, change management and re-engineering. He was appointed Managing Director of Deloitte Consulting UK in April 1995.

Keith Ferrazzi

Keith Ferrazzi is the Chief Marketing Officer for the Deloitte & Touche Consulting Group, where his responsibilities include building the brand equity on a global basis and developing new lines of business. In 1997, he launched the firm's first advertising campaign. Prior to joining Deloitte & Touche he worked for ICI where he was responsible for creating the company's total quality management programme for North America. While attending Harvard Business School, he established a consulting firm specialising in service quality.

Orit Gadiesh

Orit Gadiesh is the Chairman of the Board of Bain & Company, where she continues to advise top-level management in structuring and managing portfolios, developing and implementing global strategy, executing turnarounds, improving organisational effectiveness, determining channel strategy, and designing cost reduction programmes. She is a frequent speaker on issues of strategy around the world, and is also an active board and council member at the Harvard Business School, the Wharton School, and the Kellogg School, as well as various not for profit boards.

Crawford Gillies

Crawford Gillies is the Managing Partner of the London office of Bain. Having joined the firm in 1982, he has extensive experience of working with clients on issues of strategy, acquisitions, performance investment and organisational change across a wide range of industries.

James Hall

James Hall has been Managing Partner of Andersen Consulting UK since 1994. He is also Managing Partner of the firm's global business in the

Automotive and Industrial Equipment and Transportation and Travel Services industries. Mr Hall joined the firm in 1976 as a graduate trainee. He became a partner in 1987 and has been head of the Products and Technology Integration Services divisions in the UK. During his time with the firm, James has worked with clients in a wide range of industry sectors and has managed some of the largest and most complex engagements undertaken by the UK practice.

David Harding

David Harding is a Director of the Boston office of Bain & Company, where he is an expert in the areas of corporate strategy and organisational effectiveness. Mr Harding has led corporate strategy work for a broad array of clients in diverse industries, focusing particularly on the organisational challenges involved in implementing strategy. He also speaks and writes frequently on strategy issues; his latest article, 'Brand versus Private Label: Fighting to Win' was published by the *Harvard Business Review* in 1996.

Brian Harrison

Brian Harrison is a Vice President of A T Kearney and a member of the firm's Board of Directors and Board of Management. He is currently responsible for managing A T Kearney's internal global support functions in information technology, knowledge management, research and development, human resources, professional development and marketing. He also oversees the firm's global strategy consulting practice. Previously, Mr Harrison managed A T Kearney's Canadian practice as well as the firm's global Business Process Re-engineering practice. Mr Harrison has been a consultant for 24 years during which time he has lived and worked on all five continents.

Mick James

Mick James was the editor of the UK magazine *Management Consultancy* for five years, and is now its consulting editor and an independent writer and consultant. *Management Consultancy* is the world's first professional title aimed at the consulting industry. The magazine also publishes market reports (*Current Trends in Management Consultancy* and *Future Markets in Consultancy*) and produces the annual *Careers in Management Consultancy Guide*.

Michael de Kare-Silver

Michael de Kare-Silver is a leading consultant on business strategy. For many years he has worked with a number of major European and US multinationals. He is a senior partner with the Kalchas Group, now part of CSC Index Consulting. He was previously with McKinsey, worked for four years as a marketing manager with Procter & Gamble, and is a qualified commercial lawyer. He is also the author of the best-selling *Strategy in Crisis* and has a new book, *e-shock*, published in November 1998.

Jean-Pierre Le Calvez

Jean-Pierre Le Calvez joined A T Kearney in 1997 as Director of Marketing – Europe and is based in Paris, France. Previously, he was the European Corporate Affairs and Media Relations Manager at Apple Computer. Prior to joining Apple Computer, he held the position of International Strategic Programs Manager – Europe, at Texas Instruments in Nice, France. From 1983 to 1986, Jean-Pierre taught Marketing and Advertising Research at the William Alan White School of Journalism at The University of Kansas in the United States.

David Maister

David Maister is the leading authority on the management of professional service firms, consulting to many prominent firms in a broad spectrum of professions. He has a global consulting practice, which covers all professional firm management issues from human resource strategies to practice development, from profitability improvement tactics to multinational practice strategies. Formerly a professor at the Harvard Business School, he taught for seven years in the school's MBA and executive programmss. He is the author of *Managing the Professional Service Firm*, and *True Professionalism*.

Richard Measelle

From 1989 to 1997, Richard Measelle was the Worldwide Managing Partner at Arthur Andersen. When he took on this role, as a result of the reorganisation of Andersen Worldwide and the establishment of Andersen Consulting, the firm was characterised by low morale, and little or no growth. Richard Measelle presided over the reinvention of the business and the period of his tenure saw the firm's revenues increase from $1.9 billion to $5.1 billion.

Paul Mitchell

Paul Mitchell is a vice president with The Boston Consulting Group and head of the firm's London office. Prior to joining BCG, he worked as a site engineer for Balfour Beatty and as a design engineer for Ove Arup & Partners. Mr Mitchell holds a BSc in Civil and Structural Engineering from the University of Edinburgh, a Diploma in Computer Modelling from Trinity College Dublin, and an MBA from Harvard Business School.

Eddie Oliver

Eddie Oliver is Chairman of KPMG Consulting in the UK and a member of the KPMG Board. In his ten years with KPMG, Mr Oliver has led many consulting assignments, covering areas such as strategy, organisational development and performance improvement. Before joining KPMG, he was Deputy Chief Executive of the London Docklands Development Corporation. Outside KPMG, he is the Chairman of the Pool of London Partnership and a member of the National Curriculum and Assessment Committee.

David Ogram

David Ogram is the managing Director of AMS UK (American Management Systems) and Director of Business Development, Tele-communications, Europe responsible for the development of AMS's telecommunications business across Europe. He joined AMS in 1991 and has been a key player in growing AMS Telecoms' revenues in Europe from virtually zero in 1990 to around US$200M in 1997. With the re-organisation of Telecoms at the end of 1997 David is now the deputy Director of the European Telecoms Group.

Brian O'Rorke

Brian O'Rorke became Executive Director of the MCA in 1985, and played a major role in ensuring that the Association addressed the issues that could have divided the consulting industry as it entered a new phase in its development. Prior to his appointment, Brian served first as an Army Officer retiring on completion of command of his regiment in 1976. For the next ten years he was appointed director of a number of small/medium-sized companies, which mainly concentrated in the financial sector. He retired in 1998.

Glen Peters

Glen Peters is an engineer by education, who two years after graduation, spent short tours of secondment in British Gas working in all the main functions of the organisation in their graduate training programme; an experience that was better than all the formal training he has ever received. He was a project director working on major energy projects until he joined

Price Waterhouse in the mid-1980s. There as a consultant he completed a doctoral thesis on information management, ran their energy practice for three years and launched the Market & Customer Management function. In recent years he has developed scenario planning and reputation management capabilities for the firm. Throughout his time with Price Waterhouse he managed the firm's relationship with BP.

Bruce Petter
Bruce Petter is the Executive Director of the Management Consultancies Association in the UK. The MCA acts as industry spokesman, and plays a leading role in FEACO, the Federation of European Management Consultancy Organisations, based in Brussels. Prior to taking up this role, in 1998, Mr Petter was the founder, and then Director, of the Petrol Retailers' Association, in which capacity he was responsible for representing members' interest to the government and oil companies.

Darrell Rigby
Darrell Rigby is a Director of Bain & Company's Boston office. In his 20 years of consulting experience, he has led assignments in a variety of industrial and consumer industries, where he has specialised in corporate strategy. He is a frequent speaker and writer on strategy issues, including innovation, mergers and acquisitions, customer-based strategies and change management.

Allan J Steinmetz
Allan Steinmetz has over 23 years' experience in marketing, advertising and strategy, having worked for some of the world's most respected advertising and consulting firms. He is presently Senior Vice President and Corporate Director of Marketing for Arthur D Little, where he is responsible for the firm's brand identity and positioning, business development, strategic awareness, lead generation, advertising and communications. Mr Steinmetz is also a member of the firm's senior leadership management team. Prior to joining A D Little in 1993, he was the Worldwide Director of Marketing and Communications for Andersen Consulting.

Thomas J Tierney
Thomas Tierney is the Worldwide Managing Director of Bain & Company. He joined the firm in 1980, following his graduation from Harvard Business School, and has since specialised in customer service and marketing, competitive strategy and organisational change. In

addition to his responsibilities as the senior executive of Bain & Company's multiple offices around the world, Mr Tierney also serves on the board of (among others) The Boston Symphony Orchestra and the Hoover Institution.

Vincent Tobkin

Vince Tobkin is a Director of Bain & Company's San Francisco office. He joined the firm in 1992, following eight years in Venture capital with Sierra Ventures and eight years as a consultant with McKinsey and Company. As co-head of Bain's Telecom and Technology practice, Mr Tobkin has led assignments in all areas of computers and tele-communications: systems integration, wireless, multimedia, interactive services, broadband, transmissions, LAN/WAN and data networks. A member of Dr Michael Hammer's re-engineering group (Phoenix Group), Mr Tobkin headed Bain's re-engineering practice from 1992 to 1996.

Michael Younger

Michael Younger is Chairman of Arthur D Little Limited, and until recently a main board member of Arthur D Little Inc., where he remains a Vice President. He has been with the company since 1968 and was Managing Director of the London office from 1980 to 1992. In his early career, he was with the Resource Consulting Unit in Cambridge, MA, and transferred to the UK in 1971. He has focused on consulting on strategic and organisational matters with a particular focus on resource companies. He has also had an interest in working for government development agencies in Europe and elsewhere. He is a member of the Royal Society Arts and Manufacturing in the UK.

Index